Maria Hearne's War Memories

Copyright © 2021 by Maria Hearne

All rights reserved. No part of this book may be used in any manner without permission.

This book is dedicated to Katy and to those whose encouragement was invaluable.

Preface

I decided some years ago that I would like to capture my memories for my family and friends, and others who are interested in the Romany way of life.

I have since, and over a period of many years, been jotting these memories down as they come to me, sparked off by many sights, sounds, and people talking to me. So, the events recorded here are in no way in any chronological sequence, but as I remembered them.

I hope you enjoy reading them as much I enjoyed writing about them.

Maria Hearne

Katy

Katy was diagnosed with breast cancer in 2018. Kate phoned me and said, "I hope you're sitting down Mum I've got something to tell you". I thought she was going to tell me that Kieralea was pregnant again and felt a little bit excited. However, what she told me was far from good news. She had found a lump and the doctors were going to check things out but thought it was likely to be cancer. A week later the results were back and confirmed our fears. It was an aggressive type of hormonal cancer.

Katy's treatment progressed, and she was so brave and strong throughout, always smiling, joking and putting on a brave face. From then on, we would see a difference in her health as the illness and the side effects of the treatment took hold. The doctors were still hopeful but after the treatment had finished Katy was still very poorly and made a difficult decision to have a single mastectomy. She looked so tired, but she still plodded on. I remember when she came home from the operation and, when she was able to, she enjoyed making cakes with Savanah. Tragically Katy was told she wasn't going to get better. I'll never forget hearing her scream coming from the doctor's office whilst I sat in the waiting room of the hospital. We were all taken to another room and she was given a devastating prognosis of only three weeks left to live.

Katy never told the grandchildren she was going to die. They knew she was poorly and often showed their concern and love by asking how she was. She always gave them a lovely smile and told them she was not feeling too poorly today. Shane was one of the last people she told. They were so close they could have been twins.

Her wish was to die at home and although she had to spend some time in the hospice, she succeeded in that. Sadly, Katy passed away, at home, with all her family around her at 8.20 a.m. on the 28th July 2019.

She desperately wanted to reach 50, which she did, and we were all able to celebrate with her on the 8th August 2018. Little did we know at that time the sadness and heartache that was to come. She would have been 51 the day after her funeral.

Life now feels so empty without her. We all struggle, and the little ones have been so brave. Savanah still cries for her Nanny Kate; they were so close. Kieralea has had to grow up fast as her Mum did a lot for her, and again, they were very close. She and her brother have struggled to cope but I am so proud of them both.

We'll never get over losing Kate, but we remember the good times. She was always bubbly and full of fun. Everyone who met her loved her. She is loved and missed so much. Darling Kate R.I.P. xx

A writing place

I like to think of writing as a place to go rather than something to do. Who are we after we give birth? We hope to be the same person, but with a baby. Yet afterwards, everything is so different. We find ourselves struggling with changes in our lives.

My writing is a journey inwards. In many ways, it's like mining.

We dig down into the earth and bring back moments that are raw. Yet there is a reward that comes from the work itself. When we engage in the practice for a period, our minds come alive with thoughts, images and reflections, and we begin to sense the presence of our own voice. Like any journey, there is no single road to take, no easy set of directions. We have our whole lives to write about, but the choice can be overwhelming. I usually start by focusing on a particular time, or place or thoughts, even the tiniest moment that comes to mind. I may remember a journey or a view from a window, or the colour of lights against a wall. Feelings create energy, and energy creates momentum that will carry me forward, often to a place I have been to.

My whole childhood comes alive as does our bungalow where I lived as a child, the clothes I wore and the feel of the air on my skin.

All the memories are as clear as can be in my mind, just as if I am looking at photos.

Cooking not my best subject

In the early stages of my married life, I had a dreadful time when making pastry, and don't ask me about cakes! Honestly, the only thing I was somewhat good at was boiling an egg. Well, how could I get that wrong!

Most days I would telephone my mother-in-law, or sometimes my sister-in-law Janet, for advice. I don't know what I would have done without their help. I'd have the phone tucked under my chin while writing down instructions - at the same time trying to cook. Very difficult!

Brian would not eat meat, apart from sausages. Also, he had this thing that everything had to be with sauce, so as long as there was plenty of that I was halfway there. The only problem was, the sauce wouldn't thicken for me. It was either too thick or too thin and runny. I could never find that happy medium!

Still, Brian never complained. I wonder why!

Eventually, when I did get it right, there was no holding me back. Cookery books, I think I had them all!

I wouldn't say I tried all the recipes, but I had a good go. I always knew if Brian liked the look of the dish, just by the expression on his face. If I'm honest, some of the dishes I cooked were quite nice (at least I thought so) *but others were disgusting!*

I think my mother had the right idea. When they were travelling on the road they could cook outside, over an open fire. They used to have a piece of iron which was bent over and then bent again to make a hook. This was so they could hang their pot of food on it and it could cook nice and slowly.

When my parents bought the bungalow, Mother thought she was in heaven with her cooking! Then they had their roasts and apple pies. I didn't know any different as I had never travelled and was born in the bungalow. That's where we stayed until I was thirteen and my parents moved to Warley Hill.

    Although this was still in Brentwood, Essex, I didn't like it. I much preferred Marlborough Road.

Katy's night out

Katy decided to go out with her friends down to the village. She was quite a while getting dressed. When she eventually came downstairs, she was looking very nice and smelt nice too.

'Where did you say you are going tonight?' I asked.

'Just to Herongate Village to meet up with some of my friends,' Katy replied.

'I don't want you in too late, Katy.'

'Oh Mum! I don't have to get up in the morning. It's Sunday and I can have a lay in. Shane, are you ready?'

No sooner had Katy shouted out to Shane than he was downstairs.

'Bye Mum,' they called out.

'Katy, I'd like you in by ten o'clock.'

'OK, Mum,' she said as she and Shane were walking out the gate.

'Don't worry, Mum. I'll make sure she's in by ten o'clock,' Shane said.

'Don't forget your dad comes home tonight,' I called out. All I got back from them was a wave. It took me back to when I was young and used to go out. I had to be in by dead on ten o'clock, otherwise my parents would give me a few words.

I looked up and saw Brian's lorry turning into the top of our road. When he eventually got out I noticed that he looked so tired. I had prepared dinner so all I had to do was put the kettle on.

'Hello,' he called out, 'I'm home.'

'Hello, love. How about a nice cup of tea?' I said. 'Yes please. That will go down really nice,' he said.

'I'll go and run your bath for you when you've had your tea. Would you like a glass of whisky while you're in the bath?'

'That will be lovely,' Brian said. 'And you can leave the bottle up there if you like!'

After we had our pot of tea I went upstairs and ran Brian's bath. I also put a nice glass of whisky on the small table which was placed beside the bath. After being away all week he used to look forward to his weekends so much. Sometimes he didn't have a full weekend, because he had to go away Sunday morning after we had our breakfast.

Brian loved being home but, as he used to say, he chose to be a lorry driver. Deep down I knew he liked his job.

'Where are the children then?' Brian asked me.

'Oh, they've gone out together. They said they were going down to the Green Man .'

'The Green Man! Katy isn't old enough to be drinking.'

'Don't go on, Brian. I've been through that with them, and Shane said he would look after her. Also, Katy promised me that she wouldn't drink.' All the time I was talking to Brian I was thinking to myself, please Katy don't drink!

After Brian had his bath and his dinner, he was sitting relaxed in his armchair, watching the television and half falling asleep. I didn't really want him falling asleep in the chair, because he never feels like moving afterwards. Katy was on my mind so much, and I hoped she wouldn't come in drunk.

After Brian watched his programme, he sat up in his chair and said, 'I think I'll have an early night if you don't mind, Maria?'

'No, of course I don't mind.'

All I kept thinking about was Katy, hoping she didn't drink and come home singing. Her father would skin her alive in the morning if he knew she had been drinking.

'I'm not feeling tired, Brian, so if you don't mind I'll just potter about then watch a bit of television.'

'That's OK love,' Brian said. 'In the morning I'll cook you all a lovely breakfast.'

'That sounds really nice, Brian.'

He bent over, kissed me on the cheek, and said, 'Good night and God bless, love.'

I felt so relieved that he had decided to go to bed early. I tidied up downstairs, and then made myself a cup of coffee and sat down to watch television. I looked up at the clock. It was quarter past nine. I didn't really know whether to go to bed and pretend I was asleep when Katy came in.

I drank my coffee, and decided to wash my cup up and go to bed. Katy was sixteen and I knew she would be in safe hands with Shane, but all the same, I was very worried about her being out this time of night as she was very headstrong. I knew she wouldn't drink, well I was hoping she wouldn't.

After I had done everything I wanted to do I went upstairs and cleaned my teeth. I think I was just prolonging the time really. I eventually got to bed and waited for the sound of her coming home. Oh come on Katy, I kept thinking, please don't be late otherwise I'll be in for it in the morning. That sounds as if Brian was a hard man, but he wasn't like that at all.

I must have fallen asleep, because the next thing I heard was Katy shouting out, 'Thank you, thank you.' The front gate was locked so she had to climb over the wall. It had to be the front gate. Why couldn't she have gone to the back gate as that one was always left open?

Sacha, our Alsatian, was so good because when the children came in late she never made a noise. Brian was sound asleep. Please don't wake up, I was thinking. Should I go down to let her know that I heard her, or should I pretend I'm asleep when she comes upstairs?

Here she comes. At least she isn't making a noise. She's taken Sacha into her bedroom. Sacha loves being with Katy, but she won't like being with Katy if she's sick!

The next thing I knew it was morning. As I got up I could smell bacon cooking. Oh what a lovely smell! I don't think Katy will think it's a lovely smell after last night.

'Hello, Shane,' I heard Brian say.

I turned around and there stood Shane. Then Katy came in, her hair all messy. 'Morning,' she called out.

'Morning love,' Brian said. 'Did you have a nice time last night?'

'Yes, thank you Dad,' she replied, rubbing her eyes.

Shane was just standing there, biting his bottom lip and waiting for his dad to say something about last night.

'Come on, you three. Breakfast is ready,' said Brian

It was ready all right and looked wonderful. Bacon, mushrooms, tomatoes, eggs and lovely fried bread. No way will Katy eat that, the state she came in last night. I knew she had been drinking. The look on Shane's face was giving it away. I just sat with my head down eating my breakfast.

'Is it nice, Maria?' asked Brian

'Yes, thanks. It's really nice,' I replied.

'What about you kids. What do you think about it?'

'Lovely,' they both said at the same time.

They both ate everything on their plate. Then Shane started to laugh.

'What's the joke, Shane?' Brian asked

'Nothing Dad. Just something that happened last night, I was thinking about. I'll tell you later.'

As we were cleaning the plates away, Brian said, 'I didn't think she would eat that breakfast after last night.'

'What do you mean, Brian, about last night?' I asked.

'You know as well as I do that she had far too much to drink last night. I thought by giving her that breakfast it would turn her stomach. But no, it didn't. She enjoyed every bit, which surprised me.'

I could hear Shane talking to Katy. He was saying that it was really nice of Simon to bring her home. And to bring her to the gate as well.

'Don't go trusting everyone will you, Katy. They are not all like Simon,' said Shane.

There was a pause before Katy replied. 'He brought me to the front gate, and it was locked. So he had to help me over the wall, which was so funny.'

'You're not coming out with me next time, Katy.'

'Why not. I was good.'

'You were not good, you drank, and you wouldn't let me take you home.'

'I didn't know someone else brought me home Shane. I'm sorry.'

'If Dad had heard you, you'd have been more than sorry.'

'I don't know how he didn't hear. I was laughing so much, I couldn't stop. So I sat on the log by the back door for a while. When I went to bed, Sacha followed me. She was so quiet.'

'You were really lucky, Katy, to get away with it.'

'I know. I'm going to have a nice relaxing bath.'

Little did she know that we knew all about it! It was a few weeks later when Brian told her and she went crimson.

'You might go red in the face, my girl, but don't think about doing it again, will you.'

'No,' she said.

No more was said after that for many months, and then it was a standing joke.

She never did it again though.

The dresses

While Mother was out selling flowers one day, she called on one of her regular customers who often had flowers from her, and the lady gave her quite a few dresses. When Mother came home after selling her flowers, she gave me these dresses to look at.

'Oh, Mum! They're lovely. Can I try them on?'

'If you want to. Celia can try some on as well, so after you've finished you can go and get Celia.'

I came out of the bedroom with one of the dresses on. I thought it fitted me, as well as looking good on me.

'Oh, my lord, Maria. You'll have to grow a lot more before you can fit into the dresses,' said Mother.

I tried to push my chest out and my shoulders back to see if it would make any difference. I thought it did. By this time, my sister Anne had come in and there was I twirling around in this dress that I thought fitted!

'What have you got on?' Anne asked.

'Mummy has brought home some dresses and I've tried one on, as she thought they might fit me,' I replied.

'Mummy!' Anne shouted out. 'Have you seen Maria in this dress? She looks awful!'

'I told her it didn't fit her, but she was happy just twirling around in it,' said Mother.

'Just come and have a look at her. You can see her salt cellars.'

'You're horrible, Anne,' I said. 'You pick on me all the time.'

'I'm not picking on you,' she said laughing. 'I would much rather you had a nicer fitting dress on than those. None of them will fit you.'

'Can I go and get Celia to try on the dresses?' I asked Mother.

'Yes, of course you can,' Mother said. 'And Anne, you can stop laughing at her.'

'But Mum, you must admit it was too big for her.'

The next thing I knew, Anne had gone to get my cousin Becky to look at the dresses.

Once I had told Celia, she and I were running up the road as fast as we could. As soon as we got back, the dresses went on again. We liked them and we thought they looked really nice on, but all we could hear was laughter from Anne and Becky. 'They look like old grannies dressed up,' they said.

Celia and I just took the dresses off and stomped out. When we got outside, we looked at each other and just burst out laughing.

'Do you think they looked that big on us, Celia?' I asked.

'Well yours did,' said Celia. 'It hung off your shoulders. In fact I think you could have got another person in with you.'

'I didn't look that bad, did I? I didn't like it when Anne said I had salt cellars, whatever that means. You wait, Celia. Anne and Becky will have them on in a few days' time.'

'Oh shut up, Maria, and stop moaning will you.'

With that, I never said another word and started to hop and skip down the road with Celia.

The Gypsy

The world has always been fascinated by the shadowy ambiguity of the Gypsy people, or Romany, as they call themselves. They have been shrouded in mystery as they travelled the world perpetuating many myths.

Gypsies still keep their customs, and local people still regard them with curiosity and suspicion. They are very reluctant to share their secrets with other than their own people.

Gypsies have been persecuted for many years for lots of reasons. Their lifestyle is totally different to a *gaje*, or non-Gypsy. Their lifestyle causes them to be outsiders.

Gypsies are normally dark skinned with dark, bold, flashing eyes. However, it's not unusual to find golden or crimson haired Gypsies. They are very proud and independent, life loving and passionate people. Gypsies are best noted for their occult skills, healing arts and storytelling abilities. It's still said that Gypsies can cast a Gypsy curse!

Gypsies are wanderers, never staying too long in one place. All Gypsies are considered part of one great family. From time to time they will permit a *gaje* to be accepted into their clan. This is usually done by marrying into the family.

I don't think a non-Gypsy would like the Gypsy way, as it's not an easy way of life. It's hard with all the moving around they have to do.

The time Becky's husband came home by horse and cart

My cousin Becky's husband Billy decided to go out for a drink. He took his horse and cart as it was such a nice summer's evening.

'Cheerio, Becky. I won't be long.'

'Cheerio, Billy, and don't have too many beers.'

Away he went on his horse and cart. I suppose it's about five miles down to the pub - not that far, but far enough. It's quite a busy road, but Billy had a lot of experience with horses, and when it came to driving the horse and cart he was good.

Becky had decided not to go that evening, as she would rather be busy cleaning her caravan out (especially her brass and her Crown Derby) than drinking beer.

I don't suppose Billy will be too long, thought Becky, as it was getting quite dark. He's got the horse and cart tonight, not the car. So she sat down with a cup of coffee for a well-earned rest, intending to watch television.

Within seconds she fell asleep in the armchair. The next thing she knew, there was this loud banging on her door. She jumped up with such a fright she felt quite dizzy. She staggered towards the door.

'Is that you, Bill?' she called out in this soft voice. She knew no one would get into the yard, as they had eight-foot wrought iron fences all round as well as the eight-foot iron gates. Who could it be at this time of night? She stood upright. It must be Billy. I'll kill him, she thought!

'It's alright, Becky. We're the police. We've got your Billy here with us,' came the reply.

At that very moment she was thinking she didn't really want to see the state he was in. 'Is that you, Bill? Where's your bloody key? If you're drunk, lord help you. Billy, what are the police doing with you?'

Becky turned the key in the door and opened it slightly. It shot open and Billy promptly fell in.

'How come you've brought him home?' asked Becky.

'Oh, we found him heading towards the traffic lights,' replied one of the policemen, 'and he didn't look that good. Plus the fact it was not safe for the horse either. So we pulled him over, and the other officer sat with him on the cart while he drove the horse and cart home. I drove behind and gave him a police escort!'

'I'll give him bloody police escort,' shouted Becky. 'Billy you said only a couple of beers!'

'I've only had a couple, Becky!' said Billy.

'Good night and thank you, officer. I'll sort him out now.' She turned around and yelled, 'Billy, where are you?'

'I'm here,' Billy called out.

'Who's that now?' said Becky, hearing another tap at the door. Opening the door, she saw the same two officers.

'We just want to say that Billy's horse and cart is in the yard, still harnessed up. Can you manage to unharness the horse?'

'Yes, thank you, officer,' she replied with a half smile.

Once Becky had unharnessed the horse, she fed and watered it. After this she walked it into the field, which was next to their caravan. Then she went indoors shouting, 'Billy, where are you? I told you last time what I thought of you when you came home drunk!'

When Becky eventually found him, he was not in bed and where do you suppose Billy was? Not in bed, but asleep in the armchair. Becky didn't attempt to speak to him. He was snoring away and wouldn't have heard her anyway. Besides, when he was awake it only went in one ear and out the other.

Billy stayed in the armchair all night and Becky went to bed without him, and as far as I know, things haven't changed to this day, except that Billy takes the horse and cart out in the afternoons, rather than in the evenings. What's more, he's watched very closely these days by the police!

When Becky told me the story she was laughing about it all the time.

Summer evenings

I used to love the summer evenings. After Dad had come home from work and we'd had dinner, we would sit on the back step just talking. I must have been such a questioning child! I loved Dad to tell me stories about how they all slept, especially in the bender tents, and what they used to eat. I didn't mind hearing about the rabbit. It was the hedgehog that made me feel very sad.

'Don't tell me how you kill any of the animals, Dad,' I used to say.

'It was all we had in those days to eat. We never thought about it. We just killed it,' Dad said. The rabbit was put into a pot for a good old stew with vegetables. But, Father explained, the hedgehog was cooked in a different way (which I say more about in the chapter "Just a Few Weeks Away from Anne's Wedding Day").

The thought of this was making me feel quite sick. 'Are you alright my girl?' asked Dad.

'No, not really,' I said. 'I feel sick at the thought of the poor hedgehog. It's funny, Dad. The rabbit doesn't make me feel sick. I suppose it's because we eat rabbit quite a lot.'

'I suppose so, my girl, but how do you know we haven't just been eating hedgehog?'

'We haven't, have we, Dad?' I said with this sickening feeling in my stomach. 'It's disgusting, Dad, and horrible. In my mind I've got a picture of the ones that are squashed on the roads.'

'Never mind, me girl, be happy for them, as they're the ones that got away.' I looked up at him, and he has this smile on his face that I felt I could easily wipe away with one blow. But I couldn't as he was my father.

Mind you, I did in a way get my own back on him. He used to put a small cage out, which really was a bird trap. My dad wanted bullfinches to go into the cage. He used to keep these birds as they were really good singers, which he liked. He also had canaries. I would sit with a glass and keep pushing this cork around the glass to get the canaries to sing.

This I didn't mind doing as they had nice large cages for them to fly around in. But the bullfinches were wild birds and used to being outside. So I used to lie in wait for the bird to fly down for the bait. As soon as it was caught, I used to let it go again.

Then I would leave the trap down so no other birds could get into the cage.

Before Dad came home I always laid the trap door so it had fallen half way down and with the bait gone. Every evening Dad would say to Mother, 'Well I don't know, but that damn door is down again but there aren't any birds inside.'

'Never mind, Ambrose. Perhaps tomorrow you'll catch one.'

My dad never did, because every morning I would either let the bird out or I would have left the trap door down so it looked as if the bird had knocked it when trying to get the bait. In the end, Dad gave up trying to get bullfinches. He just concentrated on his canaries.

Marlborough Road

I decided to visit Marlborough Road, just for old time's sake. I still feel I was so happy living there, although I understand why my parents wanted to leave the bungalow. We would be moving into a cottage, which would have a bathroom, and the kitchen would be bigger for Mother. In addition, we would have a separate dining room and a nice sized lounge, whereas the bungalow had only a lounge come dining room.

There would be a bus stop right outside the cottage. I knew this was going to be wonderful for Mother, as most days she caught the bus to go to Romford, to sell her flowers. This would save Mother lots of time as there would be no more walking to the bus stop. The only thing was that Mother and Father had never lived in a place which had stairs.

The nicest thing of all which we were going to enjoy was the toilet. It would be indoors, and not outside! I was sure they would adapt and knew they were looking forward to the move far more than I was, but I would be leaving all my friends behind.

Suddenly there was a car hooting at me. I turned around, and there was this chap leaning out of his car window, not looking very pleased, and shouting out, 'If you stand there too long like that you'll get knocked over, love.'

I just stepped out of his way and didn't feel like saying anything. All I could hear inside my head were my cousins and friends playing in the road, just as we used to, many years ago.

I started to walk down the road looking from side to side, thinking not much had changed really. Then I noticed no street lamp outside Mrs Dale's house. The fun we had had throwing an old bike tyre up, and trying to get it over the top of the lamp-post. We used to play for hours.

'Hello, it's Maria Hearne isn't it?' I turned around, and there stood Mrs Dale. I hadn't seen her for years.

'I'm looking for the lamp-post. Where's it gone to?'

'Oh, they took it down, after you moved away,' she said standing there laughing. All I said was, 'I bet Hilary missed throwing the old tyre up and trying to get it over the lamp-post.'

We both looked at each other and laughed. After a long chat about the past, I said good-bye and carried on walking. I eventually got to the end of the road, turned around, and thought of all the fun we had had.

If only we could turn the clock back!

Nowhere to go

My father used to say you had to have a very strong caravan, and a good horse to pull it. You would always see them travelling in a line, and there would be quite a few of them. All the caravans would be painted in different colours, glittering in the sunshine. It was very rare that you would see one caravan on its own. Camping together they could help each other.

Generally they liked to park outside town. They had usual stopping places including ground where farmers allowed them to stop. Then they used to go into town where the women would sell their lucky heather and do the odd fortune telling.

It was very hard times in those days. When it was cold, we would feel so frozen that our bones would feel sore and our hands would be very rough. In the evenings we would sit outside around the fire telling our stories of the day while cleaning our horse brass. We were very proud of our brass, and it was so important to us that it should be kept clean and sparkling like our caravans, Dad said.

Night in Ireland (Brian)

'Well, I give it to you Mac. Ireland is certainly a pretty place. Everywhere is so green and the people are so friendly. The Guinness tastes good too. It's going down and it's not even touching the sides of my throat. That's what I call a real smooth drop of drink.'

Brian and Mac were on a driving job in Ireland.

'The people over here talk to you as if they have known you for years,' continued Brian. 'That man over there has asked me to come back again and he'll take me fishing, I don't like fishing so I just said thanks and walked on!'

'You ungrateful bugger. What do you like?' asked Mac.

'I like lots of things.'

'Such as, Brian? On second thoughts I don't want to know! I tell you what, I'll have another Guinness. This one's empty.'

'A few of these, Mac, and I won't need any rocking. I'll sleep like a baby.'

'There's another pub down the road. Do you fancy trying it?'

'How far down the road?'

'About a mile and a half. The walk will do us good.'

'No thanks. Let's stay here. By the time we get there it will be time for us to be getting back. And we don't want to lose any drinking time, do we?'

'You old sod, Brian. You're always telling me off for drinking too much. Now who's calling the kettle black? Here, get hold of that, and get yourself up to the bar and get another drink. Brian, how does that song go, "*let's have another one?*"'

'Why not Mac. That'll be good and everyone will join in. Are you going to have something to eat?'

'Yes. What about a good bowl of Irish stew?'

'On your bike, Mac. This is summer not winter. Still, I forgot you always do things back to front! No offence Mac, but you are Irish.'

'What do you mean by back to front, Brian?'

'Arse about face. Come on Mac. Let's see what they have to offer us to eat. I could do with a nice piece of steak.'

'If that's what you want you shall have it. Come on, let's go and get it.'

'Mac, what time are we leaving for the ferry in the morning?'

'Just eat your dinner, Brian. I'll tell you later.'

'You bloody won't. You'll tell me now. I know you. We could be here all night, and then back to the lorry for just a few hours sleep. So what time is it that we leave for the ferry? Tell me before I throttle you!'

'Stop panicking. We're leaving at seven in the evening.'

'That's more like it, Mac. Now be a good boy and get me another Guinness.' Then as Mac got up to go to the bar, Brian adds, 'I tell you, Mac, God knows what I'll be like in the morning with your roads. The way they're built here makes me feel as bad as if I'd been on the booze!'

'Whatever has the standard of the roads got to do with you feeling bad, Brian?'

'The roads are on the piss!'

'That's not nice to say about our roads. We Irish lads are noted for our buildings. Well the roads do lean a bit, don't they? Perhaps when they built them, they've been out on the Guinness the night before.'

'Oh, you're agreeing with me then, Mac.'

'Don't worry, Brian. I'm thinking of something that the British can't build. I don't think you Englishmen are very good at getting up in the morning!'

'I tell you what, Mac.'

'What are you going to tell me now, Brian?'

'I think I'm going to have to get my bucket out tonight instead of my usual lemonade bottle, because after all this Guinness I could be up most of the night. And no way am I getting out of my lorry to do a wee!'

Brian's sheepskin coat

I first started going out with Brian in December 1963. I can remember it was a very cold winter, and Brian had bought himself a light sheepskin coat. It was rather nice and I must say he looked good in it.

He used to take me to London quite a bit just to see the sights, and I loved it. We would go and see a show and then afterward he would take me round to the back door where the actors would come out. The very first time I saw an actor come out the back door I was expecting someone very smart. But no. He had on an old coat which looked as though the cats had been laying on it.

Saturday afternoons were nice because Brian would take me to London and we would just sit outside one of the coffee shops, drinking our coffee and having a cake. Nothing really special, but I enjoyed just sitting watching people go by with their different ways of dressing.

We would have to queue to go into the afternoon matinee when we went to a show. It was quite cold sometimes and Brian would unbutton his coat so I could stand closer to him. Then he would button it up to keep me warm. That was in those days but I don't think it would happen now.

Brian always kept his sheepskin coat and although he has died I still have it hanging up in the wardrobe. I couldn't part with it. It has so many warm memories.

My sister Anne had a sheepskin coat the same time as Brian, but I didn't like them myself. I preferred leather coats. My mum bought me a really nice light green three quarter length leather coat. I loved it and wearing that and my short skirts and high heels I felt the bees' knees.

I had that coat for many years. I don't know why I got rid of it; I suppose it was no longer in fashion really. You know what us girls are like. If only I had kept it, as they are in fashion again. Only one thing, I wouldn't be able to get into it. Mind you, the weight I'm losing at the moment it won't be long before I can get into it again. High heels are also back again. If only I'd kept mine. Mind you, I wouldn't be able to walk in them now. I would probably fall over and break my neck, like my father said I would when I had my first pair of high heels. I'm still a size five, but my feet have got wider! So I wouldn't get them on anyway.

When Brian was courting me, there I would be in my bedroom making myself up to look really nice. Then suddenly I would hear his car pull up, followed by the sound of his shoes. He used to have steel caps on his heels which used to make this wonderful noise. My stomach used to turn with excitement and my face would flare up all red in places. It used to upset me so much that my make-up was all spoilt.

Once I was outside in the fresh air the redness would disappear, so on would go the powder and lipstick once again.

I was so fussy about my hair. It had to be just right, and if I didn't feel it was right I would comb it through again. I used to love my hair. I loved having all the different styles.

I never wore anything to keep me warm. I didn't have to as Brian would put me in his sheepskin to keep me nice and warm if we had to stand around anywhere.

What lovely days. Still never mind, I have the memories now to keep me warm.

My garden

Since Brian died, my garden has been such a comfort to me. I didn't do anything in the garden when Brian was alive, except water it with the hose. I found it so relaxing. It helped me to think of many things which I wanted to do, especially my book. I still find it relaxing, but with sadness in my heart.

It's such a pretty garden, with lots of lovely colourful shrubs. When I'm watering it, I'm always talking to Brian, and I know he's with me. As I look out of my office window, I can see the summerhouse. I have everything I want in it.

On the right I can see many different colourful plants. Then, to the left of the summerhouse, I have the fruit trees which Brian put in. He grew them into a superb fan shape. Looking at them I can see I will have quite a task on my hands when it's time for pruning. Shane and I have been to our local nursery to ask about this, and when is the best time to start on it. Not only do I have two large pear trees, I also have two fan-shaped apple trees as well. I have so many shades of green which blend in with the colours of the other plants which are flowering.

I have so many different kinds of birds in my garden, and I have put many seed containers all around the garden. They are hidden in the trees in the back garden. I have also hung containers for the grape vine, which is outside my back door. Brian put that up four years ago and it's beautiful. Brian and I used to sit under it and have our meals on nice days. When the grapes are out they are the large black ones and very sweet.

Many people used to say to Brian, 'Are you going to make wine with them?'

'No,' he used to say. 'They are for the birds.'

Brian and I used to sit under the vine having our coffee, and the blackbirds would dive into the vine to get their grapes. The birds are so tame. They come right up to the back door, and when I'm gardening they are all around my feet for food. They are not even worried about my little dog Betsy. In fact, they hop right up to her, which is wonderful to see.

Brian used to love gardening and found it very relaxing. So he was ever so upset when he had very bad arthritic knees and could not do it. He could hardly walk some days and it was so sad to see. Then the surgeon decided to operate on one of his knees. Brian was so glad he had it operated on, although for a good few weeks afterwards it was very painful. After Brian had got through the pain, his specialist asked him if he would like the other knee operated on.

'Can I go home and have a think about it?' Brian asked.

'Of course you can,' said the specialist. 'When you feel ready, just ring the centre and leave a message with the nurse.'

I could see he thinking about it while he was driving home. When we got there he said, 'I don't think I'll have the other knee done. Having this one done was so painful.'

'I know it was painful Brian,' I said. 'But look at you now. You're walking around beautifully with that knee.'

We didn't say any more after that. I just left him to mull it over. Anyway, he did have the other knee done. For a few weeks it was painful, but once he had got over the pain again he was up and doing quite a bit in the garden. This was lovely to see, because for many weeks it was a struggle for him.

Now the garden is mine to do, although I do have help from my grandson Shaun. He cuts the lawn for me, and I have my son Shane to do the extra bits and pieces for me. I don't know what I would do without them both.

Once it is all tidy, I go and get myself a cup of tea. Then I sit in the garden and just look at it. It's such a pretty garden, thanks to Brian. As I'm drinking my tea, the birds are coming right up to my back door. They are looking at me and chirping away, asking for food. So I'm going to feed my little friends now.

I was so shy

When I first started to go out with Brian I was so shy, especially when we went for a meal. I would be sitting there thinking, don't move your mouth too quickly - he'll hear you chewing.

'Come on, Maria. Eat up. I've nearly finished.'

'Would you like my other piece of steak?' I asked him. It was the daftest thing to order, really. Steak gets in the mouth and no way can you get rid of it, especially if you get a tough piece. Mine wasn't tough. It was my shyness that put me off eating.

My shyness got worse when Brian took me home to meet his parents. This was a Sunday afternoon, and I was dreading it!

When he introduced me to his parents, his dad and I got on straight away, but I was so scared of his mother. I knew his sister Janet and his brother John. Not really that well, but well enough not to be shy with them.

I don't know how many butterflies I had in my stomach. In fact they felt like elephants going round and round.

Every time his mum asked if I would like tea with them, I said no thanks as I was not really that hungry. It was bad enough sitting at the table with Brian when we went out for something to eat. I certainly couldn't face having afternoon tea with the family, as much as they were nice to me. It took me weeks before I actually sat at the table with them all. It was one Sunday afternoon when I was over at Brian's. I knew his mum was getting tea ready and, any minute now, she would be coming to the lounge door and calling out, 'Tea is ready.' Janet was sitting with me and we were chatting away. I looked up and there was Brian's mum poking her head around the door. I was beginning to feel sick at this point.

'Tea everyone. Come on, Maria. Come and have tea with us.' I looked at Janet.

'Yes, Maria. Come and have tea,' she said.

With that, I got up. Well, I didn't have a choice. Janet had hold of my arm and walked me through to the dining room. As I sat down my legs were trembling. They were going ten to the dozen and I hoped no one had noticed.

The table was laid out beautifully. There were sandwiches, tomatoes, celery, cucumber, and all sorts of cakes. Everyone was chatting away, and Janet was chatting to me. I couldn't take it in, I was feeling so nervous. If I'm going to stay with Brian I'm going to have to buck my ideas up.

'Would you like a piece of celery, Maria?' Brian's father asked.

'No thank you.' I couldn't risk that. It would certainly make a lot of noise in my mouth. Whenever am I going to get over my shyness? It seemed as though we were at the table for hours.

'Has everyone had enough to eat?' Brian's mother asked.

'Yes thank you,' I said in a soft squeaky voice.

Brian's mother started to clear away the table. I got up and started to help her. It was only right, I thought, even though I didn't eat enough to keep a mouse alive.

'Thank you,' she said. 'Just put the things on the side, and I'll do the rest.'

'That's alright. I'll help you clear away the things.'

'Thank you, dear,' she said with a smile.

I looked at her and smiled back. I was still very frightened of her. I don't know why.

As the weeks went by it did get easier when I went to Brian's for tea. His dad used to make me feel relaxed. He would be sitting at the top of the table, making jokes and laughing all the time. In fact, apart from Janet, he was the one who made me feel at home.

I didn't go many Sundays as Brian would come and pick me up in the evening, and then we would go out. Often, we just went for a quiet drink, as I had to be in by ten o'clock sharp. If I wasn't in by then my parents were there to let me know that I was late.

They were quite strict with me getting in on time. I had to get up early in the morning, and I wasn't that good at getting up. In fact I hated mornings. I still do to this day. Shane takes after me, but Katy loves mornings.

I come alive after eleven in the morning, and I love evenings. I'm quite happy to do whatever I have to do in the evening and don't seem to get tired at all. I much preferred Brian to come and pick me up from home. That way I didn't have to sit at his parents table and have to try to eat. I think it took me nearly a year before I felt really comfortable having meals with his family. Once I got over the actual fear, there was no stopping me. I enjoyed and loved every meal with them after that.

About the children

When the children were born they were so different. Shane was born on the 2$^{nd.}$ March 1966. He weighed seven pounds, and had lovely long black hair down to his shoulders. It was very thick and there was lots of it. I used to put it into a lovely curl on the top of his head, and I was so proud of that curl. My parents called it a quiff. It was like boys had in the early sixties. He looked so much like my dad.

One day while I was out shopping I saw my cousin Jenty.

'Oh let me have a look at your baby, Maria.' As she was saying this, her head was under the hood of the pram. 'Maria, he is so much like your dad.' That made me feel really good.

As he grew up, he had the features of my dad, but a lot of Granddad Everett's ways. If we were visiting Granddad Everett he always went outside with him, messing around with the car. Granddad would be laying underneath and Shane would be doing the same as they chatted away to each other. I could never send him over in good clothes. When they came in Nanny would say, 'Go and wash your hands the pair of you.'

Granddad would be laughing all over his face. It was fun to watch the pair of them. They were great friends.

Shane loved playing with his cars. He would play for hours with them. When it was time for bed he would put all his cars very gently back into the box where they belonged. He never threw any of his toys around. He was so good with them.

He never slept much, but when Brian took him for a ride in the van he hadn't got down the road before Shane was fast asleep. The problem was getting him out of the van without waking him. He managed it most times though, thank goodness.

He used to have one of those steering wheels that stuck on the dashboard. He would be steering away quite happily thinking he was driving the van. He must have been about two at this time. I was always happy when he was doing something, but bedtime was certainly another matter.

He was very curious as a child, and always thought things through before he did anything. He loved his little old bike, and used to ride around our garden for ages. But one thing he didn't like was heights.

I remember one Christmas time. My in-laws and Janet, my sister-in-law, and her husband and children were down at our house. Like me, Janet had two children. Heath was born two days after Shane and Donna was born two months after Katy. We had eaten our dinner and played pass the parcel, lucky dip, and many more games with the children. We were all in the front room except the children who were playing in the conservatory. As Janet and I were getting afternoon tea ready we could hear them laughing.

'It's nice to hear them play nicely,' Janet said. 'Yes,' I replied.

We laid the table, and thought it would be better for everyone to help themselves rather than sitting back down at the table. Everything looked really nice.

'Shall we call everyone in so they can get something to eat?' I asked. 'Or we could lay the table in the conservatory for the children to have their food. We can sit with them. It will be fun, Janet. What do you think?'

'Yes,' she said. 'I'll go and lay the table for them.'

I was washing up at the sink, when Janet put her head through the window. 'Come out here quickly,' she said.

'Oh my God! Whatever have they done?'

'They've been drinking the beer, Maria, that's what they've done, and they're drunk, all four of them.'

'We'd better get Brian and Mick,' I said. I didn't know whether to laugh or cry at this point.

'Brian! Mick! Can you come out here for a minute,' I called out. Brian and Mick were standing in the dining room. 'What, do you want?' Brian said. 'We're watching a film.'

'You'd better go and have a look at the children in the conservatory,' I said biting on my lip. With that Brian and Mick walked out to the conservatory. By this time I was beginning to feel quite sick, and very worried about the children's condition.

'Bloody hell! What's been going on out here?' asked Brian.

'It looks as though they've been on the beer,' Mick said, trying not to laugh.

Brian, grinning all over his face, turned and looked at me and Janet. 'Well, we'd better sober them up. There's four of them and four of us. So we can have one each. Come on, don't just stand there looking at them. We're going to take them for a nice walk.'

So that's what we did, although all they wanted to do was sleep. Mind you, after a while they did show signs of sobering up and we decided to take them back home.

They certainly didn't want anything to eat. I shouldn't think they would after the beer they'd drunk!

Moving into the flat

I was nine months pregnant with Shane, and the council had given us a flat at Pilgrims Hatch. The block of flats was called Elizabeth House, and we lived at number thirty six.

Elizabeth House was in fact comprised of two blocks of flats. On the top floor of our block was a long balcony which went from one end to the other, which was rather nice. Also, the grounds were well kept.

Our flat was lovely. It had two floors, with a bathroom and separate toilet. The main bedroom, which was ours, was a good size. So was the second bedroom. It was great, and it meant that we had to go upstairs to bed. Downstairs, we had a bay window in the front room, which was lovely because it let in a lot of light.

The only thing which I didn't really like was that there were so many stairs to climb to reach our flat. Once I had the baby, pulling the pram up those stairs was quite hard going. Most of the time I would take the baby out of the pram and carry him upstairs. I used to leave the pram outside a friend's flat downstairs. When Brian came home from work he would come and get me. Then we would go down and collect the pram and carry it upstairs. No way was I going to bump my pram up the stairs and damage the wheels. Whenever I wanted to go out there was always someone around to help with getting the pram downstairs for me.

Our washing line was downstairs, so when we had done our washing and wanted to peg it out we had to go all the way down the stairs yet again. Then when it was dry, we had to go back down to fetch it in. I always made sure I was up nice and early so I could get my washing out early, that's if it was a nice drying day. I tell you what, it kept me fit. I always had to keep my eye on the weather, as it wasn't like just stepping out into the back garden.

After Shane started school, I got to know most of the people who lived in the flats because many of them had young children who went to the same school.

Our Katy was in fact born at Elizabeth House, although when she was nine months old we moved to Gloucester Road. I was so pleased to be moving and having a back garden for the children to play in.

Mick, my brother-in-law, helped us move. He turned up in one of the lorries from the farm where he worked.

'I do hope he has washed the lorry out well!' I said to Brian.

'Of course he has,' said Brian. 'You don't think for one minute, do you, that he'd bring a dirty lorry to us?'

We had so many people to help us. The move to our new home was completed in no time. From where we lived to where we were going wasn't that far. In fact it was a short walk for me. So I put the children in the pram, and off I went.

I was so excited to be moving into a house with a garden. Brian was as well. He was itching to start on the garden. But he had made up his mind to decorate the house first. That was with the help of his brother John, and Mick, his brother-in-law. By the time they had finished it looked really nice. When the decorating was finished, Brian worked in the front garden for a couple of hours every evening after coming home from work.

We had stocks and many other flowers in the front garden, including dahlias under the two front windows. We also had beetroot growing in the front garden, as well as other vegetables. Brian said they made colour, which they did, and very nice too, in many ways!

Going to get my wedding dress

I decided to buy my wedding dress, but I couldn't afford the one I wanted. It had beautiful lace with lots of petticoats. The dress had a lovely train with wonderful layers of Spanish lace. I fell in love with it the moment I saw it in the shop window. But how could I get a dress like that? My wages were low, and I had just seen the dress of my dreams.

The next day I went into work and told everyone all about the dress. I was nearly in tears just talking about it. Every time I closed my eyes I could see the dress displayed in the shop window. I sat down, putting my hands to my head and trying to think where I could get a dress like it, but at a much lower price.

My friend Mavis, who I was working with, called out, 'Maria, I know where you can get a dress like the one you saw.'

'Where?' I asked.

'In Hornchurch. When we finish our shift we could go if you like.'

'I'm up for that,' I said.

I couldn't wait for my shift to end. All I could think of was the dress. Half past two came and Mavis and I were out the door so quickly we nearly fell over each other. We ran all the way down to Brentwood railway station. I don't think we even stopped for breath. Once we were at the station, we got our tickets and went straight to the platform to wait for our train to take us to Hornchurch. We were both pacing up and down like school children.

Eventually the train arrived. We jumped on and sat down on the nearest seats. Mind you, the train was empty so we could have had a pick of many, but we chose the seats by the door. We chatted all the way there, mainly about the dress. No sooner had the train arrived at

Hornchurch than we were off towards the shop. We were both out of breath by the time we arrived.

Mavis had said it was a big shop and it certainly was. I had never seen so many wedding dresses before, all hung up with plastic covers over them. As soon as we got in the door a shop assistant came over to us.

'Can I help you?' she asked with quite a nice smile.

'I'm looking for a wedding dress with lots of petticoats and with a long train, but I would like to have lots of layers,' I replied.

'If you'd like to come over here I can show you the dresses which we have in the range I think you're looking for.'

We followed the shop assistant very slowly, both of us glancing at the wonderful dresses. It was breathtaking just looking at them. I hadn't even got to the stage where I'd tried any on!

'I'll get some from the rails and put them over here for you to look at,' the assistant said.

Mavis and I were sitting in these two very nice chairs, and I was thinking that there was no way I was going to be able to afford one of the dresses out of that shop. My mouth was beginning to get quite dry with the prices.

'Would you like to try this one on, madam?'

I was so deep in thought that I jumped when she spoke to me. The poor lady must have thought, what have I got here!

I tried many dresses on, until at last I found the one I wanted, 'Oh, Maria!' Mavis said. 'It's beautiful. Is it like the one you were looking for?'

'Yes, it's just what I was looking for,' I said, holding the dress and swaying from side to side. I was too afraid to ask how much it was.

'Do you want to buy or hire, madam?' Hire? I hadn't thought of that.

'Well, people usually hire when they come here, although you can buy if you should wish. To buy you would be looking at nearly £500. To hire for the weekend it would be about £150, with a mink cape.'

I looked at Mavis. Then I turned and said, 'I would like to hire it please.'

'Would you like the cape as well, madam?'

'Yes please,' I replied.

'When would you like it for?' the shop assistant asked me.

'I'm getting married on the 27$^{th.}$ March, at two thirty.'

'Oh that will be fine. If you like, we can deliver.'

'That would be great.'

'There will be a small charge of ten pounds for delivering. If you like, we can pick it up. The amount would be twenty pound.'

'Yes, please,' I said with no hesitation. 'No one else will be wearing the dress will they, as I would like to think that I was the first one to wear it?'

'This one is new. It only came in last week. As you can see, it has the designer's name on it, and new dresses are on a separate rail. It hasn't even been tried on by anyone else. I'll put it out the back for you and we will deliver two days before your wedding day. There's also a lady who goes out to people's houses to help them dress for their wedding day if you wish.' 'How much does she charge?' I asked.

'Twenty pound. As well as helping you dress, she will see you to your car with your father. Then she will follow behind the car and when you get out she will make sure that your dress is perfect for going into the church.'

'Well, the church is only next door but one, so she won't have to go that far will she. I wanted to walk to church, but my father said I must have a car to take me. By the time I get in the car it will be time for me to get out.' I giggled.

'That's lovely to have a church so near to you,' said the shop assistant.

'It is, really. But I would much rather walk to church.'

Then the shop assistant put her head down to total up the cost. This is going to cost me a bomb, I thought. Still, it's a lot cheaper than buying the dress. And I have a new one, not one that has already been worn. I was so excited, I looked at Mavis and we gave each other a big smile.

'Well, only two weeks to go, and now you're all set for the big day,' said Mavis.

'Yes, I've got everything now,' I replied.

The shop assistant called me to the counter to pay. This is it, I thought. What do they say? This will break the bank. I don't care, though, as long as I look good for the day.

'In total, madam, it comes to one hundred and seventy pound.'

I opened my bag and got out my purse. The shop assistant counted the money very slowly and then gave me my change, which wasn't a lot.

'Thank you, madam,' said the shop assistant in a very soft, polite voice.

'Goodbye,' I said and walked out of the shop feeling very excited. Mavis looked pleased, since she had found the shop for me.

'Come on, let's go and have a nice cup of coffee,' I said.

'That sounds good,' she said, smiling at me. 'Are you happy with the dress then, Maria?'

'Yes thank you, Mavis. If it wasn't for you I don't know what I would have done. The shop was wonderful. Thank you.'

The trailer in the air

Shane and I were having a nice quiet evening indoors when all of a sudden the telephone rang. I got up to answer it, hoping it wasn't going to be Brian to say, 'Come and get me. I'm coming home tonight.' That would certainly mean an early morning for me, which I really loathe. Early mornings do not go down very well with me.

The next thing I heard was Brian shouting down the phone. 'Get Shane to drive down to the lay-by.'

'What lay-by?' I asked.

'It's the one near us down the road. Don't hang about. Be quick, the pair of you.'

With that the phone went dead. I promptly put the phone down, and shouted out to Shane. 'Shane, come on. We have to get Dad.'

'Whatever does he want now?' asked Shane.

'I don't know. He just said come quick.'

Well off we went. We took Shane's car, as Brian had told me to do. As we approached the lay-by where Brian had parked his lorry, Shane suddenly burst out laughing.

'Look out of the window, Mum. How on earth has Dad got the trailer in that position? It's stuck right up in the air.'

I couldn't say anything, I was so worried. All I kept wondering was how on earth would Shane's car pull him off that. The nearer we got, the worse it looked. Shane was still laughing, and I'd started to laugh myself. I think it was through worry, really.

As we turned into the lay-by, Brian was standing beside his lorry looking rather worried. Mind you, the position it was in I think any lorry driver would be looking worried.

Shane got out of the car and I could hear him say, 'What have you done, and how on earth did it happen?'

I was watching Brian very closely. He wasn't shouting, but his voice was perhaps a little bit loud. Shane was underneath the front of the lorry. 'Get out of the car, Maria,' Brian called out to me.

I got straight out and walked towards the grass verge. No way were they going to get me to drive the car, and I wasn't having them shout at me. But by this time they were in quite a mood.

'Shall I walk back home, as I don't think you really need me, do you?' I said.

'You stay there. We might need you for something,' Brian said. I really didn't like the thought of that. It was at this point that Shane got into his car and started it up. How on earth was Shane going to pull that thirty-eight ton lorry with his Mazda, I was thinking to myself.

'Go on, Shane. Take it easy, and when I tell you to stop, stop straight away,' Brian called out.

Poor old Shane didn't answer. I reckon his throat was too dry to talk. Suddenly, I noticed that the lorry was moving. Oh, my God, I thought. It'll pull Shane's car in half. Every so often I could hear, 'Stop!' and then, 'Bit more!' I just didn't like what I was seeing.

'That's it Shane. We're all done,' Brian eventually called out. 'You won't do that again, will you Dad? You'll have to be more careful at that corner.'

Shut up Shane, I was thinking, and please keep your opinions to yourself.

The sweat was running down Brian's face so badly it looked like someone had poured a bucket of water over him. He was such a hard-working man and all he got was kick back. But he never moaned about it.

'What time are you leaving in the morning Brian?' I asked.

'About four. Shane will get up, won't you, and take me down to the lorry?'

'Mum's better at mornings than I am,' said Shane.

'You're both the same. You hate mornings, the pair of you.'

I'll take you in the morning, Brian,' I said.

'Well done Mum,' said Shane. 'Don't wake me up when you come in, will you.'

It wasn't long before we had all had our dinner. Brian watched some television and then went to bed as he was getting up early. Brian didn't sleep that well. All he kept doing was moving around in the bed. He had the lorry on his mind, and I often wonder why he used to come home when he had to get up so early in the morning. He could have easily stayed in the bed in the lorry and let the men who were going to unload him in the morning wake him up. That way he would have a far better rest.

Anyway, I took him down to his lorry at four o'clock in the morning. I waited while he started the lorry up, and waved him off. Then I went straight back home to my bed.

As I lay in bed I kept thinking about the trailer up in the air. Brian wouldn't forget that in a very long time. I must say, thinking back over the years, it did give us a good laugh. Even Brian saw the funny side.

Strawberry picking

It was a beautiful July morning. The sun was shining and we couldn't have wished for a nicer day. Brian had got a day off work. We had decided to go strawberry picking.

I had taken the children to school, and before I got back to our house I noticed that Brian's good friend Peter Brown's car was in our driveway. What on earth does he want, I was thinking to myself, as he was supposed to be at work. I hoped we were still going out as I was so looking forward to picking strawberries, as well as eating them at the same time. I think that's the best part about it, one for the basket and one for the mouth.

There the pair stood drinking tea.

'Hello. What are you doing here?' I asked Peter.

'I thought I would have a day off and see what you two were up to,' said Peter. 'Brian said you were going strawberry picking, so I thought I would come with you if you don't mind.'

'I don't mind,' I said.

'Come on, then. Let's all go otherwise there won't be any left,' Brian said as he was walking out the door.

We climbed into our motor, with our tubs on our laps. I looked down at my tub, and thought to myself, I've got rather a large tub. Goodness knows how much it will cost me to fill up. Brian and Peter were chatting away. I was quite happy to just sit and be quiet. I was so looking forward to the day in the strawberry field.

'Ok, we're here. Out you get,' Brian said.

I jumped out of the motor, and started to walk over to the place where we had to weigh our tubs. Once mine was weighed, off I went to pick my strawberries. Brian and Peter went their own way, and I was quite happy to be on my own. Every so often I could hear them both laughing away.

It wasn't long before I had filled my tub up. 'I'm done,' I shouted out, 'I've got some real nice big ones. What about you two?'

'I've filled mine too. I can't say the same for Peter. He's only got a couple in his tub,' Brian called out.

I walked over to Peter and noticed that his tub was almost empty. 'Couldn't you find any, Peter?' I asked.

'Yes, but they were too nice to put in my tub,' he replied.

'Don't worry. We've got plenty. You can take home some of ours.'

'I don't think so, I've eaten enough today.'

'What about Linda? Wouldn't she like some?'

'I couldn't look at another strawberry for a good few days. I don't think I could even bear the smell of them in the car going home.'

By the look of Peter and Brian, they had both certainly had their fill. Mind you, so had I, which was very nice. I couldn't get fed up with eating strawberries. They taste so nice when they have been picked straight from the field. The ones you buy just don't taste the same.

When the children came home from school and noticed the nice large dish of strawberries, they were two very happy children.

I took some round to my mother-in-law. The first thing she said was, 'Oh thank you, I'll make some jam with those.'

I wasn't into making jam. Strawberries and cream, yes. I must say we did have a wonderful time. We even caught the sun, which was rather nice.

'What time is dinner, Mum?' Katy called out. I don't think it was so much the dinner, it was the dessert that the children were wanting.

The icicles

When I was a child I can remember the winters being ever so cold, not like they are today. The snow used to be really deep, whereas nowadays if we have snow it doesn't stay around for long, thank goodness.

I would walk to school so wrapped up that I could hardly breathe sometimes, with the layers that my mum had put on me. No way was she having me catch a cold. Mind you, I used to take cod liver oil. It was so thick I would push my spoon into the jar and get out a lovely dollop. Then I would put it into my mouth and savour every bit.

It would take me ages to take off my coat and scarf, especially the way that my mum had put my scarf on. She used to wrap it around my neck and across my chest and then tie it at the back. Mind you, I was warm as toast, and my cousin Celia would be wrapped up just the same. No wonder we never got cold. The cold never had a chance to get through.

On the way to school we would get a long stick so we could knock the icicles down. This was very dangerous as they were rather large. They could have fallen on us and cut our heads open. They could have killed us.

We would be warm as toast by the time we got to school, but our hair would be so wet from bashing the icicles down. Being plaited though, the water couldn't really get into my hair. Most of the girls had plaited hair. All we did, when we got to school, was squeeze our hair tightly so the water would come out.

Every so often I would feel water dripping on my neck. It couldn't have got further as I had too many layers on. One thing about my mum, she always insisted on keeping me nice and warm.

Mind you, come play time I never put my scarf on the way Mum did. Well, I just couldn't. All I did was tie it around my neck. If I could have got one of the teachers to help me put it on the same way as Mum I would have missed half the lesson just getting myself out of it!

I can laugh about it now. Look at the children these days. They don't even wear coats to school, and that on a really wet, cold morning. No wonder they have so many coughs. In our day the cold couldn't get to us. Coughs and colds, we never had. I only had to cough slightly and out would come the Vicks to rub on my chest. What with liking the cod liver oil, and not minding the Vicks, no wonder I didn't get any coughs.

The cesspit

One of the houses we lived in had a cesspit. It used to worry me silly. All I kept thinking was, I hope it doesn't fill up too quickly and spill over the top and run down the garden. No way was I lifting the lid. Not that I could anyway!

'Stop worrying about it,' said Brian. 'With only two of us in the house there's no way we'll fill up something that size, providing we keep a check on it.'

We used to have it emptied about every three months, and it cost us seventy-five pound a time.

Every weekend, when Brian came home from being away, I always asked him to check the damn thing.

'It can't fill up in one week,' said Brian, 'unless you've been doing loads and loads of washing.'

'Why on earth couldn't we have bought a place without a hole in the ground, like other people? I hate it, Brian. I have nightmares of waking up one morning and smelling it.'

'Stop worrying about it, will you. Nothing is going to happen.' No way was I convinced. I had got it in my head that something nasty could happen.

One Saturday morning, Brian and Shane were working on the lorries. The oil had to be changed and all the other bits and pieces had to be done as the lorries were due in for a full service first thing Monday. All day long they were out there under the lorries.

Every so often I would see Brian walk by the kitchen window, and go towards the bottom of the garden. I didn't take much notice really, being busy myself sorting out the dinner for the evening. Suddenly I noticed that Brian was carrying a bucket which seemed to be rather heavy. Then along came Shane, who didn't look happy. So I thought it was time for a nice cup of tea.

'Cup of tea,' I shouted.

'Ok, we'll be there in a minute. I hope you've got some nice biscuits, Mum. You know me. I can't drink a cuppa without a biscuit,' Shane was looking through the window.

Before I knew it, they were in and smelling of oil. I quite liked the oil smell as they stood there having their tea. Shane was dunking his biscuit.

'What are you taking to the bottom of the garden in a bucket?' I asked. 'Is it from the lorry? And if so, where are you putting it?'

Brian and Shane looked at each other. There was no smile on their faces.

'Ok, you two. What are you up to?'

Shane was looking down at his boots, and Brian was hovering from one foot to the other.

'Don't worry. It's the oil. We've put it into the cesspit,' said Brian.

'You've done what?' I said. 'It won't sink. It'll stay on top of whatever's in there. When the man comes to empty it, he's not going to like what he sees, and I bet we'll have to pay more to get it emptied.'

'He won't notice it. He only lifts the top of the tank enough so he can get his hose in. You don't think he lifts the lid to have a look what's inside, do you?'

'Well, we'll see, won't we? The cesspit man is coming this week to empty the tank. So let's see who is right or wrong.'

No more was said after that. They finished their tea and away they went. 'I told you what Mum would say, Dad. The oil will float, and you'll have to pay a hell of a lot more.'

I wondered how much it would cost us. A bloody packet, I reckoned.

Well, the cesspit man came the next day. When he knocked at the door, I opened it with a smile.

'Hello,' he said. 'I've come to empty your cesspit. Is it OK to do it now?'

'Sure,' I replied. 'Would you like a cup of coffee?'

'Yes please. Milk and two sugars.'

To allow the man time to check the cesspit, I put the kettle on. A couple of minutes later there was a knock at the door.

'I can't empty your tank out love. You have oil in it, and it's more than my job's worth. It will have to be emptied in a different place to where I usually tip. It's going to cost you a lot more.'

'How much more?'

'Four hundred pound.'

'Bloody hell. Four hundred pound?'

'Sorry, love, but that's what it is.'

'Oh, no!' I said.

'I won't be long. I have to empty what I've got before I can put yours in.' He turned and walked away.

This is it. I'm going to telephone Brian now, and tell him that Shane and I were right.

No, on second thoughts I'll wait until the man has emptied it. Then I'll know exactly how much it will cost us.

I went indoors to make myself a cup of coffee, which I really needed. While I was sitting quietly, the telephone rang.

'Hello Brian. What can I do for you?' I asked.

'I was wondering if the cesspit man has been yet,' Brian replied.

'Oh, he's been alright, but he's got to empty his load first before he can empty our tank.'

'Why can't he do ours then?'

'He saw the oil.'

'Ok then. Let me know when he's done it. Talk to you later, darling.'

I was left holding the phone, as he obviously wasn't going to talk anymore. Still, I'll speak to him later, when the man's been.

Well, it wasn't long before the cesspit man came back and emptied the tank. I took him out a cup of coffee, for a sweetener really. I was thinking he might take a few pounds off the bill!

'I'm finished, love,' I heard. I went straight to the door.

'Four hundred and fifty love.'

I had my cheque book all ready. I wrote the amount and gave him the cheque, and away he went.

Well now it's time to tell Brian the damage. As I was telephoning him I was thinking, no more whisky for you, Brian, for a month.

'Hello,' said Brian.

'It's me, Brian. The man's been, and the total was four hundred and fifty pound.'

'What! I thought it was four hundred pound that he was charging us. Where has the fifty pound come from?'

'That's because he had to tip his other load first. Don't start, Brian. You did it.'

'I'm sorry. I didn't mean to shout,' he said.

'Let's just say that your whisky will be cut out this month due to the cesspit,' I said, laughing.

'Oh well, I suppose we can only laugh about it now. It's done and we can't do anything about it.'

'Don't worry, when you come home at the weekend, Brian, I'll have a nice dinner ready. And your favourite whisky will be waiting for you as usual.'

'That's nice, darling. But what about my nice hot bath, like you always have ready for me?'

'Don't push it, Brian, you're getting your bottle of whisky,' I said, smiling all over my face.

Thank goodness be couldn't see me. I was really trying not to laugh out loud. What else could I do? Crying certainly wouldn't make things any better, would it? Life is too short for that. I know who will laugh when Brian tells him, and that's Shane.

We did have a nice weekend. I got Brian his bath ready, and then we had a lovely dinner. We had plenty of laughs, but not all at poor old Brian's expense. Then we sat back in our chairs, Brian with his whisky and me with my martini, and enjoyed our weekend.

The man next door

When we lived at Bulphan in Essex there was an elderly couple next door. Well, I thought they were old anyway. They had one son, John, who was at the time going to school. I never did know their last name as they kept to themselves quite a bit. The husband used to talk only to say good morning or good night. The wife never spoke, only to be nosy! Well that's what Brian used to say!

Enid, that was the wife's name, often called out, 'Toby, come and get your drink,' or 'Toby get your dinner.'

I thought it was her husband's name, until one day I happened to say, 'Enid, it must be teatime. Your Toby is home.'

'Toby,' she said with this sharp looking expression on her face. 'That's not my husband's name, it's the dog's. My husband's name is John.'

'Sorry,' I said in a squeaky voice.

With that, she turned and walked away. Oh, I thought. I'd better get my facts right next time before I open my mouth!

There was also an older man who lived with them whom they called Uncle. God knows how old he was, but he looked really old. I only ever saw him when he fetched the coal in from outside for their fire.

It was quite funny to watch because they used to store their coal at the bottom of the garden behind their shed. It wasn't that far but nevertheless far enough for an old man. In fact, I never did see John carrying coal up to their back door. Uncle only ever carried one shovel of coal at a time. I used to sit in my dining room sometimes and watch him. Up and down he would go. Never mind, I suppose it got him out of the cottage, and gave him something to do as well.

Around this time Brian had bought me a black poodle, which we named Tops. He had quite a character, did our little Tops. When Uncle used to do his chore of getting in the coal, Tops would sit by our back door and watch. He would wait for Uncle to make another journey down to the bottom of the garden, and as soon as he turned his back, Tops used to pinch lumps of coal from the shovel which was outside their back door. Then he would bring them in and place them by our fire.

This used to be quite a game for our Tops until Uncle noticed what Tops was up to. He then put the coal inside the back door in an old cardboard box away from Tops.

I don't think they really liked Tops, because they were always moaning about him. He was always running after their ducks and they were fenced in as well! Tops used to jump the fence and get in with the ducks. He would chase the ducks round and round their pen. Then the ducks would turn and chase him.

When he had had enough, Tops used to jump back onto the fence, trying to balance, and tormenting the ducks. He used to look so funny. The ducks would be hissing at him, and he would be barking at them. This seemed to be great fun for Tops and they never bothered him at all. Uncle was always shouting out, 'One day those ducks will get him, and kill him.'

'I'm so sorry, but I can't catch him,' I used to say with a half smile on my face.

We didn't live there that long. I bet when we moved away they were so glad to see the back of our Tops. They did come to the gate and wave us off, probably saying under their breath, 'Thank goodness they've gone.' It wasn't us so much. It was our Tops really who caused all the trouble!

The Romany flag

The flag, which was officially approved in 1971, is blue at the top and green at the bottom, with a sixteen spoke wheel in the middle.

The blue signifies the sky, and the green signifies the land. If there hadn't been great people like my forefathers there wouldn't be anyone to tell the stories of the Romany life.

The travelling people are having hard times now, because they don't have the places to pull onto. Although it was also hard years ago, there was plenty of field work which meant they had places to stop.

Water always was a problem, and they had to be very careful not to waste it. I can remember my mother saying that once they had moved into their own place it was heaven having running hot and cold running water.

I have travelling friends who come and visit me and they still live in trailers, as they call them these days. The have hot and cold water, but they have to go to the washing area to get all their water. I couldn't live like that.

I wonder what my parents would have thought of having a flag. I would probably have heard more stories about the wagon, and the things they got up to. They had to be very cunning in those days to get on in life. It turns my stomach really when I think how my parents had to work from a very young age.

I never started work until the age of fifteen, which at the time was school leaving age. That was when I went out and got myself a job. It was wonderful as I had money to spend on myself. To be able to buy shoes and clothes was heaven. Mum also bought me clothes, which was very nice. My sister did as well and my brother Patsy gave me money to go and spend, so I was very lucky.

I loved buying clothes and looking in shop windows at the shoes. If I didn't have enough money one week I would put off buying until the next week when I could afford it. My wardrobe used to be packed with clothes, and my shoes were all in a straight line at the bottom.

I still like my wardrobe neat and tidy. I can't bear anything untidy. My mum and dad were the same.

Weekends at Priestfield

Brian and I had weekends on the odd occasion at John's house. Janet and Mick live there now with John and Malcolm.

There have been a lot of changes to the house since Granddad and Nanny died. When I first married, I never knew what to call them. However, when my first child Shane was born I found I could call Brian's parents Nanny and Granddad. I wonder what I would have called them if I had never had children.

I got on well with Brian's father when we first got married, far better than with his mother. Although we talked and she was very helpful and kind to me, there was always that edge to our relationship. But after a few ups and downs we aired our differences, and then we started to get on well.

John has his father's features. His face is quite long with smallish eyes and a sharp nose. His mouth is also small, but plenty comes out at times when he gets going. *Sorry John. No offence taken I hope!* We tell him that if his stomach gets any bigger we will have to cut a piece out of the table so he can fit closer. He just sits there and laughs about it. Poor old John. He loves his food. Still, who doesn't these days?

Brian is totally different from John. He looks like his mother, more rounded in the face, although he also has put on a lot of weight over the years. Even I have, come to that. I've lost my waist!

Janet is very much like her mother to look at. In fact I would say she is the spitting image of her. Janet also takes after her mother as regards cooking. She is brilliant at it. In fact, she taught me a lot. I have much to thank Brian's mother and Janet for when it comes to cooking.

As I sit in their lounge this luscious smell of baking is coming from Janet's kitchen. Tonight Janet is preparing a dinner party for ten. Heath, Janet's son, is helping to cook. He is also in the profession, so I think we are in for a good meal. Heath has certainly followed in his nanny's and mother's footsteps.

Then of course there's Mick, Janet's husband. He hasn't changed either, apart from getting old, but that's one thing none of us can get away from, can we? He's still as thin. In fact, I think he's slimmer and still very quiet, happy doing things in the garden or cleaning his car.

Mick has still got this enormous appetite. I can hear John saying now, 'I don't know where he puts it all without putting any weight on. These days I only have to eat a small piece of cake and I've put a pound on! Well, that's what it seems like anyway.'

I looked across the room and there was John with this rather large piece of cake in his hand, eating away quite happily and laughing all over his face.

'You have to start somewhere, John, if you want to lose weight,' I said looking at him, half smiling and thinking, Do I go and get a piece of cake or do I suffer and wait until dinner time?

'I know, girl,' he replied. 'I can't let it go to waste, can I? The chocolate will have dried up by tomorrow, and I can't let that happen.'

He had this expressionless face while he was eating the cake. I never said another word to him. I just left him alone to enjoy his chocolate cake!

Caravan days

We had had our caravan for quite some time. Then one weekend Celia, my cousin, and her husband Tony decided to get a caravan, so we could all go away for weekends, which we did. Cousin Jenty and her husband Bryan also came along and stayed in Celia's caravan.

Their first time away was to Cornwall. The children were on holiday and this meant we could have a week away rather than a weekend. We parked up at this rather nice caravan site, which was right beside the sea. This was lovely as we didn't have far to walk.

Most days we would be down by the sea as the children really loved being there. It wasn't really fair for them to be walking around town looking at shops. Who would want to at that age?

Celia's boy, Tony, was only about sixteen months old. My Shane was ten and Katy was nine. So for a quiet life it was down by the sea. Mind you, we all enjoyed it really.

I loved being by the sea. Feeling the gentle breeze was really wonderful, especially on my face. The children were beginning to get a lovely tan, in fact we all were. Celia just changes colour in the summer and goes a nice brown.

The bit I liked was when we came off the beach in the evenings and washed the children and got them ready for their tea. They all used to look so nice.

One afternoon, Tony and Brian had bought these two enormous crabs for our teas. Brian laid the table while I got the salad ready, scraped the new potatoes, and put them on the stove to cook. Brian sat and played with the children, which was a great help. Then I ventured to clean and get the crabs ready. They smelt so nice while I was pulling them apart. That's one thing you can guarantee when you're by the sea. The fish is fresh. (Well it should be!)

Once everything was ready and on the table, we decided to start having our tea. It did look lovely.

'Come on, everyone, tuck in,' Brian said. With that we started eating and it went quiet as we and the children enjoyed our food. Suddenly, there was a tap at the window and there stood Tony and Celia.

'Our crab didn't look like that. What did you do to make it look that nice?'

'We just pulled it apart and dressed it with lots of seasoning, that's all we did,' said Brian.

'We just pulled ours apart, and then we put it on a plate and ate it,' Tony said.

'What about a nice cup of tea and a cake,' I said to them. No sooner had I spoken than they were all climbing into our caravan. Little Tony came up to our table.

'Get him a plate. I think he would like some of our dinner,' Brian said.

'That looks really nice, Maria. Can I have some?' my cousin Jenty called out.

'No, you've had yours. If you wait a minute you can have a nice cuppa and a cream cake. How about that?' I said.

With that Jenty was up and making their tea.

'Where's our cake Maria?' Jenty called out, laughing all over her face. 'Oh you have loads in here Maria.'

'Yes. We bought some for you lot as well,' Brian said, still eating his dinner.

'Maria, is little Tony eating the food you gave him?' Celia asked.

'Yes he's eating all his crab, new potatoes, crusty bread and salad. He's really enjoying it. Well, there isn't much left on his plate shall we say.'

Once we all had our dinner, I cleared the table away and put the kettle on. I laid the table for our cup of tea and our cream cakes. The cakes were heaven. I sat in dreamland, eating my cake slowly.

'Are you sure you can manage it all, Maria? It's rather a large cake,' Jenty said.

'Did you manage to eat all yours, Jenty?'

'Yes, thank you. Every bit. I didn't even leave a crumb. None of us did.'

'Well, leave me alone then,' I said, laughing away, my hand over my cake.

'If we buy a crab another day, Maria, would you dress it for us and make it look nice on our plates?' Celia said.

'There's four of you. Why can't you try? I'm sure you could make it look nice if you all took your time at it.'

'Oh go on, Maria,' Celia said, smiling all over her face again.

'Well if we have crab again we'll do it for you, but we're only cleaning the crab for you. You can do the rest of the meal,' Brian said.

Jenty leant across to the others and said smiling, 'Well, do we agree with that?'

The next thing I heard was, 'Yes, we agree.'

'But we could get ourselves in a mess. So would you come and help us if we should need any help, please?' I said.

'That's very kind of you both,' Tony said.

Well we did get another crab, and we did dress the crab for them and made it look nice on their plate. Their caravan was alongside ours which meant that we could see them having their dinner. They looked as though they were enjoying every bit, and so were we.

That evening, after we had our meal, we decided to sit outside with a few drinks.

'Tony, have you emptied your toilet bucket yet?' asked Brian.

'Bloody Hell, no!' Tony said, putting his hand up to his mouth.

'I tell you what, Tony. When you lift it out you'll need to put your hand over your mouth. And you'll have to hold it very steady as you're walking over to where you have to tip it,' Brian said.

'Oh, come on, Brian. Give us a hand. You've done caravanning before. We've never done this type of thing.'

With that, Brian was up and helping. All we could hear was laughing, and Brian saying, 'Hold the bloody thing level, otherwise we're going to tip it out all over the place. Then they'll be chucking us off the site, and we'll never be able to come back again.'

'We won't be coming down here again anyway, will we Brian?' said Tony. 'There's plenty of other nice campsites to visit.'

'Any more wine anyone?' Jenty's Bryan asked.

I looked up, and there he stood holding the bottle of wine. 'Why didn't you go with them?' I asked

'Three people can't hold the bucket, can they?'

'No, but you could have lifted the lid where it had to be tipped into,' I replied.

'Look, they managed alright. They're walking back now.'

'Thanks, for all your help, Brian,' Tony and Bryan said as they went into the caravan to put the toilet back.

'Well it's all nice and clean, so don't forget to empty it before it gets too full, the pair of you,' said Brian.

That was a really nice week's holiday away with my cousins. Jenty bought my Brian a large wooden spoon as he was always stirring people up. I have still it. I often look at it and laugh, and think of the lovely time we all had that week.

Peter Brown being towed

It was a very hot afternoon. Brian and Peter had this old car that needed going to the scrap yard, which was at Raleigh in Essex.

They had their cup of tea and off they went. Peter was in the towed car which was roped up to Brian's lorry. As I looked out of the kitchen window, I noticed that Brian had smashed the windows of the car. What on earth is he doing that for, I thought. There must be a handle to the car window. Still he ought to know what he's doing.

I watched them drive off and disappear around the corner. Oh well, this won't do. I must get on and finish what I'm doing, I thought to myself. They had been gone quite some time, when suddenly I heard the lorry pull up. Cup of tea time, I thought, as I heard them coming up the path, laughing.

'Well, if taking a car into the scrapyard makes you laugh that much, you have obviously got quite a bit of money for it,' I said.

'No,' said Peter.

'What is it then?' I asked.

Brian stopped laughing and started to tell me. 'While we were driving down the road the sun was shining through the windows of our motors and it was hot. Suddenly, out of my lorry window I noticed that Peter was slowly creeping up the side of me, with his head back. He's asleep, I thought. I immediately slammed on my brakes, which gave Peter's car a good old jerk and woke him up, thank God. We were lucky that nothing was coming the other way.'

I just stood there with my mouth open wondering how could they stand there drinking a cup of tea and laughing about it.

'You could have killed yourselves, and others as well, you bloody fools.'

I just walked away shaking my head and thinking, I'd rather not know what those two got up to.

Still, I shouldn't moan. The money does come in handy.

Falling down the stairs

I was seven months pregnant with Katy. I was upstairs getting Shane's clothes ready for the morning. Afterwards I would have a lazy bath while it was nice and quiet. Brian was downstairs watching television. I used to find the evening time after dinner so peaceful, and to me it was the best time of the day.

After I had my bath I decided to get ready for bed. Then I thought I might as well go and watch television with Brian for a while. I looked in at Shane first to see if he was OK. He was tucked up in bed, fast asleep, and looked lovely and snug.

I pulled the door to, turned and walked towards the stairs. I put my foot on the first step and away I went, bang, bang, halfway down. I hit my head on the airing cupboard door, and then rolled the rest of the way down. I was holding on to my tummy and thinking, please God don't let anything happen to my baby.

I sat at the bottom of the stairs for a while, feeling quite sick and shaky. I kept shouting to Brian for help, but he couldn't hear me because the television was on so loud.

'Brian,' I kept shouting. 'I've fallen down the stairs. Help me!' Oh well, I might as well try and get up by myself, as it doesn't look as if Brian is coming to my assistance. I rolled myself over onto my knees and held on to the banister and pulled myself up. I then made my way to the front room where Brian was happily watching television.

With that he turned and looked at me. 'What did you say you've done? You've fallen down the stairs? How on earth did you do that?'

'I tripped on the top of the stairs.' By this time I was sitting down in my chair, still feeling dreadful.

'Would you like a cup of tea, Maria?'

'Yes please. I thought you were never going to ask me.' Brian went out to the kitchen and made me a nice cup of tea, which was well needed.

'Maria, I'm still confused how you could have fallen down the stairs, from top to bottom as well. Our stairs are not straight. They're an L shape. How come you didn't stop halfway down?'

I just sat drinking my tea. I didn't want to answer him, for what I might say to him.

'If you feel rough in the morning you ought to go and see the doctor.'

'Yes, all right,' I said rubbing my head.

After I had my cup of tea I decided to go to bed. I just said good night and off I went. I didn't sleep that well and was so restless all night long.

In the morning I decided to go to the surgery just so I could be checked over. My doctor said I would have some nice bruises up my back. Well, he wasn't far wrong as I certainly had some discoloration. After he checked me over, he confirmed that I was alright and so was the baby. I felt so much better after hearing him tell me that, but I still hurt all over my body.

After a few days the soreness got better, thank goodness, and the bruising started to fade. But I was still surprised that Brian hadn't heard me fall down the stairs. I did know that he wasn't deaf!

Katy has always hated stairs. I often wonder if it was because of my fall. When I watch her sometimes I notice that she hovers before she starts to make her way down the stairs. I have to smile to myself. It brings it all back what happened to me that night.

They say a bump doesn't hurt the baby when you fall when you are pregnant. But I don't know how Katy survived that night, with all the bumps I had. I wasn't that big, but she must have been well packed in my tummy, thank goodness.

The things Katy got up to

While I was cleaning upstairs one day, Katy was quite happy playing with the baby bath. This was the bath that I used for bathing our children. I used to put a certain amount of water in it so she could wash her dollies. She would sit there singing away to herself. It was lovely to watch her wash them and then wrap them in a towel. Then she would take them through to her bedroom to finish wiping them.

Out would come the cotton wipes to clean her dollies eyes out, and once they were dry she would put pretend powder all over them. Then she would dress them in her old baby clothes.

Suddenly I heard, 'Mum you can empty the bath out now.'

I went and emptied the bath and wiped it out, but I didn't put it back into the bath like I usually do for her to play with again. I was in our bedroom putting away our clothes, which I had just ironed. I could hear Katy singing.

'Row, row, row the boat gently down the stream merrily, merrily, merrily down the stream.'

The next thing I heard was this almighty bang. Katy had gone down the stairs in the baby bath. She had hit the front door, and there she sat holding on to the sides of the bath, laughing away.

'Katy, you must not do that. It's dangerous.'

'But it's fun.'

'Promise me you won't do it again.'

She was only three, and a very tiny child at that. This incident was on my mind for days and days. When I told Brian in the evening he said to put the bloody bath away so she couldn't use it anymore. We didn't put it away but we left it downstairs so in the summer she could still play with it.

Mind you, there was another time when she was upstairs again playing with her dolly. I had clean forgotten about her pram. Then I heard this bump, bump down the stairs. There she was, coming down the stairs holding on to her pram with her bum on the stairs, once again laughing all over her face.

'What are you doing?' I said to her.

'Getting my pram down the stairs, Mummy.'

I didn't say anything. All I could think about was whether there was anything else up there which she might bring down.

A lazy day in the garden

It was a beautiful summer's day. Brian and I were sitting in our garden relaxing with a nice cup of tea.

'Look at those legs, Brian. Not bad for a fifty-six year old woman, are they!' I said with a smile on my face.

'Not bad at all,' he said with a half-hearted smile. 'Pity you have those veins though.'

'Everyone has veins, Brian.'

'I know that. What I mean is your varicose veins. If it wasn't for them your legs would be smashing, just like years ago.'

'Look Brian. They disappear when I put my legs up in the air. If only they'd stay that way! I don't know what shape you'd call them these days. They certainly don't have the same shape as they did have, do they Brian? I don't even walk the same though. I'm beginning to think I walk like I did when I had my first pair of high heels. I waddled like a duck then. Well, that's what my cousin Celia used to say.'

Brian made no reply.

'Brian did you hear me?' I asked.

'Yes I heard you,' he replied. 'There's a few years gone by. I used to be able to put my hands around your waist. I certainly can't do that now, but I can put my hands around your ankle.'

'That's not funny Brian.' I just sat there biting my lip, and trying not to smile. 'You can't talk Brian. You wouldn't be able to stop a pig in a passage as the saying goes.'

We all know about gravity, don't we girls? Everything shifts and moves, downward and sideways and all on its own. When we get to a certain age I think we can all say that we have tried all the diets on the market. They all work for a while and then suddenly we are back where we started. It's a pity our bodies don't go back to our younger days. They've lost their way on route. Well that's what I tell the grandchildren, which makes them laugh.

When I passed my driving test

The day I passed my test, Brian was in hospital having his toe operated on. Janet and I and the children had a lovely day out. Well, I think they did. They never really said much. That evening, while I was washing up our dinner things, Mick my brother-in-law came in.

'Hello Maria. How long are you going to be?' he asked.

'Not that long. I'm nearly ready.' Janet was going to look after Shane and Katy while Mick was going to drive me to the hospital, or so I thought.

We dropped the children off at Janet's and out we went to my car. I opened the door to get in. Then I heard Mick shout out. 'What do you think you're doing, Maria?'

'I'm getting in the car. Why?'

'Not that side. Come round here. You've passed your test so you can drive it now.' Mick spoke in this rather deep voice, which I hadn't heard before.

'Oh no, Mick, there are too many people on the road this time of the night.'

'Don't be silly. You've been driving on the roads for quite some time, and at all times of the day. So come on you, get behind the wheel.'

He just looked at me and pointed at the door. I felt like one of the children being told off!

I walked around to the other side. Mick had already got the door open. As I got in, I heard, 'Don't just sit there. Start it up. We want to get to Harold Wood Hospital and we won't sitting there like that, Maria, so shake yourself.'

I don't know about shake yourself; I was already shaking all over. I hadn't heard Mick talk to me like that, even when he was teaching me to drive. There were many a time when he could have. There was this particular time when we were going over quite a busy road. Mick said it was clear his way and to go when I was ready, which I did without looking my way. I went straight in front of a tanker lorry.

I started the engine up and away we went. I didn't speak much. I just listened to Mick and did what I was told. When we got to the hospital, the car park was full except for one space.

'Go on, then', Mick said. 'Reverse into that space. All you have to do is position yourself right and away you go.'

I looked at him and thought, I'll never get into that space. Out of the corner of my eye I could see Mick looking at me. I'd better get moving, I thought, otherwise I'll be here all night. With that I positioned myself and started to reverse. Then all of a sudden I heard Mick shout out, 'Stop.' It was too late. I had mounted another car.

'What am I going to do Mick?' I said.

'Well, first we have to get out and try to dismount our car from the other car.'

I slowly got out of our car, wondering what the hell I was going to see.

'Well, Maria, you've mounted the car too much. I don't know what the damage looks like underneath.' I hadn't said a word from the moment I mounted the car. All I kept thinking was that I didn't want to drive anymore. I was never getting behind a steering wheel again!

The next thing I saw was that Mick was lifting my car off the other car. I turned around and there stood a hospital porter. I didn't say a word I was so frightened. We're in for it now, I'm thinking.

'Just lift it off and park it over the back,' said the porter. 'I won't say anything.'

'Thanks, mate,' said Mick.

'Get in, Maria, and drive it over there, where he told us to go.'

'Don't be horrible, I feel really bad. I don't feel like driving.'

'All right then. Get in the other side and I'll drive for you.'

'Do you know, Mick, we'll only have a few minutes left to see Brian,' I said laughing. I think the laugh was more a nervous giggle.

'That's better. You're having a laugh now, but you still look green though.'

'Do I?' I said.

When we eventually got in to see Brian, there he was sitting up in the bed waiting for us. The first thing he said was, 'Well, did you pass?'

'Yes,' I said in a rather squeaky voice.

'Well done. I thought of you this morning,' Brian replied. 'Clever isn't she, Mick.'

'Yes.' Mick looked up at me and winked.

The next day Mick came home with the paint to brush up the paintwork on my car.

My poor little car. Brian bought it for £140, and when he came out of hospital it was only worth £40, he reckoned. Brian never said a word about the markings on the car, which he noticed. All he said was, 'Just as well I didn't buy a new car, wasn't it Maria?'

'Yes,' was all I said.

Father's drinking days

One Saturday Father had been in the pub all afternoon and he had 'one too many drinks'. When he eventually came home, Uncle Joe was waiting to take him out again, but he was not in any state to venture anywhere. He had obviously fallen into a load of cement, and it was all over him. Patsy, my brother, could not stop laughing. He wanted to put the hosepipe over him. He said it would be the only way to get it off! All Father wanted to do was to wash his face, change his clothes and then go back to the pub with Uncle Joe.

'Don't worry about going to the pub tonight, Ambrose,' said my uncle, laughing. 'We can go another night.' But it took some time to persuade my father not to go.

Patsy managed to get his clothes off and clean him up, even without the hosepipe, and eventually managed to put him to bed.

If my memory serves me right, he only had a couple of hours sleep. Then he was up and feeling nicely, or so he told me! But he didn't ask to go to the pub. He just sat quietly in his armchair by the fire.

Some weekends Dad and Uncle Riley would go out together for a drink. They very often went to the Rose and Crown pub, which was on the estate where we used to live. This was a good thing as it meant that they didn't have very far to walk home!

We always knew when they had been to the pub, because you could hear them in the distance, Uncle Riley playing his penny whistle and my father singing. Uncle Riley used to play very well - far better, in fact, than my father sang! 'I'll be your sweetheart if you will be mine.' While this was going on, I would be in bed laughing.

When they had finished their duet they would start saying good night to one another, which took quite some time. After they finished the verse, one of them would say, 'Let's sing it again!' Then, laughing away to themselves they would sing the same old song again. Eventually Uncle Riley would go home, still playing his penny whistle. Then Dad would come in - or should I say fall in - via the back door. From my bedroom I could hear quite a lot which went on. My father would still be singing away to himself - well, trying!

'Hello love!' I would hear him say to Mum.

'I'll give you hello love,' said Mum. 'Drunk again!'

Then I would hear him say, 'No, I'm not drunk, love. I've only had a couple of drinks with Riley.'

'Only a couple of drinks! By the sound of you both, I would say more than a couple. I can hear Riley from here, and he must be nearly home. Lord help him when he gets indoors!'

Father always knew when to keep quiet and this was one of those times because he was losing the battle! On one occasion, after Father had gone to bed, Mother came to my room to say goodnight and tuck me in.

'Are you still awake, babe?' she said to me.

'Mum has Dad had too much to drink?'

'No dear. He didn't have enough money on him. He only had ten shillings to spend. No way could he get drunk on that, unless the people who he meets in the pub gave him extra drinks.'

'I saw Dad and Uncle Riley carrying flowers, so they had them to sell as well.'

'Oh did they now?' Mother said. 'Tomorrow is Saturday, and Dad will probably want to go out again.' Mother had a smile on her face.

The next evening as I was sitting by the fire reading I heard Father say, 'Luvvie, have you got any money?'

'What have you done with last night's money?' asked Mum. 'You said you never had that many drinks, so you should have money left over.'

'I only had ten shillings, love,' Father said.

'What about the flower money which you had last night?' Mum replied. 'If you haven't got any money left you'd better pick some flowers, hadn't you!'

Father didn't say a word. He just went outside and picked some of his flowers. I got up from my chair, put my book down and followed Father outside. I decided to sit on the back doorstep and watch Father picking his flowers. When he'd got enough, he laid them out on the lawn into bunches and tied them up with string. Then he picked them up, laid them in his arms and walked over to me.

'Be a good girl,' he said, giving me a kiss goodbye.

'I will,' I said, smiling at him, as I walked with him to the front gate.

'Bye Luvvie,' he called out to Mum.

'Bye, Ambrose. Don't be too late coming home tonight,' Mum replied.

As Father was walking up the path towards the gate, Mother then came to the front door. 'Have you got enough money, Ambrose?'

'I've got a few bob in my pocket. I've picked some flowers to sell, thanks.'

'Here take this with you.' With that Father walked back to Mother, and she handed him some more money.

'Thanks, Luvvie, I won't spend it all.'

'Just don't come home too drunk.'

'You know me better than that, Luvvie, after yesterday.'

When I think back, I realise why Father grew his flowers. Not only because he liked them, but also for his beer money. Mind you, my father and Uncle Riley did have the best gardens in our road. I think my Father had the best carnations and Uncle Riley had the best tulips. They were lovely and no wonder they got plenty of beer money!

Reading this piece it must sound like my father had to ask every time for some money. Well, usually it is the woman who holds the purse strings. However, the men do have money in their pockets as well!

I know my father liked his beer, but he only ever went out Friday nights and Saturday, and this wasn't every weekend. Father was such a hardworking man. He never complained about going to work, and we never went without much either. I was a lucky child.

Vinegar and olive oil

It was a very hot day, and I decided to visit my mother-in-law. She had been listening to a programme on the radio. Katie Boyle had been talking about the sun block which she used. It was one part vinegar and one part olive oil, mixed well together.

Brian and I and the children used to go down to Walton-on-the-Naze quite a bit, and always went to the beach. This is when I would use vinegar and olive oil. I would be putting the lotion on one of the children and Brian would be putting it on the other.

We never had a bee or wasp around us as it didn't smell that good, and the children never got burnt. I used to put it on as well and we all had a wonderful tan, thanks to Katie Boyle.

Mind you, we wouldn't be able to do it these days with the rays like they are. The oil would fry us and the vinegar - well I don't really know what that would do!

After our day on the beach, I would take the children for their shower while Brian would get their tea ready. The vinegar and oil came off them really well and also helped the skin. Once they had their showers, we were back at the caravan and having our tea. I used to look at them in their pyjamas. Brown as berries, they were.

After they had their tea, they would get down and play with their toys. Shane would be playing with his cars, and Katy would be playing with her dollies and writing books. They had such a full day on the beach they never used to ask for anything else.

Sometimes we would walk up to the town and have a glass of beer, and the children would have their lemonade. Occasionally, Brian would put some of his beer into their glass which would make a shandy for them. They used to really enjoy that with a packet of crisps. Then we would make our way back home. Even Tops, our little dog, enjoyed his walk, and he had a packet of crisps as well! The bar girl always brought a dish of water for him, which he would lap up with real enjoyment.

The children used to walk around with sunglasses on, and so did Tops. He wasn't going to be left out. He liked wearing them. People would walk by and have a chuckle to themselves.

Once we had had our drink, we would walk back to our caravan. By the time we had got back the children were always tired and ready for bed. It was never long before they were tucked up and fast asleep. This was when I would get on with my jobs for the next day. Brian was really good and always helped me.

I liked to get the children's clothes out for the next day, and they looked so nice laid out neatly. In the morning the children looked so lovely and fresh with their little soft brown bodies. The thing was, they never got burnt. Not that we didn't keep an eye on them though.

Katy loved the water and we had a hard job keeping her out of it, but Shane wasn't overly keen on it. He was quite happy playing in the sand and making sandcastles. Most of the time Tops would wait until he had finished them and then he would jump all over them.

That's when we would hear, 'Tops, get off!' Then off he would go to find the next sandcastle to jump on.

Most of the children on the beach would make sandcastles for him, just so they could see him jump on them. If there weren't any sandcastles for him to jump on he would run around barking. This was his way of saying, 'Please make more sandcastles.'

He would stand beside the children and wait for his sandcastle. He was so funny to watch. He used to have everyone laughing.

Oh what fun days they were.

The little mini pick-up

Our little mini pick-up was so versatile. If it wasn't carrying the children in the back, it had a load of tot in it. The tot earned us a few bob, but the children used to cost us money! Still, they were worth it.

This particular Sunday I decided to go down to our local dump with Brian. We had some rubbish to take, so we piled it into the back of the mini, quite tightly I might add. The children didn't want to come so they went to Brian's parents, just around the corner from us.

With my roast in the oven cooking nice and slowly, I had plenty of time to go to the dump and get back to get dinner ready for the family.

When we arrived at the dump, Brian's mate Peter started to unload our rubbish from the back of our motor. I wasn't going to sit in the motor, so I decided to have a look around.

'Maria, over here,' I heard. I looked up and there was this chap, Bill Parkins, I'd known for many years. All I could see was his head poking out of this skip.

'Do you like large dinner plates, the ones you put the Sunday roast on? There's some really pretty ones in this skip, and lots of other things as well.'

The voice was rather muffled, and I walked over to the skip so I could hear what Bill was saying more clearly. By then his head had disappeared and I waited for it to pop up again. Then all of a sudden Bill jumped up and gave me such a fright.

'Look what I've found, Maria. It's in a box as well, not a mark on it,' said Bill.

'What is it then?' I asked.

'It's a bible. What a shame. It's been thrown away.'

'Can I have a look at it?'

Bill passed it to me, and sure enough there wasn't a mark on the box or the bible.

'Can I have it, Bill?'

'Of course you can. What about these three dinner plates. Do you want them as well?'

'Yes please,' I replied.

With that he handed them to me, and I walked back to the motor. I got in and started to look through the bible. It was in perfect condition, as if it had just been left on a shelf. I was so pleased with it.

'Look what I've got, Brian. Bill found it in the skip over there, with these large dinner plates.'

'I'll have a look in a minute,' said Brian. 'At the moment I'm putting things in the back of the motor.'

I didn't take any more notice. All I could hear was a thud and I could feel a pushing movement. Brian and Peter were very busy loading our motor up. With not too much, I hoped, as it only had small wheels.

'Well that's the lot,' said Peter eventually. 'See you this afternoon.'

With that Peter just did a couple of bangs on the roof of our motor, and away we went. We didn't hang about and we soon got home.

'I'll go and see to the lunch,' I said. 'I'll telephone the children to say that they can come home now.'

With that I went indoors and checked the oven to see how our lunch was getting on. That looks nice, I thought. Now I can turn the oven up. As I was preparing the vegetables, I heard Shane and Katy.

'Hi, Mum. What's for dinner?' they shouted out.

'Roast beef and roast potatoes with a nice lot of fresh vegetables.'

I turned around and neither of them were there. They'd gone upstairs. Oh well, I thought. They'll be down those stairs quick enough when I shout out, 'Lunch!'

Brian unloaded the motor and put it into the garage for him and Peter to clean in the afternoon.

'Come on kids, your lunch is ready.' Down they came, five steps at a time by the sound of their feet. I could hear Brian washing his hands in the cloakroom.

'Have I got time to change for lunch, Maria?'

'Yes, if you're quick.'

As I turned off the television, I noticed Brian race upstairs. It didn't take him that long before he was down again, helping me with the dinner like he always did.

As we were eating our dinner, I mentioned that Bill Parkings had found me a bible in one of the skips, and it was in wonderful condition.

'Where are you going to put it, Mum?' asked Katy.

'I'll put it beside my bed, so every evening I can read it,' I replied. 'I'm so sorry, Katy, that we didn't get to church this morning, but Dad wanted the motor so he could go to the dump.'

'We can see that, Mum, with all the plates outside the back door. We're not going to use them are we?'

'Of course we are. They're lovely meat plates.'

'Well, you can count me out, because I'm certainly not eating meat off them,' Katy replied with a scornful look on her face.

'You can count me out as well, because no way am I going to eat off anything which comes out of the dump,' said Shane.

'Don't be so silly. They'll be washed. And you'll see, they'll look superb on the table.'

All the time I was trying to keep a straight face. I looked up at Brian and I noticed he was having difficulty not to smile.

Well, I thought my best bet was to wash them and just put them away for a while. Then I would bring them out at

Christmas and see if they noticed them. They shouldn't with a nice turkey on them.
   And that's what I did.

Shane growing up

Shane loved watching television. Once Katy had had her bath in the evenings, she would call out to him, 'You can have your bath now, Shane. I'm finished in the bathroom.'

'Ok. I'll be there in a minute,' Shane used to reply, as he carried on watching the television. His minute was half an hour, even more if he could get away with it.

When he decided to have a bath, he would go upstairs, run his bath, and then he would come back downstairs and sit in his chair.

I would call out, 'Shane, don't forget the water is on.'

'I know when it's ready. Don't keep on, Mum.'

'If you flood the bathroom, Shane, I won't be pleased with you.' After a while he would get up and run upstairs. He would be there for five minutes at the most. Then back down he would run, hair soaking wet. He used to try and have a bath while the adverts were on. He used to make it every time. I don't think he ever missed the next part of the programme he was watching.

'I hope you've washed behind your ears,' I used to say.

'Yes, Mother. Of course I have.'

My parents bought Shane a television for his bedroom, but most evenings he would watch with us downstairs. I don't know about resting. His body might have rested, but his eyes didn't. Shane could watch the television until he fell asleep, if he had the chance.

Mind you, when girls came on the scene, Shane and Katy would argue who would have the bathroom first. He never caught Katy out. She made sure of that. She was there before him every time. But now it was more than five minutes for Shane - more like an hour!

Shane used to go round to see his uncles, John and Malcolm, to find out what sort of deodorants they used.

(Malcolm always bought the expensive ones.) So Shane always smelt really nice.

After his bath, off Shane would go on his bike. I knew he had a girlfriend because Katy was always pulling his leg. One evening, while we were all sitting at the dinner table, Katy started to sing, 'Hey, hey, Paula.'

'Shut up, Katy,' said Shane. Katy just laughed at him and they both started giggling. I tell you, when they started they would get on my nerves. Like most families, really, I suppose... Still, I wouldn't want to be without them.

I can remember once, when I was downstairs clearing away the dishes, there was this almighty shout from upstairs. 'Mum, Shane has got his television in the bathroom.'

I ran up the stairs, I think four at a time. There he lay in the bath with loads of bubbles, television in the bathroom with him.

'What the devil do you think you're up to? You could electrocute yourself, you fool.' With that I started to take the television out of the room.

'Don't do that! I was watching it,' Shane shouted.

'I'll plug it in on the landing. Then you can watch it in safety.'

'I won't be able to see it this end of the bath. I'll have to go to the other end and the taps are there.'

'I don't care. You're not having the television in the bathroom.'

I plugged the television in on the landing and I never heard another word from him that night. After that he always plugged it in on the landing.

The garage full of tott

Every afternoon after work, Brian and Peter would be in our garage cleaning off the tot for extra money. On this particular day, when they arrived home from their usual work on the dustcarts, I called out to them, 'Would you like a cup of tea?'

'Yes but can you bring it out here please,' Brian shouted out.

To have their tea in the garage, and not come in, they're getting up to something, I thought. Anyway, I took their tea out, and as I was doing so I noticed that their truck was backed into the front of the garage as far as they could get it.

'Whatever are you doing, the pair of you? You're working like beavers. Are you throwing the tot on the lorry before its cleaned?' I spoke rather loudly. I had to shout because of the noise they were making. Neither of them answered me, so I just walked away and went indoors.

It must have been a good hour later when I heard Brian shouting out, 'Maria!'

I ran downstairs. 'What do you want?' I asked him. 'And where are you going?'

'We're off to get rid of the tot in the garage. If anyone from the Council should come and ask about the tot, just say there isn't any. They might want to see the garage. Just show them, but don't say anything else.'

With that, Brian and Peter jumped into the lorry and off they went. Oh dear, I thought. This could get complicated. Still, all I have to do is what Brian told me. In other words, keep your mouth shut!

It wasn't long before there was a rather loud banging on my front door. I went and opened it, and there stood two men. I knew who they were, and they knew me. One of the men I went to school with.

'Hello,' I said with a rather nice smile. 'Can I help you?'

'Yes. Is Brian in?' one of the men said.

'No, I'm sorry but he isn't. Would you like to leave a message?' I said.

The one who knew me said, 'Can we have a look in your garage?'

'Why do you want to look in my garage?'

'We've been told that Brian is cleaning tot in there.'

'Cleaning tot?' I said. 'There's no tot in our garage.'

'Then you won't mind us looking, will you,' one of the men said sarcastically.

I opened the door wide so they could look in. Brian had put our Land Rover in. Even the bench was clean where they had cleaned the tot off.

'Thank you,' they said as they stepped back. I closed the door, turned around, and started to walk towards the house.

'Tell Brian everything is OK. We won't be coming here anymore,' they said.

'Thank you,' I said.

I went indoors feeling quite cold. Now they will have to get somewhere else to clean their tot off.

It wasn't long before Brian and Peter were back with an empty lorry, big smiles all over their faces. I'll give them smiles, I thought.

'Have they been?' Peter said. 'We've been worried about you.'

'Oh yeah, they've been alright. They looked in the garage and then they walked away. All they said was to tell Brian everything is OK and they won't be coming here anymore.'

'Stop worrying,' Brian said. 'It won't happen again. We've got a yard now to clean the tot off.'

I can't tell you the relief I felt when they told me that.

'Where's the yard?'

'It's at Kelveden Hatch.'

I didn't ask any more. I didn't want to know. All I cared about was that we wouldn't have two men knocking at my door again, asking questions.

Totting days

We decided to have a holiday, or I should say Peter Brown decided for us. He had suggested going to Jersey.

One particular Saturday afternoon, Brian and Peter were cleaning their tot off in our garage, which they used to do most afternoons after work. It was extra cash for them both. It came in very handy at times, believe you me! With two young children, who wouldn't need the cash?

It was a rather cold afternoon, and I thought it was time I called them in for a cup of tea. 'Tea up,' I called out.

'Right oh, coming,' Brian shouted back.

I left the tea on the kitchen side for them to help themselves. I was upstairs washing my hair, as we were going out that night to a dance at Keys Hall with Peter and his wife Linda. Hopefully it would be a good night.

'Maria, have you got a minute?' I heard Brian call out.

'Yes. Hang on a minute.' I wrapped a towel around my head and went downstairs to see what they wanted. They were probably going to ask me to drive so they could drink. They normally didn't like my driving, but that didn't bother me. Mind you, perhaps I'd given them cause to not like my driving in the past!

I went into the kitchen. They were both laughing. 'OK, then,' I said. 'What's the joke? Let me in on it.'

'Oh it's no joke,' Brian said. 'Peter was asking if we would like to go on holiday with them.'

'Holiday? Where to?'

'Jersey, for two weeks, in June,' Peter replied.

'Very nice. But where are we going to get that sort of money, and what about the children?'

'Oh, I'll sort that one out. My mum will have Shane, and perhaps your mum will have Katy.'

'All sorted then, is it? Then you can ask them,' I said sharply. 'And how are we going to afford to go?'

'Plugs,' said Peter rather quickly.

'Plugs? And plugs to you, Peter Brown!'

'No. That's how we are going to get our money, Maria.'

'Well the best of luck. I think you'll need to clean a lot of plugs to pay for us to go on holiday,' I said with a smile.

'Oh, we will,' Peter called out.

'Well, it's February now, so if you intend us to go away in June you'd better drink up and get cleaning those plugs,' I said as I walked away.

The next thing I heard was the back door shutting followed by the pair of them laughing. They'll be laughing on the other side of their faces if they don't clean enough plugs. They've told me that we're going on holiday.

I finished doing my hair and went back downstairs to wash up the cups. The kitchen window faced the garage; and I looked out towards the garage where they were working. How on earth are they going to make money just cleaning plugs! Oh well, that's not for me to worry about. I'm going to just think about my holiday.

Over the weeks, Brian and Peter kept up the plug cleaning. I used to ask them from time to time how things were going.

'Not too bad,' was always their reply.

I think they had been cleaning for two months when Brian broke the news that we wouldn't be able to go away for two weeks. I didn't mind a week, as a week in Jersey is better than nothing. We did go away, and it was a smashing holiday.

Linda and I can remember everything. I can't say the same for Brian and Peter. I don't think I need to explain the reason why. (Too many hangovers.)

Lorry driving

Brian once said he couldn't have been in his right mind when he decided to be a lorry driver.

At night, although the lorry was nice and warm, the sleeping bunk was so narrow that Brian's face was pressed up against the driver's seat. He used to say that if he turned over it wasn't any better because then his nose was squashed up against the cab wall. So he used to lie on his back, which was fine until he moved in his sleep!

When he stretched out, his feet were pressed against the bottom of the cab. He used to say it was like lying in a coffin - not that he'd ever laid in one! He reckoned that he was so tired that after a short while he just fell asleep.

He would put his stove out for the morning in the middle of the two passenger seats, with his tea and biscuits ready. He used to say he had all his mod cons without the wardrobe and the kitchen sink.

At night, whenever he got comfortable, he would need a wee. But all he had to do was take the top off a lemonade bottle and, hey presto, he didn't have to go outside into the cold night air. Then he would open the cab door, and tip it out under the lorry, and then screw the top back on.

He used to wonder what the lorries would look like inside in twenty years' time. Probably they would have microwaves and fridges. With those thoughts, he would curl up in a ball and drop off to sleep. Then, the next thing he knew was hearing shouting and banging on the cab door to wake him up so the lorry could be unloaded.

Well that's it, I'm going to sleep, good night all, and with that Brian curled up in a ball and went to sleep.

May Day

Mother always made the headdresses for Pilgrims Hatch School May Day.

One evening she would be bending pieces of wire so they would fit each girl's head. Then she would twine green tape around the wire.

The next evening she would be making the flowers for the headdresses. This would be crepe paper flowers, usually roses. Mother would cut the crepe paper in various places, and then unfold the paper. Then with a sharp knife where the cut was, she would put the piece over her knee and roll the knife on the crepe paper so it would curl up. This would be done where all the cuts were. After she had finished curling the paper she would twist it around her fingers to make a rose. Then she would twine the roses around a small piece of wire. They would be placed very close together, not a space to be seen. For many evenings, she would be there until very late at night making these headdresses. When they were finished, Mother would put them very carefully into a box.

Mr. Davis, the headmaster, was so pleased with the headdresses. On the day, we would all dress up looking rather pretty. Oh, it was so lovely. In fact I can't remember it ever raining. Only the sunshine do I remember.

Holding on to our ribbons, we would dance around the maypole. Over and then under each other's ribbons we went as we skipped away to the music. Once our ribbon was plaited in the correct way, we would then dance the other way to unplait the ribbon. It was lovely. The ribbons were all different colours, which helped it to look pretty.

This was always at the front of the school, in the playground. Many people would be standing outside the school gate and others were sitting on chairs around the edge of the playground.

I would be dancing holding on to my ribbon and feeling so proud that my mother had made the headdresses.

I don't remember how many years Mother made the headdresses. All I know is she made them for many, many years, and with so much pride.

The girls used to ask me if I could make the paper flowers, and I always replied by saying, 'Of course I can.'

'Can you show me?' they used to ask.

'One day,' was all I said in reply.

Mother used to show me how to make the flowers. Like most Gypsy children, I was shown many things which would one day give them a living.

The christening

Shane was christened six weeks after he was born, on a Sunday at two thirty. Brian and I thought it would be nice for Shane to be christened at the same church where we got married two years earlier. We made the appointment to see the vicar one evening. He said it wouldn't be a problem. In fact he agreed with us that it would be nice to do the christening as well as our marriage.

Looking around, the vicar's room hadn't changed much. He still had the wonderful rather large armchair. As I sat in it, it didn't seem to be quite as large as when Brian and I saw the vicar to arrange our wedding day. We were so pleased to be able to fix the date for when Shane was only six weeks, because we didn't want him to be any older.

'Goodbye then,' the vicar said, 'and I'll see you five weeks' time at two thirty.'

As the church was only next door but one to where my parents lived, we were able to leave Shane with them. When we walked through the gate I could see my dad cuddling Shane. He was stroking Shane's face.

'Hi! We're back,' I called out.

'You weren't that long. I was just warming Shane's bottle up for Dad to give him,' said Mum.

'Has he been good for you?' Brian asked.

'He's been as good as gold,' Dad replied.

I was so glad, because when Shane started to cry there was no way of stopping him unless he had his bottle, and he was due for his bottle while we were at the vicar's. I was quite expecting Mum to come round to the vicar's saying that she couldn't stop him from crying.

'You haven't been worrying, my girl, have you?' Mum asked.

'No, I never gave it a thought. I knew you could cope,' I said.

The next day I went over to see my mother-in-law. It was quite a walk, but I enjoyed it. I was loaded up with all my feed for Shane, nappies and all the other things that we mums would have to take with us. Plus I had my little dog Tops. He loved coming out with me for walks. Once I got to my mother-in-law's the kettle was put on for a cup of tea. Janet, my sister-in-law, had her baby just two days after me.

While I was having my cup of tea I told her that Brian and I had made the arrangements for the christening, and could I ask a big favour.

'What's that then?' my mother-in-law asked.

'Well, you know your tea trolley. I was wondering if I could borrow it.'

'Yes, you can, but it has a back to it.'

I sat there looking at her, thinking the trolley hasn't got a back to it. What on earth does she mean? I didn't ask her. I thought I'd leave it until I saw Brian and ask him.

'What about a cake?' Janet said.

'Yes please, Janet. I would love you to make the christening cake.'

'I'd better get started then, hadn't I,' Janet replied with a big smile.

'Anyway, when is the christening to take place?' my mother-in-law asked.

Oh dear, I thought, she's going to have a go at me now. I was still a bit afraid of her, although I was warming to her slowly.

'Four weeks' time,' I said rather quickly.

'Four weeks' time? Why four weeks? Couldn't you have made it later?' Janet asked.

'No. It means Shane will be six weeks old, and that's when Brian and I would like him christened.'

It went quiet. Say something I thought.

'That's alright. We'll get there, won't we?' Janet said.

All Brian's mum said was, 'There isn't a lot of time, Janet, to get the cake done.'

'Oh, I'll get it done. We can't have Shane without a cake, can we?'

I didn't say a word. I just sat there. Well, this won't do, I thought. I'd better get Shane fed, and that always took ages.

'I'll feed him,' Janet said. The next thing, she had got hold of Shane and was feeding him.

The donuts

In the school holidays, Katy would go with her dad in his lorry. One of her favourite places was Peterborough, about a two and a half hour drive. Katy and Brian got up around four o'clock and left without me hearing them.

After Brian unloaded, they would go and get these amazing donuts. They were not like the ones in the shop. These were special. They were large and full of cream. Once you had bitten into them, it was like bliss. You didn't have to chew them. They just melted in the mouth.

Katy wanted to go and get the donuts herself. Brian was watching through his lorry window, and out she came with this box of donuts, smiling all over her face. Then all of a sudden, down she went on the pavement. The box was broken, and so were all her donuts.

Brian jumped out of his lorry and ran to her. He picked her up and gave her a cuddle.

'Never mind,' he said. 'We can go back and get some more.' With that, he turned round and there stood the baker.

'Come on in darling and I'll give you some more donuts,' he said.

Katy's knees were all cut and bleeding, and her big blue eyes had these enormous tears coming out of them.

The baker put some more donuts in the boxes and gave Katy one extra for her to eat straight away. She looked up at the baker and said, 'Thank you so much.' Brian also thanked him and they went back to the lorry.

'Would you like some coffee with that donut?' Brian asked Katy.

They sat in the lorry for a while drinking coffee and eating their donuts. Once they had finished, they headed back home, with the rest of the donuts placed safely between them.

I was washing up at the sink when I heard the lorry coming. I watched Brian help Katy out of the lorry, and in she came with the donuts.

'Put the kettle on, Maria. Let's have a cup of tea with these lovely donuts which we have for you,' he said.

'Where's Shane?' Katy asked.

'He's around the corner with Granddad and Nanny,' I replied.

'Can I ring so he can come and get his donut?'

'Course you can,' Brian said.

While we were waiting for Shane, I was getting the tea ready. No sooner had I got the cups ready than I heard Shane coming through the gate. 'Hello,' he shouted out.

We all sat down at the dining room table with our tea and donuts, which we enjoyed thoroughly. Katy told us about her fall, and I looked down at her legs and said, 'Well it looks as though I'll have to refill Dad's first aid box with the amount of plasters you've got on your legs.'

Looking at Katy's legs I could see some rather nasty grazes around the plasters.

'After you've had your tea and donuts you ought to go and lay in the bath. That will help those cuts. Then I'll put fresh plasters on your legs.'

Katy did go and lay in a nice warm bath, and every so often I could hear a funny little noise as she pulled off her plasters.

'Katy, would you like a cup of tea?' I called out.

'Yes please,' she shouted back.

With that I took a cup of tea up to her. To be quite honest I wanted to check if she had got the plasters off alright. I also wanted to see how bad the cuts were on her legs. Brian had said they were quite nasty.

I placed a little table next to the bath for her cup of tea and put a nice biscuit on a plate for her. I could see that she had taken the plasters off.

'Oh Katy,' I said. 'Those cuts and grazes do look rather nasty. You'll have to soak those every night really well.'

'I will,' she said, looking at her knees with a very sad face.

I think Katy had been in the bath for a good hour. She came downstairs and lay on the settee, patting her legs to make sure they were dry.

'The dinner is on. It won't be long,' I called out.

Then I heard, 'Don't push on my cuts please, Dad.'

I put my head around the door just enough so I could see them. Katy was on the settee and Brian was kneeling on the floor, putting more plasters on her knees. Poor Katy. They do look nasty. We'll have to keep an eye on those cuts, I was thinking to myself.

Katy was always falling over and cutting her knees, and I was forever having to fill the first aid box up with plasters.

Katy's knees took some time to heal up. Every night she was soaking in the bath, and eventually the plasters were able to come off. She did go to Peterborough again with her dad on several occasions, and we also had our donuts, which they brought back. With no plasters on the knees either! And whenever she went into the baker's shop, he always gave her extra donuts.

In the olden days, man felt special

When my parents moved into their bungalow, Mother was over the moon as it meant no more moving around. But for Father, it didn't feel right. He thought the bungalow was dark, and becoming a house dweller made him feel imprisoned. As a child I would sit and look at him. Suddenly, he would get up and walk outside as if he couldn't get his breath properly.

One evening, my father and I were sitting by the fire. He was squatting down with one leg tucked under the other, in a crouching position. I never knew my father to sit on the floor any other way. Father was looking into the flames of the fire, and I noticed tears in his eyes. I feel it was because he was no longer able to move. Father reached out for my hand and held it tight.

'Do you know, my girl,' he said, 'feeling insecure can cause a Gypsy to lose his home, his freedom and even his life. A Gypsy needs a balanced way of life, a fountain of life which expresses itself in song and dance.'

By this time we were just quietly sitting and staring into the fire, thinking our own thoughts. Then suddenly the back door opened, and in walked my uncle Jim. He was a rather plump man of medium height, with a roundish face. Once he was in and sitting down, I got up and went outside to feed and talk to his horse. I used to love getting water for Uncle Jim's horse and feeding it. I would sit quite happily talking away to the horse, until Uncle Jim came out with Father. Then off they would go to the pub for their Saturday afternoon drink.

Traditionally, the Gypsy traveller's lifestyle was an outside one, and many travellers still maintain the country ways.

In the early twentieth century, these people had wandered more freely in Britain. Most travellers stayed together in large family groups - parents, grandparents, older children, uncles and cousins would all work and travel together. So when they stopped they needed a large enough place for all of them.

I was lucky, as I didn't have to work in the fields.

I used to hear my uncle Joe shout out, 'Luvvie, that girl is big enough to pick peas, you know.'

'Joe, you look after your own family and I will look after mine,' Mother replied. 'She pulls my bines for me. She don't have to if she don't want to - not like your children. You are evil, Joe. Do you know that?'

I can't remember my uncle Joe ever saying another word to my mother about me working. All I can remember is seeing him push his hat to the back of his head and walk away grumbling under his breath.

'Maria,' I heard Mother say. 'Don't go near your Uncle Joe today. He's not in too good a mood.'

I just looked up and said, 'OK,' and asked Mother if she was alright with her bines.

'Yes, my love,' she replied. 'You go and play if you like.' With that, I went and laid behind all the bines I had pulled for Mother. The bines were nice and comfortable and the next thing I knew was Mother calling me to have my lunch. After lunch I went straight back to my bed of bines and fell asleep. The next thing I heard was, 'Come on, Maria. It's time to go home.'

I noticed my Uncle Joe give my mother a rather nasty glare. Mother glared back, and with that Joe just got on with his packing away for the next day. Mother packed her orange box away in the corner of the field. She used to sit on this box, and it was also used for our lunchtime table.

'That's it, Luvvie, put your orange box up for tomorrow,' said Joe sarcastically.

'If I were you, Joe Webb, I would shut up.'

Without another word, Uncle Joe started up his lorry, called the children to get in the back, and off they went.

'See yer, Luvvie, Sunday morning for that nice cup of tea,' he called out with a smile on his face.

'I'll give you cup of tea!' Mother snapped, but still managed a smile in return.

When I think back, this banter was rather nice.

When I was in the fields, I used to hear parents shouting out to their children throughout the day.

'Heads down. We have to make a living so we can eat tomorrow, you know.'

In those days the boys and girls married other Gypsy boys and girls. They never married gorger-bred people. It was different for my generation. I often wonder if my family were happy for me marrying outside the Gypsy way of life. However, I did - and a happy life I've had too.

Katy growing Up

When Katy was small, she was far more adventurous than Shane. Whereas Katy would climb, Shane would think about the situation first, and didn't like heights at all. Shane would rather have his feet firmly on the ground, and he still does.

There was a time once when Brian was doing some work outside, cleaning the gutters out.

I had called them all in for lunch. After she had eaten, Katy wanted to go back outside to play, which she did. Shortly after, Shane asked to get down from the table.

'Of course you can,' I said, and off he went.

'Dad! Mum! Come quick! Katy is up the ladder.'

With that, Brian and I got up from the table and ran outside. There she was, nearly at the top of the ladder.

'Hello. Look at me,' she called out.

'Don't move,' Brian shouted. 'And don't keep looking down. Just hold on to the sides of the ladder.'

Brian started to walk slowly up the ladder, talking to her all the time.

'Mum, is Katy going to be alright, and will Dad be able to get her down?' asked Shane.

'Of course he will,' I said, holding Shane's hand and thinking, please don't move, Katy. I couldn't look up. Then suddenly I heard Brian talking to her.

'OK, Katy. I've got you. Just let me hold you and then we can get down.'

'That's alright, Dad. I can walk down.'

'All right then. I'll tell you what to do.'

With that the two of them started to walk down. Katy looked so confident at this point, but Brian was rather white in the face as he walked down the ladder holding on to Katy at the same time. Katy was laughing all the while and looking down at Shane and myself.

'Hold on, Katy,' Shane was calling out. He was squeezing my hand ever so tightly.

Eventually Brian was down, holding Katy in his arms. 'Oh Katy, don't you ever do that again. You really frightened us.'

'I'm alright,' she said as she ran around the garden.

'Don't you ever leave a ladder up the side of the house again Brian, or anywhere else come to that, please,' I said.

We went in for a cup of tea, both of us with our hearts in our mouths. It never really stopped her from climbing, but she never went up a ladder again. After we had got over the shock of Katy climbing, we did have a laugh about it. Not when she was around, mind you!

We never thought for one minute that she would do anything like that. Even to this day she won't go up a ladder, and she's forty one.

Crocken Hill

My uncle Elijah and Aunt Becky used to live at Crocken Hill, Swanley, in a very small cottage. Two up and two down, they had no bathroom. But they did have a toilet which was outside and situated at the bottom of the garden. It had a pretty plant growing over the top which made it look quite nice. The garden was very narrow with a centre path leading to the bottom.

I used to go down to see my aunt and uncle three times a year and looked forward to these times. I never did anything special but I really enjoyed their company.

Whenever we visited them my dad brought some plants for my cousin Michael's grave. He died of pneumonia when he was eight. My dad and uncle would work very hard each time to clean the grave up before putting the flowers on.

My uncle had asthma which made walking very difficult for him. It was a very steep hill to get to the grave, and each year I went I noticed that my uncle was finding it more difficult to walk up the hill.

I think I was about sixteen when I stopped going to see my aunt and uncle. They always came down to see us once a year which was really nice. That way I did still get to see them.

Helen, their daughter, was crippled, although she walked fairly well. It was very sad because when she was a young child she fell over on the ice and damaged her leg very badly. She was in hospital for many weeks, but I don't remember anything about it as I was only a young child. But every time my parents and my uncle met up they always spoke about it. It seemed as though my aunt and uncle never did get over it.

However, they had two other children who were very healthy. Their names were Nonie and Bluey, which were really old travellers' names.

I'm so glad my parents didn't choose a travellers' name. I like my name, Maria. I have always thought it was such a pretty name.

It's funny how certain things stay in one's mind so strongly. I can see things so clearly as though they are there right in front of me. I love my memories and wouldn't want to be without them.

Some are not so good, but that's life. We all have good memories and bad memories and it's good to think about the good times and the bad times.

My Uncle Elijah died in March 1966 and my Aunt Becky in September 1968. Nonie died just three weeks after her father, also in March, and Bluey died in May 1984.

My Aunt Jenty

I had thoughts today about my dear Aunt Jenty, my cousin Celia's mother, as I was putting my washing out on the line, after it had come out of my washing machine. I remembered how she used to sit on the wall in her garden with her tub and her rubbing board. There she was putting a little soap, or perhaps washing powder, on the garments, and then rubbing it up and down on her washing board. This was on fine days, but on the days that were not so good she would do her washing in her bungalow.

Aunt Jenty's washing used to be brilliantly white. Lord knows how she managed it when the whole family - herself, Uncle Riley and their six children - were at home. Then on wet days there was the problem of getting it dry and airing it all. And everything was done by hand. She probably never even used hand cream - not like we do these days, girls!

It makes me wonder what will happen in another fifty years. Perhaps, if we are lucky, they will bring a robot in to do all the housework. By then I will be with the good Lord. I won't need all my mod cons then, let alone a robot! Then I will look down and say, 'Oh my dear Lord, whatever is that thing!'

I don't know if they were good days or bad days, thinking back. My poor old mum and my aunt Jenty went through hell like most other mums. I don't have enough hours in the day now. Lord above knows how they managed. The good Lord only gave us the same amount of hours in the day.

Oh well, I had better go and put my soup on. That's done in the pressure cooker. Everything is done for speed these days, and does it get us anywhere, girls? The answer to that is no. We still say, 'If only we had a few more hours in the day.'

I bet if you were to ask your grandparents they would say the same thing. The other saying is, 'If I had had it as lucky as you, life would have been a lot easier.' What is <u>our</u> excuse then, girls!

Shane's grass cutting days

Every Saturday Shane would be out cutting lawns. He was only about twelve. He would get up in the morning, really early, but not so bright! He never went out without his breakfast of two shredded wheat and two slices of toast with strawberry jam and a pot of tea. If I ever called out, 'Cup of tea, Shane,' he always shouted back, 'Yes please.'

Once he had had his breakfast, away he would go. It was a big old lawnmower, but he pushed it. His first stop was Nanny and Granddad's, which was only a few houses away from us. I could hear the mower from our house, as it had a real old deep sound to it.

There were twenty-eight houses to our little estate, which was small and very friendly. Shane earned quite a bit of money. He paid for his own bike, which wasn't a cheap one. He even paid a lot of money towards his school trip which was a cruise for a week. Shane had this little red exercise book and all the money he got was documented in this.

Not only did he do his grass cutting, Shane cleaned windows. He would only clean bungalows, not houses, unless they only wanted the bottom windows cleaned, as Shane isn't a ladder person. When he leaves home and buys his own property I do hope he decides to buy a bungalow, Brian and I used to say.

I always knew when Shane was near the house, as I could hear him sneezing away. Then I would hear the mower. Once he was in the garden I would call out to him, 'Cup of tea?'

'Yes please, Mum,' he would call out. He took after his dad so much. He had this knitted hat which he always wore. He wore it every day. I used to get hold of it sometimes and wash it, which it needed. Katy washed it as well sometimes. Bless her, she was very domesticated.

On school mornings, I used to hear Katy shout, 'Come on, Shane. Get out of bed.'

'I'm out,' replied Shane. All the time he was still lying in bed.

Then Katy would run up the stairs. 'Get in that bathroom and have a wash and then come downstairs for your breakfast.'

'All right,' I could hear Shane shouting out.

Weekdays he was a devil to get out of bed, but weekends he was up at the crack of dawn.

Once all his grass cutting and window cleaning was done, Shane would have his lunch. Sometimes he ate with us, and sometimes he would go to Nanny's for lunch.

While he was grass cutting I'd pick apples off peoples' trees and take them to Nanny. She used to love making toffee apples for Katy and Shane. Granddad would stand beside her waiting to help dip the apples into the toffee. Shane would bring me home a toffee apple, smiling all over his face. He used to look so pleased with himself for getting apples for his nanny.

Shane used to sit with Granddad most Saturday afternoons, after he had finished his grass cutting and window cleaning. They would watch the Westerns on the television and have their tea and biscuits. Give Shane a pot of tea and the biscuit barrel and you wouldn't hear anything from him!

Granddad only had a few teeth, but he could certainly bite into a toffee apple. I sometimes went round to Nanny's for a cup of tea. As soon as I got in through the backdoor I could hear Granddad and Shane laughing away in the front room.

Brian's mum never liked Westerns but she loved cooking and there was always a wonderful smell of cooking coming from the kitchen. She was a great cook and was in service for many years when she was young, until she married Brian's father in fact.

Her Sunday afternoon tea was really nice - cheese and cucumber sandwiches and her freshly made cakes. It was lovely.

These days, families don't seem to have the time for their Sunday afternoon teas. It's such a shame really that families don't sit down together anymore.

Life was fast when I was first married but we still found time to sit together at weekends. It's quality time which everyone needs. People go shopping on a Sunday, which was never heard of. The big shops weren't open so we could only go to the corner shop, but they never seemed to shut anyway.

Shane would bring our toffee apples home to us. Brian, Shane, Katy and I would sit in the front room munching away. We certainly didn't talk that much to each other. Well, not until our toffee apples had all gone!

Just a few weeks away from Anne's wedding day

Anne was talking to Mum about her wedding. 'We only have one month to go, Mother.'

'I know,' replied Mum. 'You don't have to keep telling me. Maria keeps saying it'll soon be the twenty-fourth of August.'

They didn't like me intruding on their conversation. Father took me outside, I think to get me out of their way. We sat on the back doorstep, in the quiet darkness of the evening watching the clouds roll by. I felt like a pearl in his hand. We sat and talked about when he was a child, and how times were so hard, and how precious to him life was. He never knew where he would be the next day.

My mother came outside and sat on the step beside us. She sucked in her breath through her teeth. 'It's cold out here, you two. You'd better get inside to finish off your story telling.'

'Come on, my girl,' said Father, 'Mother is right. It's getting cold.'

My father's hands started to look frail and thin, and I could see the blue veins in them. Thoughts of Anne when she got married were going through my head. She won't be there anymore to brush my hair or shout at me - or will she! She may still want to do these things. Well I hope so. After all, she'll only be across the way from us. By this time I was sitting in front of the fire listening to the crackling of the wood. There's nothing nicer than a woody smell on a cold night.

For the next few weeks, while there was so much happening at home, I tried to stay out of the way. Mind you, it was hard to do as I was only twelve and seemed to be always getting under their feet.

I was forever asking my father questions, like what did you have to eat for meat, and how did you cook it? He told me they used to eat rabbit and hedgehog. My stomach started to turn by this point. 'How did you cook hedgehog?' I asked.

'Well,' he said, 'once it was killed we rolled it into a nice tight ball and used string to tie it together. Then we would dig a hole in the ground and place the hedgehog into the hole. Then we packed firewood over the hole and lit the fire so that the earth would get really hot and the hedgehog would bake nice and slowly, which would make it lovely and tender to eat. This is when the stewpot full of vegetables was put over the fire. (Everything except the hedgehog was cooked in the stewpot.) After the stewpot was taken off the fire, we used large sticks to drag the fire to one side. This was so we could get to the hole where the hedgehog would be lying, still curled up. We would pull the hedgehog apart to get to the fleshy meat, which was nice and tender to eat with the vegetables.

I still didn't like the thought of hedgehog, but nevertheless I was full of questions. 'When the hedgehog was ready for eating, what colour was the meat?'

'It wasn't dark meat. It was light, like chicken.'

Of the many stories which my father told me, the hedgehog story is the only one which made me sad over food.

Hard as it was, my father said that they seldom went without once they were schooled in the way of life. Hunger makes a man a crack shot, silent on his feet and fearless, and skilful and cunning. They had to be otherwise there would be no food to eat for that day, or the next day.

Another incident that my father told me about was being asked by a man how we let each other know about important events, like weddings and funerals, when none of us have telephones.

'Oh, we have our ways, and they're far better than phoning or writing,' my father had replied with a smile.

The man had a very questioning expression on his face and kept quizzing my father. 'Gypsies move around a lot, don't they Mr. Hearne?'

'Yes sir. They do, but we still hear important things on time.' My father then said good day and left the man thinking.

These days, when I am out and see Gypsy people, I usually stop and look at the gorger-bred people. (Gorger bred is the Gypsy name for non-Gypsies). I wonder what they think when they look at Gypsies. Probably the same things - and more besides - as the man who spoke to my father!

Shane's evenings

Every evening Shane would venture into the kitchen for his toast and strawberry jam. Usually he would get three slices. Then he would come back to the lounge, promptly sit on the settee cross legged with a pillow on his lap and eat his toast with great enjoyment.

Sometimes he would also have shredded wheat and his cup of tea, which he never went without. Shane loved his cup of tea - mornings, afternoons and evenings he would always say yes to a cuppa.

When Shane was in the kitchen, sometimes you would hear him shout out, 'Cup of tea anyone?' Then we would hear, 'Get out of the way, Shane. You're no good at making a cup of tea.'

With that he would be back with us in the lounge in no time, leaving Katy to make a pot of tea for us all. Mind you, she could make a nice cup of tea, even though she was only twelve.

Once it was made, Shane always got his mug of tea first. Then Katy would bring Brian and mine in on a tray with hers. After that, she would go straight back to the kitchen to get the biscuit barrel. None of us could have our cuppa without our biscuit. It doesn't taste the same. It was lovely to see Shane eating his toast and drinking his tea.

I must say Shane was very good at doing his homework. He went up to his room to do it as soon as he had come home from school and had his tea and cake. But straight after having his dinner you would find him watching television. Although he had one in his bedroom, the front room was his favourite place to be.

If something was really good on television nothing would move him. 'Come on Shane. You ought to go and have a wash and change into your pyjamas,' Brian would tell him. Shane had this timed to perfection and would be downstairs as soon as possible without missing any of his programmes. If anyone had it well timed, he did.

I used to hear Katy shouting out, 'Shane, get in this bath now!' She was a right little mum, and used to pull his bed back for him to go to bed at night. She would also put all his nice smelly bath salts in the bathroom for him. I don't think he really appreciated all the smellies. He wasn't in the bath that long. I used to say to Katy, 'Don't worry, that will change when he gets himself a girlfriend.'

Katy's tea making

It was a Sunday morning and we were all fast asleep. Well, that's what I thought! We were awoken by an almighty crash. Brian and I jumped out of bed and ran towards the stairs as we could hear Katy crying.

All I could see was a tea pot and cups and milk jug all lying at the bottom of the stairs. And there was Katy sitting on the stairs in tears.

'I wanted to make you a pot of tea. I've broken everything,' said Katy.

'Don't worry about anything being broken,' said Brian. 'Did you burn yourself?'

'No,' she said.

Brian took her back to bed, while I cleaned everything up and picked up all the broken china. Actually, there wasn't that much broken, apart from the tea pot lid and a couple of handles on the cups.

All I kept thinking was that she could have been scalded with the hot tea.

'You alright, Maria?' I heard Brian say to me. 'Yes thanks. It's nearly done now.'

'I'll go and make another pot of tea, and take it upstairs with some special biscuits,' Brian said.

It wasn't long before Brian had made the tea and taken it upstairs.

We were all in bed - Brian, me, Shane, Katy and even our little dog Tops. Katy's eyes were so red where she had been crying. After we had our tea and special biscuits and lots of cuddles we got up and went downstairs to have our breakfast.

On Sunday mornings we always had the works - a good old fried breakfast. Then the children went upstairs to get dressed.

'All I keep thinking, Brian, is that she's only nine and could have burnt herself really badly,' I said.

'I know, but she's alright. So we must not mention it to her as it could upset her again,' Brian said.

'Mum,' I could hear. Oh no, what's happened now, I thought. Katy stood in the doorway, still looking rather upset. 'The stair carpet is wet. Will it dry out alright?'

'Of course it will,' I said. 'When I put the hoover over it, it will be all nice and dry.'

'Ok,' she said as she turned and walked back upstairs. 'Poor kid. That's really upset her,' I said.

'Bless her. She was trying to surprise us,' Brian said.

Old Joe Grey

One Saturday morning, my friend June Elephick came around to ask if I would like to go and play in her dad's woodyard.

'Mum,' I shouted. 'Can I go and play with June?'

'Yes, if you like,' Mother replied, 'but I want you back by one o'clock for lunch.'

'What have we got for lunch?' I asked.

'Old Joe Grey.'

'Oh lovely, Mum.'

With that June and I started to walk out of the door. We had a lovely time at the woodyard, making wood bundles for firewood for her father to sell.

While we were playing on the piles of wood, June's brother came over to us and asked if we would make up more bundles of firewood. His dad would pay us, he said. Like fools, we fell into his trap. We were most probably doing his work for him!

My stomach was rumbling. It was telling me that it was near my lunchtime. 'I've got to go now June. I think it's my lunchtime.'

'Will you be coming back out to play after your lunch?' asked June. 'When Old Joe Grey has gone home?'

'Old Joe Grey isn't a person,' I said, 'it's my lunch!'

'Why did your mum call it Old Joe Grey?'

'It's what it's called, that's why.'

'What's it made of then, Maria?'

'Tinned tomatoes, chopped onions, sliced bacon and potatoes, with plenty of seasoning. All this goes into a frying pan and cooks slowly. We eat it with nice crusty bread. It's really lovely.'

After I had explained all that, I could see that she was about to ask more questions, and no way was I going to hang around.

'I'm off now June. I'll see you after I've had my lunch.'

With that, off I went hopping and skipping, and certainly looking forward to having my lunch.

Later, when I got home, and was eating my lunch, I asked Mother, 'Mum, why do they call this Old Joe Grey?'

'Probably after Old Joe Grey himself,' she replied.

I didn't bother to ask any more questions because it was all getting too complicated.

I never asked again and to this day I am still none the wiser!

The balcony

Patsy and Yvonne never had a handle on their balcony door. I never did find out why!

If they wanted to go out onto the balcony, they would ask me to climb out of their lounge window onto the window ledge, and then step over to the balcony ledge. From there I would be able to jump down onto the balcony and open the door for them. When I think back, God knows why I did it. I never did like heights.

One day, I was in our street talking to Celia when I heard Patsy calling out from this lounge window.

'Maria, we can't get out.'

'Yes you can,' I replied. 'You can use the front door, like other people do.'

'It's not the front door I want. It's our balcony I want to go out on.'

I just turned my back and said to Celia, 'Oh, just pay no attention to him. Perhaps he'll do it himself. I'm fed up with climbing out the window for him. I could kill myself. Come on, let's go.'

With that, Celia and I started to walk away. All I could hear was, 'Maria, don't be horrible to me. I would like to get on the balcony, and sit in my deck chair. Come on, Babe.' His voice was fading away quite nicely, and I was really happy. No more climbing on to the ledge for me.

Celia and I were out most of the afternoon enjoying ourselves. As we arrived back, I felt this almighty dig in my side.

'What do you want?' I said looking at Celia.

'Look!' she said. 'Patsy is out on his balcony.'

There he sat with this jovial smile all over his face and waving a spanner.

'I managed it in the end, Babe, so I won't be needing you anymore.'

'Good,' I said in a rather hard-hearted voice. 'It's a pity you didn't think of the spanner before.'

'What are we doing tomorrow Maria?' asked Celia. 'Shall we go to the pictures, and see who's there?'

'Oh yeah. I've got that straight skirt, Celia, which Anne and Peter bought me. Well, it's certainly straight but it's not that tight. I'll have to roll the top over to make it short. What are you going to wear?'

'I've also got a nice straight skirt, which is nice and tight. It will make the boys' heads turn.'

'Well between the two of us I think we're going to look good. We mustn't forget the high heels, Celia.'

'No. They're all in the box behind my bedroom door.'

The caravan at Walton

Janet and I were down at the caravan at Walton-on-the-Naze with the children for a week.

Shane and Katy were my two, and Heath and Donna were Janet's two children.

We had had a lovely time on the beach and the sun had shone all day. The children had been happy making sandcastles. We gave them their dinner and told them they could have half an hour outside before they came in for their wash.

Janet washed up the dinner things while I got their beds ready. 'Come on,' she called out to me. 'I've finished and I've made a cup of tea.'

We knew where the children were because we could hear each one of them playing around our caravan. Janet was saying how wonderful the day had been, and how good the children were.

'Once they've had their baths this evening they can watch television with us,' I said.

'That will finish the day off nicely,' said Janet.

Janet looked up to see where the children were as they had gone rather quiet.

'Oh no, Maria. Look at them!'

Out of the window I saw Heath and Shane carrying a window box from next door. They had tipped out half the flowers as they were carrying it across to us.

'Mum, Mum!' they were shouting out. 'Look what we've got. Flowers for you, and they're in a box as well.'

'You mustn't do that. They're not ours,' I said.

All they kept saying was that we didn't have any flowers around our caravan.

'What are we going to do?' Janet said.

'We'll have to put the flowers back into the box, and return it. Thank goodness the couple have gone home.' We looked at each other and burst out laughing.

'Janet, we shouldn't be laughing but I can't help it. The people opposite were staring at us in amazement. We've done all we can so let's get back into the caravan.'

The children were sitting on the settee quite sheepish. 'Are we in trouble?' they asked us with tears in their eyes.

'No. We've cleaned it all up, so it's alright now and nobody will notice any difference,' Janet said.

We watered the flowers every day, as it was quite hot. The people who owned the caravan only came down at weekends, so we had a week to make sure the window box looked nice on their next visit. Plus we had to drum it into the children that they must not say anything about it to the couple, as they always talked to them.

The weekend arrived and so did the couple who owned the caravan. We just stayed in our caravan, and as it was evening time the children were in bed. Janet and I looked at each other and started to laugh again. But the flowers did look nice, I must say, thanks to our watering.

It's the neighbours I'm worried about. Will they open their mouths?

Morning arrived, and after the children had their breakfast they went out to play before we went to the beach. Janet and I stood by the window watching the children talking to the couple who owned the caravan.

They suddenly turned away from the couple and ran indoors. 'Mum, Mum!' they were shouting. 'The people said thank you for watering the flowers.'

'You didn't tell them about you moving the flowers, did you?'

They stood there shaking their heads, saying. 'No, we didn't say anything.'

We didn't stay on the beach that long as Brian and Mick were coming down for the weekend. As we were all walking back to the caravan from another lovely day on the beach we noticed that the couple with the flower box were sitting outside in the sun.

'Dad's here,' the children all shouted out.

'Hello,' Brian and Mick said at the same time. 'What have you been up to?'

'See that box?' Heath said. 'We tried to carry it and put it by our caravan because we don't have any flowers.'

'But we dropped it,' said Shane.

The pair of them were jabbering away saying, 'But our mum put it all back, and we've been watering it all week. Come and see.'

'Now let's go in and have a nice cup of tea. Then you can tell Daddy all about it,' Janet said.

We were soon in our caravan drinking tea, and the children were explaining what they had done with the box. Oddly enough, the children did keep their mouth shut about the box. The couple spoke to them but the children never said a word.

Thank goodness.

We all had a wonderful week, and we still laugh about the window box even to this day.

Outside the school gate

When Katy and Shane were young I would walk them to and from school and Tops came with us. It wasn't that far, but there was a dangerous main road to cross, and I wanted to make sure they arrived safely. Also, I used to meet up with the other mothers I was friendly with.

I often walked to school with Dawn Roser. She had six children, but they didn't all go to my children's school. Her eldest one went to high school, and he caught the bus.

On this particular morning, it was rather cold. Standing around wasn't doing me any good, as I didn't really like the cold. Not that it seemed to bother Katy and Shane. They were always running around, meeting up with their friends.

'When is the bell going to go? I'm feeling bloody cold standing here,' Dawn said, rubbing her hands together.

'It's not even winter yet. It's only autumn, and I hate the cold, Dawn,' I replied.

'So do I, Maria. It's alright for the children. They're on the move all the time.'

'I'm moving about, well on the spot, like you Dawn, just to keep warm. Tops is nice and warm. He's got his coat, and that's always put on the radiator overnight for him. I like to spoil him.'

Dawn suddenly jumped up in the air. 'Oh, Dawn, what's the matter?' I asked.

'I don't know. I felt all wet going down my leg.'

I looked down and there was Tops with his leg in the air beside Dawn's leg.

'Maria, it's your bloody dog. He's just weed down my leg,' Dawn said.

'Oh Dawn, I'm so sorry. He must have thought your leg was a lamp-post or a tree. I know his eyesight is getting bad, but I didn't think it was that bad,' I said, trying not to laugh.

'Oh well, I'll have to have another bath when I get in and change my tights.' With that, Dawn looked at me and laughed.

'Come on. The bell's gone. Let's head home.'

Dawn had a wonderful sense of humour. I never saw her without a smile on her face.

Katy's cooking

When Katy was twelve, she used to cook most Saturdays. I would be doing the housework and was never allowed in the kitchen. We knew what we would be having, meat cobbler. The reason why we would have that every Saturday was because, in one of her cookery lessons, she did a wonderful meat cobbler. So every Saturday after that it was meat cobbler on the menu, with mashed potatoes and vegetables.

When Shane was sitting at the table, I could always see what was on his mind to say. I used to look at him, my eyes wide open slightly shaking my head. I wanted to make sure he wouldn't say, 'Oh, we have meat cobbler again, Katy!'

Katy was very good in the kitchen. She often went round to see her nanny to talk about cooking and what she could cook again. But our menu always stayed the same on a Saturday, until she started her Saturday morning job at the hairdresser's. I missed her cooking and I used to like doing my housework while Katy was in the kitchen.

I always had to go to work on Sunday night, so I always went to bed for the afternoon. So back into the kitchen Katy would go. This time it was making jam Swiss roll for our tea.

Brian always made the sandwiches for our tea. Katy would lay the table with her centrepiece being the Swiss roll which would look very nice too. There weren't many Saturdays or Sundays that she wasn't in the kitchen. Even these days when she makes her famous meat cobbler and her wonderful Swiss roll it's still enjoyable.

There were times when Katy would venture to make other things. I remember the time she made this wonderful upside-down cake which came out the tin beautifully. I had tried to do it many times, and no way did mine come out the tin like hers. Her sponges would rise beautifully, not like mine. I could never get mine to rise. I had a mixer, and I didn't think anyone could go wrong making a sponge with a mixer, but I could.

I used to think Katy really had a flair for cooking. But her hairdressing was closer to her heart. All she really spoke about was becoming a hairdresser.

Katy's daughter Kieralea is no way a cook like her mother. She always says, 'Mum, can you do it for me.' However, she is following her mum's footsteps because she is at college at the moment studying to be a hairdresser. She also has a Saturday morning job, plus during the school holidays she works at the hairdresser's, which she enjoys. They think very highly of her. We are so very proud of her.

Tops and ice cream

Whenever we were out and the children asked for an ice cream, Tops would want one. Brian or I would stand in the queue waiting to buy our ice cream, and the children would be sitting down waiting patiently with Tops.

With his lovely black coat Tops used to look so cute. The way he stood he could have been a show dog. But the lady Brian bought him from said that he was the runt of the litter, so unfortunately wouldn't make a show dog.

Anyway, Brian didn't buy Tops for showing. He was to be our family dog. But as he grew up from being a puppy, he became quite naughty. Whenever he had the chance to run off he would make a bolt for it, except when we were away from home. He never ran away then, even if he smelt a bitch in season. But when we got back home, his nose went straight into the air and away he would go.

When we lived at Pilgrims Hatch, there were loads of little Tops running around. In those days, dogs roamed the streets. I tried my best to keep Tops in but, once that nose went in the air, that was it. No one could catch him.

'Ice creams all round!' I heard Brian shout out.

I looked up and there stood Brian with these lovely ice creams in his hand. As Brian was passing the children theirs, Tops would be standing wagging his tail and licking his mouth.

As I was sitting on the wall eating my ice cream, Tops would be having a lick of his while I was holding it for him. He really enjoyed it, just like the rest of us. In those days ice cream tasted like ice cream.

Raspberry picking

Dad took me and Cousin Celia over to South Weald to pick raspberries. We both jumped at the chance even though it was quite a walk to South Weald. So with Dad in front and Celia and I behind, waving our baskets about and singing, we were very happy.

'How many are you going to eat?' Celia asked me.

'I don't really know. The nice red big ones, they're the best I think.'

'Come on, you two. We'll never be there the rate you're going,' Dad shouted out.

With that we started to run to catch my dad up. It didn't take us long really to get to our lovely raspberry bush, and it was loaded, great big fat red ones just hanging there for the picking.

'Mind how you go, you two,' said Dad. 'The branches are a bit prickly, and I don't want you going home all scratched.'

Celia and I were eating these raspberries as fast as we could. They looked so yummy and tempting that there was no stopping us.

'How many have you got in your baskets? By the size of them we should fill our baskets up quite quickly,' Dad called out.

'Well, Uncle Ambrose, we haven't got that many as yet!' said Celia.

'Why not?'

'We're eating them instead of putting them in our baskets,' Celia shouted out at the top of her voice.

I turned and looked at her, and burst out laughing. 'Celia, all your mouth is a pinkie red colour.'

'So is yours. Do you think it will wash off?' Celia asked.

'I don't really know,' I said.

'Hurry up,' said Dad. 'My basket's nearly full already.'

'Come on, Celia. We'd better show my dad the amount we have, plus our faces.'

As we walked round to the other side of the raspberry bush, my dad caught sight of us. 'By the looks of your faces you won't have any raspberries at all in your baskets. Still, never mind. I've got enough for what Mum needs. When you two get home you'd better try and wash your faces.'

'Will it come off, Uncle Ambrose?' Celia asked.

'It'll probably take a few days for all the stain to go away,' Dad replied. Celia and I just looked at each other with somewhat worrying looks on our faces. 'Did you check them before you put them into your mouths?'

'Why?' I asked.

'Well, my girl, they can have maggots in them. Didn't you know that?'

'You're joking, Dad!' I said, spitting and hoping that the maggots would come out. Celia was wiping her mouth on her skirt as vigorously as she could.

'Oh Celia I don't like the thought of the maggots in me, do you? Dad, I hope Mum washes them before she cooks them,' I said.

'Of course she will. She'll soak them in a little salt, and if there's any maggots in them they will float to the top. Then Mum will strain them off and rinse them well.'

'If we've swallowed any maggots, Uncle Ambrose, what will happen to us?' Celia asked.

I was rubbing my stomach, and Celia couldn't stop wiping her mouth with her skirt. 'Oh, Celia. They won't hurt us, will they?' I asked.

'Come on you two,' said Dad. 'Stop worrying about all the raspberries you've eaten, and get a move on. Otherwise Mum won't have time to make her raspberry pie.'

'Oh, Celia. I'm not having any pie tonight.'

'Why? Are you full, Maria?' Celia said, trying not to laugh. With that I couldn't help but laugh too.

'Have you had a nice time, girls? Did you pick any raspberries for me?' Mum asked when we got home.

'Well, we did, but we ate most of them,' Celia piped up.

'I can see that by the look of both your faces. You're going to have a hell of a job to get it all off at once. Anyway, I hope you checked the raspberries before you put them into your mouth. Go and sit down, both of you, and I'll get you a bowl of hot soapy water so you can wash your faces.'

Celia and I went and sat on the lawn and Mum brought out the bowl of soapy water.

'Mum.'

'Yes, Maria.'

'If we didn't check the raspberries before we put them into our mouth, and it had a maggot in, would it hurt us?'

'No, of course not. You would have chewed it with the raspberry. Why do you ask, anyway?'

'Well, Uncle Ambrose said ...' began Celia, trying to wipe away all the stain on her face.

'Oh don't take any notice of your Uncle Ambrose. He was only having a laugh with you. He probably ate plenty himself,' said Mum. 'Anyway, I must go, girls, otherwise I won't get this pie made for dinner. I expect you'll have some with us, Celia.'

'No thanks, Aunt Luvvie. I don't feel very hungry.'

'I'll save some for you tomorrow,' Mum said.

Celia didn't answer, but she whispered to me, 'Maria, I'm too frightened to eat another raspberry.'

'I'm never going to eat another one myself either. The thought of them is making me feel sick,' I replied.

'If you feel you're going to be sick, Maria, then go to the toilet quickly. I don't really want to see your maggots.'

'Don't be horrible, Mum,' I said. Then I looked at Celia and all I could see was white soap around her face. I just burst out laughing, and Celia started laughing as well.

With that we carried on with trying to wash off the pinkie red stain from our faces.

Katy being bitten

Katy was always dressing Tops up, and playing in her bedroom with him. Mind you, he was always with her. They were great pals.

One particular day she was playing in her bedroom with him as usual. I was downstairs getting on with my housework quite happily. Every so often I could hear Katy telling Tops to sit still. She could do anything with him.

Then all of a sudden I heard this almighty scream. I ran upstairs and there was Katy with her doll's blanket in her hand, wiping her mouth, and Tops looking rather sad with his ears down.

'What on earth has happened?' I noticed that she had blood around her mouth, and her top lip had started to swell up.

'Tops bit me. He didn't mean to,' said Katy.

'Why did he bite you, Katy?' I asked her.

'I put the doll's blanket over his head and then I put my head under it as well. I thought we could call you and then hide from you.'

'I'd better get you to the doctor's so he can have a look at it.'

'I don't want to go and leave Tops here on his own, Mum. He looks so sad.'

'Come on. He'll be alright.'

With that we were in the car and on our way to the doctor's with Katy holding a gauze to her mouth. Once we arrived and parked-up we went straight in.

I was dreading asking whether we could see the doctor without an appointment. The receptionist was so stern.

'Can I see a doctor, please? My daughter has been bitten by my dog.'

The receptionist didn't say a word. She just turned and walked away. That's nice of her, I thought. Then she replied, still with no smile on her face, 'Sit down and the doctor will see you shortly.'

Katy and I sat on the seat and I held her hand. 'He won't hurt me, Mum, will he?'

'No, he'll be very gentle and anyway I can't really see much of a mark on your lip.'

Katy's little face was so white. I put my arm around her to give her extra comfort.

'Come this way Maria and Katy.'

I looked up and there stood our doctor. I was so pleased to see him. Katy liked him, and I knew she would be relaxed with him.

'Well, now, what have you been up to?' he said as he lifted her up onto his couch.

'She was playing with our little dog when she put her dolly's blanket over their heads and he bit her mouth,' I explained.

'I hope you're going to have the dog put down after this.'

'It was my fault. I put it over his head and he didn't like it,' Katy shouted out with tears rolling down her face.

'There's not too much damage done,' said the doctor. 'To be on the safe side, I would like to give her an injection to kill off any nasty germs which your little dog might have.'

'He doesn't have germs, Mum. He's our dog,' Katy said.

'Anyway, this dog of yours ought to be put down as he could do it again,' the doctor repeated.

'What's put down mean, Mum?'

I was just about to explain to Katy when the doctor interrupted. 'Oh they'll put him to sleep, and then he dies.'

'You're horrible, you are. I don't like you anymore.' Katy jumped off his couch and put her arms around me.

'You must bring Katy back to me in a couple of days so I can check her lip,' said the doctor.

'I'm not coming back here,' Katy said, walking towards the door. The doctor knelt down beside her and said, 'You need to come back because we don't want your lip to turn nasty, do we, Katy?'

By this time he was holding her hand. 'I'm sorry for what I said about your little dog. You don't have to put him to sleep.'

'We weren't going to, were we Mum?' She stood there looking up at me with her big blue yes. They were full of tears. The look on the doctor's face wasn't too good either.

'Come on Katy. We have to go now. Tops will be wanting his dinner,' I said to her. With that we walked toward the door.

'Don't forget to make that appointment,' the doctor called out.

'I will,' I said.

'I'll come only if you're nice to me and my Tops,' said Katy.

'I promise I'll be nice to you and your Tops,' the doctor said to her.

I made the appointment, and then we made our way to the car. Once inside I looked at Katy's lip and by this time it was looking quite nasty. 'Katy, you'll have to bathe your lip in nice warm water two or three times a day,' I said.

'I will,' she said.

Once we were home and indoors Katy was calling out for Tops. 'Don't worry, Tops, I'm alright.' She was on the floor stroking him. His ears were still down, but I noticed that his tail was wagging slightly.

'Dad, Tops bit me today but I'm alright. Look,' she said, showing her lip to Brian. I told him I'd explain what happened later.

Then we all had our dinner, even Tops.

'Can I get down?' Katy asked after she had eaten.

'Ok,' I replied. 'But if you're going to play with Tops, don't put the blanket over his head, will you.'

'No, I won't.' Katy ran upstairs with Tops running behind her.

'Shall I go and watch her?' Shane said.

'No, she'll be alright,' I said.

'Now then. What's been going on? Is anyone going to fill me in on this?' Brian said.

I made a pot of tea and explained everything to Brian. Even he was against putting Tops to sleep.

'But if it had been any worse, or if it happens again, he will have to be put to sleep,' he said.

Well, Tops never did bite her again. It was just a one off. And thank goodness for that, otherwise it would have broken Katy's heart if he had been put down.

Most days he was dressed up in her doll's clothes and put into her doll's pram. Then she would lay him down and cover him up, this time with no blanket over his head!

Away they would go, Katy pushing her pram around our block. How Tops loved it. Especially when they got to Nanny's as there were always goodies there.

The famous vest

I arrived home from work around 5:30. As I was walking down the path I could smell my dinner cooking. By the aroma which was coming from the kitchen, it was meat pudding - my favourite! No way was I going to miss my dinner tonight, even though I had to catch the seven o'clock bus into Brentwood to meet Mick Smith outside the Odeon picture house.

I ate dinner far too quickly, although I did enjoy it. I was hoping I had not eaten too much, as I wanted to get into my skirt! I got up from the table and took my plate into the kitchen.

'Mum that was lovely. I really enjoyed my dinner. Thank you.' Then I added, 'Mum, do you want to use the bathroom?'

'No, dear. There's plenty of hot water, so you can have a good long soak,' Mum replied.

'I don't really have a great deal of time. I'm meeting Mick at 7:30.'

'7:30! You'd better get a move on. It's six o'clock now.'

'I know, Mum. It won't take me long to get ready.'

'If that's the case, Maria, that will be a first! You'll have to run for the bus, my girl.'

Mum was still talking to me, but I couldn't hear very well, what with the bathroom door shut and the water running. Eventually I was in the bath, soaking up the wonderful smells of essence of white lace, and wishing I could stay longer. This won't do, I said to myself. I'll be late if I don't get a move on!

As I came through to the dining room to go upstairs, I noticed Dad and Mum sitting at the table having their dinner.

'Hello, my girl. Alright?' said Dad

'Yes thanks,' I replied. 'I can't stop and talk, I'm going out tonight.'

'Don't forget I want you in by ten o'clock!'

'Yes, I know.' I didn't dare say what I was thinking, otherwise he would have grounded me forever!

At least my skirt fits, which is surprising after the amount of dinner I ate. As I was sitting on my bed doing my cardigan buttons up, there was a knock at my door.

'Maria, can I come in?'

'Yes, come in.'

I noticed that Mum had something in her hand. I wasn't really bothered as I was too busy trying to do my buttons up. Well, just enough so I could put my cardigan over my head. If you can remember, girls in the sixties used to wear their cardigans back to front. This was all the rage then.

'Do you want anything, Mum?' I asked.

'Here's your vest,' said Mum. 'It's cold out there. You ought to put it on, otherwise you could catch your death of cold.'

This so-called vest leapt out of my mum's hand just like a spring! 'Oh, Mum, you are joking. I'm not wearing that! I don't care if it's cold!'

'Who's going to see it under your cardigan? It's dark in the pictures! So come on, take your cardigan off and put it on.'

I knew not to argue with Mother, so I put the blessed vest on. Sure enough, it showed under my cardigan. Oh well, I knew just what to do with it! Right, I'm ready. One last look at myself. Yes, very nice.

'Dad, Mum. I'm off now. Bye.'

'Don't be late. Ten o'clock remember. You've work in the morning,' Dad called out. 'Did you hear me?'

'Yes, I heard you,' I answered.

Good God! Mother was right, it's cold. I'd better hurry up if I'm going to catch my bus, otherwise I'll be late.

As I was walking down the road I noticed my friend Janice. 'Hi! Has the six-forty bus gone yet?' I asked.

'Yes, it went about five minutes ago Maria. Would you like to walk with me?' said Janice.

'I don't know about walking to the station. I think I'm going to have to be late if I don't run, Janice.'

I could hear Janice behind me trying to keep up with me. 'Slow down Maria.'

'Sorry, Janice, I have to get a move on. I'm meeting Mick at 7:30. I'm going to call into the Essex Arms pub first. I haven't got time to explain now, Janice. See you some other time.'

I could hear her in the distance saying something, but there was only one thing on my mind at that moment. I had to get to the pub, and then catch the bus from the station. To run down Warley Hill would take me five minutes, at least!

My hair won't move, with the amount of lacquer I'd put on! Do you remember the sixties, girls? The lacquer was just like glue wasn't it? It was that old sticky stuff which we used to pour into our spray bottles.

Here at last - the Essex Arms. Let's hope there isn't anyone in the toilets. Smashing! There isn't. I wish they'd made these toilets bigger. Coat off. Oh, these blessed buttons on this cardigan. Right - off with this goddamn vest! Back on with my clothes again! I bet Mother's ears are burning.

I was struggling to get my vest into my clutch bag, but it kept springing out again! Oh, to hell with it, I'll leave my bag open. I'll try to shut the bag once I'm on the bus. How the devil did Mother hold this damn vest in her hand, so I couldn't see it?

Eventually I was on the bus, and on my way. I'd still got to put this vest in my bag. Believe you me, every time I tried to push it in, it popped out. In the end, after a lot of pushing it did go into my bag, thank God!

There he was once again, with a lovely box of chocolates. Mum will be pleased! 'Have you been waiting long, Mick?'

'No,' he replied, handing me the chocolates. Then he leaned forward and gave me one of his breathtaking kisses, which used to make my legs go weak!

I made sure he didn't see my handbag, as it looked like a potbellied pig! If I were to open the bag, I knew for sure the vest would pop out. God knows where it would land, I dread to think!

I didn't see much of the film. I knew I wouldn't. Well, to be honest, I didn't want to! The two and half hours that I was with Mick went too quickly. I had to leave at nine thirty to catch my bus home.

I was standing at the bus stop, cuddling up to Mick so I could keep warm.

'Oh, that's all right. You needn't see me home,' I said. 'The bus stops outside my house, doesn't it?'

'Maria, if we get off the bus at the station we can have a drink at the Essex Arms. Perhaps your dad will be there.'

'That's a good idea,' I said as we were jumping on the bus.

Once again I was on the bus, this time wondering how the hell I was going to get my bloody vest on again! And get back by ten o'clock. Sitting on the bus, I had everything crossed, so to speak, hoping that my dad would be at the pub. If he wasn't I had to get one hell of a move on!

Eventually we were there and I looked around the pub for my dad. I was beginning to panic. Hearing Mick laughing, I turned around.

'What are you laughing at?' I asked him.

'You look like you're going to be sick,' Mick said.

'I won't be a minute.' With that I quickly walked off in the direction of the toilets, to put my vest back on. Then I hurried back into the bar to have a quick drink. Mind you, I did need it!

'Over here.' I could hear Mick calling me.

'I can't stop that long. You know I have to be in by ten, or have you forgotten?'

'No,' he said laughing. 'Look, there's your dad behind you!'

I turned around and there stood my dad with a pint in his hand. 'Hello, Dad.'

'Hello, babe. Did you have a nice evening? I'm going home in a minute, my girl. So if you wait we can walk home together.'

Thank God for that. If I'm late, I won't be told off if Dad's with me. 'Are you coming, Dad? I'm walking home now.'

'Hang on, Maria. You're not walking home on your own,' Mick called out.

'I'll stay and have another pint if Mick is walking home with you,' said Dad, 'When you see your mother, Maria, tell her I won't be long.'

The walk home was nice! 'You're not cold are you, Maria?'

'No, how could I be cold cuddled up to you,' I replied, even though it was rather cold. It was October and the leaves on the ground were filling the air with this wonderful smell. I felt like picking them up and throwing them in the air. There was no time for that as I had to be in very soon.

We were nearly home when we both spotted my mum. We quickly turned into the side road called The Drive - just to say good night!

'Maria,' I heard. 'It's gone ten. Your father won't be pleased with you. So come on in.'

I had to break away from this wonderful kiss. His arms were wrapped around me. My legs felt as though they were floating!

'You'd better go, Maria,' said Mick. I turned and walked away. My heart was pounding. I could still smell Mick's aftershave on me.

'Good night, Mrs. Hearne,' Mick called out.

'Good night, love. Mind how you go,' Mum called out. Then turning to me, she said. 'It's a good job you put that vest on tonight. I told you it was cold, didn't I, Maria?'

I looked at Mum, my mouth wide open. I couldn't say anything. Then I turned around, hoping that Mick hadn't heard. He was still standing in the same place. Oh no, I thought, he didn't did he? By the look on his face, grinning as he was like a Cheshire cat, he had heard!

'See you tomorrow night, babe,' he called out.

'Good night,' I called back and with that I walked into our house with Mum.

'Good night, Mum. I'm going straight to bed. Oh, by the way, I saw Dad in the pub. He said he won't be too late home.'

And off I went to bed with my lovely thoughts of Mick - but certainly not of the vest!

Our pets

I couldn't say that our cat Twinkles was a nice cat, yet we were all very fond of him in a funny way.

One day, I was washing up at the sink, humming away to myself quite happily, when suddenly I heard the cat flap open with an extra bang and Twinkles making this growling noise.

'Hello Twinkles,' I called out. 'Have you come to see me?' I turned to look at him and I couldn't believe my eyes. There, lying on the floor, was this enormous fish flapping about and gasping for air!

'Oh, my God, where did you get that from?' I opened the back door to see Twinkles running across the lawn with another large fish in his mouth.

I put my hands up to my mouth, thinking that they belonged to the couple in the bungalow across the way. They were their prize fish which cost a fortune. I could see our neighbour Ron in his garden.

'Ron,' I called out. 'Can you come over here?'

'Yes,' he answered and was straight over.

I took him indoors and showed him the fish, still lying there flapping about and gasping for air.

'What are they doing there? Don't you think you should have them in a pond?' asked Ron.

'Don't be funny. My cat has just brought them in.'

'What do you want me to do then?'

'Take them back for me, Ron.'

'Where to?'

'To your pond. I think that's where they come from,' I said.

'How on earth am I going to do that?' said Ron.

'Just lean over and throw them in the pond. Your arms are longer than mine and no one will see you.'

'Do you realise, Maria, how much these fish cost?'

'Yes, Ron. Just hurry and get the bloody fish back into the pond. Here's my washing up bowl. You can shove them in there.'

With that, Ron dumped the fish into the washing up bowl. I watched him go through our gate and then lost sight of him because of our high hedge, and no way was I going to follow him.

I went back into my kitchen and just stood there waiting for someone to shout out, 'What the hell are you doing!' But, thank goodness, it didn't happen.

The next thing I noticed was Ron walking through our gate, with a smile on his face.

'Did you put them back into the pond?'

'Yes I did. You were lucky. I don't think anyone saw me.'

'Thanks, Ron. I really appreciate it.'

'Well, don't let it happen again.'

'Alright Ron. I'll make sure they're herrings next time. I prefer them!' I just gave a half smile, but I was wondering how the devil I keep a cat away from fish. It's their favourite meal!

Nevertheless, Twinkles never did bring any more fish. I have my own ideas why!

Our other cat, Jemima, didn't get up to any tricks. But one of the things she would do was call out 'hello' every time she came in from outside. Well, we thought she said 'hello.'

She did like water. The only way I could do my hoovering was to put her in the basin with warm water and some bubbles. In she would jump and quite happily lie there while I was hoovering.

Even Twinkles liked the water. There was a particular day when Ron's wife, Gloria, was lying in her bath having this wonderful soak as you do, with lovely bubbles and oils.

I was sitting in the garden with my friend Jackie. All of a sudden there was this almighty scream. We both jumped up and looked around, but couldn't see anything.

Then we heard, 'Maria, come and get your bloody cat. It's sitting on the edge of my bath, playing with my bubbles. When I went to pick it up the bloody thing went for me.'

There stood Gloria by her back door with a bath towel around her, all red faced and not looking very happy. It took me all my effort not to laugh but Jackie was rolling around with laughter, which wasn't making this any better.

'Oh look, there he is,' Jackie shouted out. 'He's all wet. Come here Twinkles and I'll dry you.'

'Dry it! I'll drown the bloody thing if it does it again,' Gloria shouted out.

'You'll have a job to catch it,' said Jackie. When I turned around, there was Jackie trying to catch Twinkles to dry him. No way was he having any of that! He was growling and spitting, his tail up in the air like a telescope.

'Leave him Jackie,' I called out. 'He'll lie in the sun and dry off.' He promptly laid himself on our blanket, rolled on to his back and just stayed there with us.

'Ah, you ought to come and see him now Gloria. He's all fluffy and smells lovely. What were those oils you had in your bath?' Jackie shouted out.

I just looked at Jackie and burst out laughing. Well, it was all we could do really. We looked up at Gloria's bathroom window and it was shut. No way was she having Twinkles in her bathroom again.

When we first had our cat flap, we put a sign on the outside of it saying, 'Beware of the cat'. Brian decided to put a hook just inside the cat flap, so we could hang our back door keys on it.

We never put our hands straight inside. We always kicked it first. This gave Twinkles time to come out. If you didn't he would have got hold of you, just like a dog.

One day he become ill and I took him to the vets who said it looked as if he had been poisoned. The vet kept him overnight to see if he would pull through, but unfortunately he didn't.

It was a terrible death. Thank goodness for the products of today. Most of them are harmless to animals. People are far more educated these days in caring for their pets.

Being pregnant with Shane

I felt so sick every day, really awful. Not in the mornings though, but last thing at night. Around nine o'clock was my worst time, when I was lying in bed at night. It felt just like I had been out and had one too many drinks.

One Sunday we decided to go to see Brian's mum. Janet and Mick were living there at the time, and I thought it would be a good opportunity for me to ask Janet if she would come to the doctor's with me.

'Janet, would you come to the doctor's with me tomorrow?' I asked. 'I might be pregnant, and I don't really want to go on my own.'

'Maria, I think I could be pregnant as well!' Janet replied.

'You're joking!' I said, smiling at her. 'How far do you think you are then?'

Janet just laughed and said, 'It looks as if we are the same time as each other.'

Janet and I met at the doctor's next day, as we said we would, feeling excited and apprehensive or, to be honest, very frightened. We sat there like a pair of bookends, not saying a word, both looking at old magazines. I say 'old' because there are never new magazines in any surgery waiting rooms, are there?

I wasn't really looking at the magazines at all, just flicking through the pages, trying to take my mind off things.

I had heard such stories about the first visit to the doctor to find out whether one was pregnant or not. I was not looking forward to it at all!

'Maria Everett,' I heard the receptionist call. She was peering through a hatch and had a smile on her face.

'Mrs. Everett?'

'Yes,' I said in this very soft voice. In the background, I could see my doctor looking over the top of his half-moon glasses.

'Go to the yellow room please.' I heard the receptionist's stern voice.

The way she called my name out and said yellow room made me feel as though I was back at school again, and had done something wrong. I expect we can all relate to those times, I know I can. Thank goodness doctors' receptionists have changed their manner these days.

Janet looked at me and said, 'Well don't just sit there. Off you go.'

Oh very funny, I thought. It's easy for her to speak. She hasn't made her appointment yet. I know what she's thinking. She wants to make sure she is pregnant first. Mind you, I don't know if I am yet! Well if not I'd love to know what's making me feel so sick.

These thoughts were whirling around in my head as I started to walk toward the corridor. It led to the 'yellow door', which must have heard an awful lot of people's secrets.

I stood outside the door for a few seconds just to take some deep breaths and to prepare myself for the unknown. 'Right, here goes.' I quietly knocked on the door.

'Come in,' I heard the doctor call out in an authoritative voice.

I turned the knob very slowly, trying to prolong the situation, but the next thing I knew I was standing in the open doorway, staring straight ahead and trying not to look at the doctor.

'Good morning Maria. Come in and sit down.'

It was only three paces to the chair, but I was shaking. The doctor peered at me over the top of his glasses. He seemed very professional and quite frightening. Yet when he spoke he had a lovely soft Irish voice that made me feel much more relaxed.

'Well, sit down Maria, what can I do for you?'

I was so nervous. I looked straight at him, but all the time I was fiddling with the buckle on my handbag.

'I think I'm pregnant!' I said very quietly.

'You do, do you? What gives you that idea?'

'I'm feeling sick and awful.'

'Right then, I suppose I'd better examine you. If you'd like to get yourself ready and get on to the couch, I'll be with you in just a few minutes. OK?'

As he walked towards the door, he turned and smiled. 'Don't look so worried,' he said in his reassuring Irish accent.

When the examination was over, I sat in the chair beside his desk and waited for the news. I didn't really know how I felt.

'Well, Maria,' he said, peering over his glasses again. 'You're certainly pregnant. I would say about six weeks. End of February, early March baby for you.'

All I could say was, 'Oh, thank you!'

'I would like you to come up next Thursday to see the nurse and to make an appointment to go to Brentwood maternity hospital. You know where that is, don't you?' As we walked back to reception, I felt his hand on my shoulder. 'Do you feel alright? Would you like to sit down for a while?'

Although I had guessed I was pregnant, I suppose I still looked a bit shocked.

'No, that's alright. Janet's waiting for me,' I replied.

'Take care, Maria. I'll see you on Thursday when you come to see the nurse.'

'Thank you,' I said, smiling and walked toward the waiting room.

Janet got up from her seat. 'Well, what did he say?' she asked, but one glance was enough to give her the answer.

'Congratulations,' she said.

Then I heard the receptionist's voice again. 'Mrs. Dunsford, go to the yellow room please.'

'Wait for me,' said Janet. 'I won't be long.'

I sat down, my head whirling. The next thing I heard was Janet saying, 'Come on, you. We can't sit here all day.'

She was walking towards the door.

'How did you get on with the doctor, Janet?' I asked.

'Oh, I'm pregnant too,' she replied. With that we both smiled and hugged each other.

'When is yours due, Janet?'

'The same time as yours. End of February, beginning of March.' After that we both caught our buses. She went to her mum's and I went to mine. I didn't tell my mum. I thought I'd better not until after Brian had called at my parents' home for a cup of tea and a chat, and taken me home.

I told Brian the good news on our way home, and he was thrilled to bits. Afterwards we told John and Malcolm, but I don't think they were too pleased. They were very kind in letting us share their flat, but I don't think they'd bargained on us having a baby so soon.

'Where are we going to put a baby?' Malcolm said.

'Oh, stop worrying, Malcolm,' John said. 'It's a long while before the baby's due.' Then, turning to me, he added. 'You must go to the council, Maria, and make sure they have your name down. Tell them that you're expecting a baby.'

The next day, after work, I went to tell my mother the news. She was in the kitchen making a meat pudding, one of the old fashioned ones you make in a cloth.

'Mum,' I said.' I'm pregnant.'

'What? Pregnant? You've only been married a few months. Don't you think it's too early?'

By the look on her face she didn't think it was good news. I was only nineteen and to her I was far too young to be having a child, and my dad agreed with her.

We were quite lucky because we were not at John and Malcolm's flat that long. Brian managed to rent a cottage in Bulphen, Essex from Mr. Parmer, a farmer who Brian used to do some work for at odd times. I did feel lonely at the cottage at times, but I tried to keep myself busy.

With Brian and me both on shifts, we managed quite well. Sometimes Brian would pick me up from my parents' house. I was so fortunate to be working opposite to where they lived. This made life easy for me on late shifts. This went on for quite a few weeks, and I was beginning to feel awful. The pregnancy was not going too well. Well, the baby was fine. It was me. I was so tired, I could sleep all day if you'd let me.

The doctor was very understanding and suggested that I gave up work. I don't think my mother-in-law was pleased about that and I felt that I wasn't getting the right support from people.

Although she was kind in many ways, Brian's mother always seemed distant towards me. I felt it was because of my background. Brian's father, however, was more understanding.

Leaving work gave me plenty of time to practise my cooking, and I needed that without a doubt! I always had trouble preparing the right quantity of food. Poor Brian had to eat for two people with the amount I put on his plate.

It should have been me eating for two. I didn't have that good an appetite in between 'fancies.' I always thought that as the months went by things would get better. Not with me, they didn't. I felt sick every day, my moods were terrible, and all I wanted to do was sleep. Overall, I felt rotten.

I couldn't wait to have the baby. Everyone kept saying, 'You won't get any sleep once the baby's born.' That didn't bother me. I was having enough sleep now! All I wanted was to feel better than I did.

Short skirts

Mac thinks, how can Brian sit there and look so cool? I have sweat running down my back, seeing Katy's short skirt! Dear God, Brian has his arm along the back of the seat, and I can see his fingers every so often touching her shoulder. How can I give him the nod that we ought to be going, and that this is totally wrong? I wish she would stop crossing and uncrossing her legs. I can see a light perspiration on Brian's forehead. I don't know how he can sit there and just talk about what kind of day she has had, when he doesn't know her!

'Mac, do you want to climb down from the side of the lorry so Katy can get out?' asks Brian. Then he turns to her and says, 'I'll meet you around eight. You know, the yard at Claydon.'

Oh, Mac thinks, so he's meeting her at Claydon. Whatever did he talk to her about before I got near the lorry? Doesn't he realise we could get the book thrown at us for this. All the time I've been driving I've never been in this situation, and I certainly don't want to be in it again. I'm feeling sick! Mind you, I could easily get to know her myself if I had the chance! I wouldn't mind, but she's not saying much. She's just agreeing with him. I've never seen such beautiful big blue eyes - sky blue, just like on a summer's day.'

'Mac, have you had enough of looking at her, and would you just help her down from the lorry?' Brian asked.

Mac ponders; as Katy opened the door and turned around to climb out, I just guided her down as I didn't really know where to touch her. As I got back to my lorry I'm sweating, and I haven't had a good wash today. So I'm not going to stand too close to her or hang round her too long, as much as I want to.

'Goodbye, love. Nice to talk to you,' Mac says.

'Yes, you too,' she said. 'But I can't say that we spoke much. Dad did most of the talking!'

'No doubt we'll meet up again sometime,' Mac replies, smiling all over his face. I'll kill Brian I'm thinking! It's his daughter. He could have said, the old devil. I watched her get into her car and drive away. 'She's a nice little thing Brian. How do you know her, then?'

'She's my daughter Mac,' Brian says laughing.

'Yes, Brian, she just told me. I'll get you for not telling me while we were in the lorry. You never even said you had a daughter.'

'You never asked me. Now, come on Mac, you f****r we've work to do. You can't sit around daydreaming, as you know we won't earn money that way.'

'I'm here, Brian, right behind you. So get a move on. My engine's running and I'm ready to go. I can't believe you have a daughter like that. She's one good looking girl. You old bugger, Brian.'

'Yes, Mac. I heard your engine. Just get in your lorry, and shut up. And you can keep your eyes off her as well! I know what you Irish men are like!'

'What's the matter with Irish men?' says Mac. 'I know we like our drink, but so do you, Brian. I've heard about your bottles of whisky, and the way you drink it laying in the bath with the bottle beside you. I know for sure that's not full when you go downstairs. Talking about whisky, Brian, shall we have a drink this weekend?'

'You're going home Mac. I know what you're thinking, and it's not going to work.'

'No Brian, I thought I'd have a little drink with you and Maria, that's all. Well, that's put paid to my ideas and plans hasn't it, Brian. Perhaps there will be another time.'

'Perhaps, Mac. But in the meantime, we have our lorries to drive, and they certainly won't drive themselves.'

'Yes sir. I'm not going to say another word to you, Brian.'

That will be the day when he shuts up, thinks Brian. Mind you, there's one way of shutting him up. I'll turn my CB off. That way I won't be able to hear him. No. I'm going to just drive and listen to my radio. 'Bye Mac.'

In the 1960's

In the 1960's we used to backcomb our hair. It was so fashionable for women. After backcombing we would spray our hair with this very thick hair lacquer. This would be done quite a few times until it was really high.

We also had high heeled shoes, the higher the better, we used to think.

I came home one day from school, and there stood Mum with a bra in her hand. I was so pleased I immediately went and tried it on, shouting out, 'Thank you, Mum. It fits perfectly.' I was so over the moon with my bra that I asked her if I could go and see Celia.

'Of course you can, darling.'

I kissed Mum, and said thank you again. I opened the back door, jumped down the back steps, and away I went.

Once I was at Celia's, I stood there smiling away and pushing my shoulders back so my bra would be more noticeable.

'Oh, Maria! You have a new bra!' said Celia.

'I wanted to tell you that. How did you know?' I replied.

'They're so obvious,' Celia said. 'They could poke someone's eye out.'

My Aunt Jenty sat peeling an orange, and smiling away to herself. 'Celia, where is your bra?' I asked.

'I've got it on. Why?'

'I never noticed your bra being as pointed.'

'Shut up about bras. Let's go out.'

'No comments, Celia, when we're out.'

'Would I, Maria!'

I must say she didn't say anything when we were out, bless her. After many years living away from each other, Celia is now living near me, which is really nice.

The apron

It was a Sunday morning and Brian was getting the children ready to take them to his parents. They lived at Ingrave, not far from us. By car it only took us about ten minutes.

The children used to look so nice when they were all ready to go. They were always so excited when they were going to see Nanny and Granddad Everett. Shane used to run up and down the hallway shouting, 'Are you ready?' Katy, who was only about nine months old, used to get very excited watching Shane.

Once the children had gone with Brian, I would start getting on with the Sunday lunch and the other things that us ladies have to do in the house. As soon as everything was done - the dinner smelling lovely and everywhere looking divine - I used to sit down and have my well-deserved cup of tea and a biscuit. It was only a couple of hours that Brian was away, and in that time I did get a lot of things done, plus I had a little bit of quiet time which I really looked forward to.

On this particular Sunday, when Brian came home he had a parcel tucked under his arm. He laid the parcel on the table, and no way was I going to ask what it was. No sooner had we taken the coats off the children than Shane was in the front room playing with his cars. Katy was put in her play pen for safety!

'Coffee, Brian?' I called out.

'Yes please. That would be lovely,' Brian replied.

We sat in the front room drinking our coffee and watching the children playing. Then all of a sudden Brian said, 'Oh, my mum has made you something. It's on the kitchen side.'

I was wondering what this parcel was. I started to unwrap it. Oh no, I thought. It's one of those wrap around aprons that tie at the side. 'Did your mum make this this morning?'

'Yes. She got her sewing machine out and made it for you. Do you like it?'

'It's really nice,' I said, standing in the front room with this apron on. No way am I going to answer the door in this, I was thinking.

'It will keep you nice and clean, Maria,' Brian said as he was sitting in the armchair.

I think he knew I didn't really like it. But I really felt awful in it. Like one of those grannies years ago. Why couldn't she have made me a pretty one that goes around my waist, with a nice frill around the side?

As I had this apron on, Brian was looking at me with a smile on his face. I was trying to smile as well.

'It's nice, Brian,' I said. 'It will keep me nice and clean, won't it? I'm going to tell you one thing, Brian. I'm not going to open the door with it on.'

'Why ever not? It looks good.'

'Oh you can sit there smiling. You don't have to wear it.'

'That's not nice, Maria. My mum sat for a good hour making it.'

'I'm sorry, Brian, but it's a bit old fashioned, don't you think?' With that Brian burst out laughing.

'You look like one of those kitchen maids in the forties!'

'Oh Brian, do I really look that bad?'

'Well it doesn't compliment you in any way,' he said with a grin on his face.

I took it off, folded it neatly and put it back into the bag which it came out of. This won't see much daylight if I can help it, I thought to myself.

The rag bell

Katy used to be a Saturday girl in a hairdresser's shop. She really liked it, even though she was shy. I knew the owner of the shop, and the other young girl who worked there. They were very nice people, but the message I kept getting back was could I ask Katy if she would talk to the customers a bit more.

However, they really liked her and the girls in the shop used to do her hair every Saturday. She looked so nice when she came home. Katy stayed at the shop until she left school, by which time she had come out of her shell.

One thing that used to get to her was when Brian and Peter Brown collected the rags from various places. They used to pick up Katy and as they arrived at the shop one of them would ring the bell and shout out, 'Old rags!'

My poor Katy. She was so embarrassed when she heard the bell, and yet the girls in the shop never took any notice of it.

When Katy got home she would be blazing with anger. It was some time before any of us could approach her.

'I don't want you ever to pick me up again, do you hear?' she would shout from upstairs over the banister.

'What have you done Brian? I do hope you haven't been ringing the bell outside the shop where she works,' I said.

'We only rang it a couple of times,' Brian and Peter said.

'You shouldn't do that. It really upsets her.'

With that no more was said and I made a pot of tea for them. 'Oh, Maria, there's plenty of work shirts on the lorry,' said Brian. That meant he wanted me to pull out the good ones and wash them. Mind you, I didn't really mind. Sometimes I found some really nice clothes for myself out of things which people had thrown away.

You would certainly be surprised at the quality of some of the pieces of clothing. Some of the clothes were new or nearly new, which saved me money. However, I never used to get the children's clothes from the cast offs. I bought these from Bom Marsh and the Co-op in those days.

Some people had it hard then. But maybe it's not so different now, except that we don't have the rummage sales like we used to.

It was fun to see the people poke around in the clothes. It was how some of them survived in those days.

One thing Katy did like was the smell of lorries. She loved it when her dad came home when he started driving articulated lorries.

Also, that drop of coffee in his flask that he saved her, she would drink with great enjoyment.

Moving on to another hospital

I only stayed at Brentwood District Hospital for about a year. Not because I didn't like it. I was just fed up with working every Friday and Saturday night.

We had a caravan at Walton-on-the-Naze, and the children were missing out on their weekends. I knew Warley Hospital was looking for nurses, so I decided to go and see if I could get a job.

Well, I got the job and started the following week. It wasn't like these days, when you have the interview and don't know if you've got the job for a few weeks.

The hours were far better. Well I thought so. Every evening from 5:30 p.m. until 8:30 p.m., Monday to Friday, with every other weekend off. I didn't mind. It got me out and gave me a break from the children. Brian didn't mind having the children. They were always ready for bed before I left in the winter months. In the summer months it was different. They used to stay up and help Brian in the garden, as it was too light for them to go to sleep.

Brian would get in around 4:30, and I would leave straight away for work. We used to say, 'One in the back door and one out of the front door.'

My parents lived opposite the hospital, which was great because it meant that I would be able to see them most evenings before going into work.

By this time we had moved from Elizabeth House to Gloucester Road, at Pilgrims Hatch, into a two bedroom house. It was the last house in the road, with a lovely large garden.

Although we had a boy and a girl, they were very young at this stage. Katy was only a few months old and Shane was only three, so this meant the bedrooms suited us quite well until we could get a three-bedroom house.

All we could think of was that we were out of the flats, and I wouldn't have to try to get my pram up the two flights of stairs. This was going to be heaven to me. Having the garden was wonderful, not only for the children but also for my little dog. At least I would know where he was instead of him roaming the streets.

In the flats we really hadn't been able to keep an eye on him as there was no garden. Believe you me there were a lot of little Tops lookalikes. Whenever he could, he used to get out at the first opportunity, to find himself a girlfriend.

My sister lived opposite on the estate where we grew up and of which I had fond memories.

Brian really worked hard in the house and in the garden to make everything look nice for us. He even built a conservatory, which was wonderful for the children.

We were there for three years, until we moved to Priestfield at Ingrave, Brentwood, Essex.

The lorry driver (Brian)

My week doesn't start on a Monday. It starts on a Sunday - well, early hours of Monday morning.

Here I am, nice and comfortable in my bed, when the blessed alarm goes off! It can't be three o'clock yet. I haven't been in bed five minutes - well, that's all it seems to be. Still, never mind. Out you get. Once you're up you're half way there.

As I'm sitting on the edge of the bed, I'm looking at my wife lying there curled up in a ball.

'Bye, darling,' she calls out. 'Mind how you go!'

Mind how you go! Well, that's an understatement. If I'm not careful I could fall over before I get to the bedroom door the way I feel. My head feels as if it don't belong to me and I can't see out of my eyes. They certainly aren't stuck together with sleepy dirts. I wasn't in my damn bed long enough. Me arms feel like lead. Me hands have got pins and needles. I'm starting to make a few noises by this time, and I've woken the wife. Well, that won't do, will it?

She turns over, taking the rest of the quilt with her. Well, there wasn't much I had anyway, quilt or bed. The cat is allowed to sleep on the bed. In fact she takes up most of it.

'Don't disturb the cat, darling. She's asleep. Doesn't she look lovely? Come on, pussy. Snuggle up closer to Nanny. No you haven't got to get up yet. It's Granddad who's getting up, not us.'

My wife pulls the cat's blanket up so it's closer to her. 'Granddad,' I'm thinking to myself. 'I wouldn't mind if I was a granddad, but I'm not. It's my daughter's cat and she's married so why can't she have the blessed cat. Oh! Maria's found her tongue again!'

'Yes, dear? Did you say something?' she mumbles. By this time I'm beginning to start to focus.

'Yes, I've got pins and needles in my hand.'

'Oh, come here and I'll put a cross on your hand for you.'

She has already wet her finger, and she places it onto the back of my hand and makes a cross. Yes, you may laugh, but it does work. The pins and needles have gone. Sometimes when I get cramp in the night, I call out, 'Quick, wet your finger and put a cross on me leg,' and it works.

I think it's about time I started to make for the bathroom to have a wash. Once that's over it's downstairs to make the flask of coffee. Ah! Little darling. She has done me sandwiches and filled me kettle up, so all I have to do is press the button down and wait for it to boil.

Now I can be putting me boots on. Why on earth did I choose boots with laces in? Whoops! That didn't do me any good - bending down. Ah! The kettle has boiled. Now I can make me coffee and be on my way. Have I got everything? Flask, bag and me sandwiches that my little darling wife has made me.

Outside the dawn has just started to break through. It's not a bad morning. In fact it's quite nice, once you get outside.

Keys to me lorry? Where are they? The best thing I can do is set me bag down onto the floor, and go through my pockets. They say a lady's bag is always full up with everything. Well, you ought to see a lorry driver's bag! Not in any of the pockets. Ah! Here they are, right at the bottom of the bag. Well, they wouldn't be on top, would they?

Right. Door's open and I'm in me cab. Me eyes are feeling better now. I expect it's the fresh air. I'm still having to squint to fill me tacho in. Have I filled it in right? Have I put where I'm going, but most of all have I put me name in the right place? Now, come on Mr. Sleepy Boy. Check your tacho, because if you don't, sure as ninepence, you'll get stopped by the police or Ministry man.

They'll look to see if you've filled it in, and we don't want to be questioned now do we? Right! I'm on me way. And it's just 3:30 am. Nice and slowly does it. We don't want to wake the neighbours, do we, otherwise I'll be in their bad books. Ok, now I'm rolling, where did I say I was going? Where did I put those notes? Ah there they are, hanging up in the window on me clipboard. Oh yes, I remember now. Liverpool with a ten o'clock booking. Here we go for a long journey. Let's hope we meet some more lorry drivers on the road. Still, it's a nice earner for the beginning of the week. That's as long as I don't get stitched up by having to stay up in Liverpool. Then I won't be saying, 'Nice earner.' I'll be saying a few more savoury words.

I arrived at Liverpool, dead on eight o'clock. I've made good time. Now if I'm nice to them here, hopefully they will unload me quickly. I notice a man in blue overalls walking across the yard, so I unwind me window and shout out, 'Hello, mate. Any chance of unloading me?'

'What time is your booking for?' he asked.

'Ten o'clock.'

'It's only a quarter to nine, mate! You're a bit early.'

Bit early! I've been up since three. What does he call early? I've done half a day's work before he even thought about getting up. Still, whatever I do I mustn't shout me thoughts out, or he won't unload me and I could be up here until tomorrow morning. So I might as well get out of the lorry and see if I can get a cup of tea in the canteen. As I go into the canteen I notice that it's nice and clean, not like last time I was here. The woman behind the counter seems quite pleasant. I order me tea.

'Fifteen pence, love,' she said.

I handed her my money, said thanks, and go to one of the tables. I'm enjoying me tea when the door opens and in walks the chap I had just spoken to. He has just started work. Surely he isn't going to have a break! I feel like saying something, but I thought I'd better keep my mouth shut. While he was having his cup of tea, he saw me and walks towards my table.

'Do you mind if I sit with you, driver?'

'No, mate, feel free.'

All I hope and pray is he don't say too much to me. I'm just beginning to feel my three o'clock start, and he looks as if he has just got out of bed.

'You look tired, driver.'

'Knackered's more the word I'd use,' I replied.

'I tell you what, driver. I wouldn't mind your job. Start when you want, finish when you want. That don't sound too bad to me.'

Keep your comments to yourself Brian, I thought, otherwise if you say something now you could be stuck up in Liverpool. That could end up being hours.

'I'll tell you what, driver,' he said.

Wait for it, I thought. Here it comes. I can definitely see myself having a night here. I lifted me head and said, 'What?'

'Don't be like that, driver. All I was going to say was, if you like, when you've finished your tea I'll unload you.'

With that he got up and walked out of the canteen. I quickly finished my tea and went back to me lorry. To my surprise he's waiting for me.

'Ok, driver, back up over there and I'll unload you. Then you'll be able to head back home.'

I don't answer. I just nod and start to back me lorry. It's not long before he has the back doors undone and I'm unloaded.

'Ok, driver. Sign me bit of paper, and then you can be on your way.'

I signed his paperwork, thanked him, and once again I switched on my engine for the drive back.

I drove away from the loading bay so I wasn't in anyone's way. I looked at my watch and thought, well I've had my rest period, so I can now head back to Felixstowe to see what I've got for tomorrow.

Do I telephone Harry in the office and ask if he's going to give me another good one, or is it going to be a short run? I'll give it a while. Let's see who I can talk to on the C.B. It'll make me journey shorter.

'One nine, one nine for a copy. Hello. Anybody out there?'

'Copy'

'Copy.

Oh, I've got somebody.

'Hello driver. What's your handle?' he said.

'Tiger,' I reply.

'Where have you come from?'

'Felixstowe.'

'You must have had an early booking?'

'Yeah. I had a ten o'clock booking.'

'You done well. You're making good time. It's only 11:30 now.'

'Where are you then driver?' I asked.

'If that's you with the white Volvo I'm right on your back door.

I'm going to stop for a minute for a cup of tea. Do you fancy one? There's a nice little cafe just up the road.'

'That will do well. I've got to have a break around twelve thirty, so I might as well have it with company. Then I can be on my way once again. Where are you going to stop then, driver?'

'About thirty miles up the road near Cannock there's this nice little cafe. They make a smashing cup of tea, and the best bacon roll you ever did taste.'

'Sounds good to me. Do you want to go in front so I can follow you?' I asked him.

'No, that's alright, driver. I'll tell you when to turn off.'

I didn't talk much after that. Well, I didn't get a chance to. He was one of those drivers who must do all the talking, and half an hour of him would be long enough out of any man's day!

'Chuck a left, driver, at the next turning,' I heard him call.

I noticed as I turned into the cafe that there were other lorries parked up. That's always a good sign. I parked me lorry so I could get out, put me tacho on break, and switched off me engine. I got out of me cab and started to walk towards the cafe door where the other driver was waiting for me.

Once inside I asked for two cups of tea and a bacon roll. 'What about you. Are you having a bacon roll?' I asked him. 'No thanks, mate,' he said.

With that I handed him his mug of tea, which did look good, I must say.

'Your bacon roll will be about five minutes sir,' said the girl behind the counter with a lovely smile.

'That's OK, love,' I replied and with that I looked around the room to see where the other driver was sitting. Once I found him, I sat down and started to drink my tea.

'You're right, driver. It's a nice cup of tea,' I said, and then he started to talk about everything and anything. I wasn't really listening. I was enjoying my tea too much to listen to anything. After a few minutes the young girl called out, 'Bacon roll, sir?'

I get up and go to the counter to collect my bacon roll. It sure does look good. My mouth is watering and I can't wait to get my teeth into my roll. I look around as I eat and notice that everybody is eating bacon rolls. Mind you, they are good. In fact, I think they're the best I've tasted in a long time.

'I shan't forget this place,' I said to him.

'So you'll be telling all the other drivers about it,' he said. 'Would you like another cup of tea?'

'No, thanks. I must head back now, otherwise I won't get me hours in.'

I said cheerio and thanked him for letting me know about the place, and walked out of the cafe,

'Driver.'

I heard somebody shout out. I turned and there is another driver waving my hat in the air.

'I think this is yours.'

'Thanks, mate. Where are you going?' I asked.

'Bury St. Edmunds.'

'I'm going to Felixstowe. If you like, I'll run with you.'

'Ok, driver. What's your name?'

'Brian,' I replied. 'What's yours?'

'Mark,' he said. 'Now we know each other's names we'd better start moving.'

I get into me lorry and once again switch on me engine and then switch me tacho over from break to drive. Then I switch me CB on and start to call for Mark.

'Ok, driver,' he shouts and we started to roll.

'That's not a bad cafe,' I said. 'I've seldom tasted a bacon roll as good as that. A driver who I met up with recommended it to me. He said it was good and he wasn't far wrong.'

'Yes, you're quite right. It's a good cafe, But he wouldn't say anything different would he. He owns it. Mind you, I give him full marks. They do make a good bacon roll.'

I didn't say anything. I just laughed to myself and think that of course he would say it's the best for miles. Who wouldn't?

Our run back isn't too bad. Mark isn't a chatterbox like the other one. Just as well because we have much further to go. It's not his own lorry so that limits us to what we can talk about. I ask him what he's got on. He said he was empty.

'I'm going for collection, and then I'm going straight back with it,' he said.

The journey goes quite quickly. I don't know what we talked about - anything and everything. Then I noticed a sign which read Bury St. Edmunds.

'I turn off at the next exit, driver. Down here is the slip road to the Sugar Bowl. It's been a pleasure to run into you,' he calls over the CB. 'What's your handle, driver?'

'Tiger,' I called out.

'I'll give you a shout next time I'm down again,' he calls over. We both shouted, 'Cheerio!' Then I carried on my way towards Felixstowe.

I turned me CB off because I didn't feel like talking to anybody else. I just fancied a bit of peace, because when I got down to the dock it would be one mad rush. All I hoped is that I wasn't going to be stuck on the dock for hours. Still, if I am I'll just put me head back and have a well-deserved sleep.

Ah! Here's the yard. Now let's see if we can get in somewhere to park me lorry. There's a space. Lovely, do me well. I get out of me lorry and start to walk towards the tiny office. As I get near I notice there are several other drivers waiting to see what they've got for the next day, and they squeeze up to make room for me. Lucky it's the beginning of the week so we all have clean clothes, and don't suffer from BO. I tell you, you wouldn't want to be here in the middle of the week, and certainly not the end of the week. Harry and the others behind their hatch probably don't mind anyway. We depend on their good will as they are the ones who give the notes out to where we are to go for the next day.

Maybe it's the witty remarks that get bandied about, but this time it isn't long before we all get our notes.

Once I get outside the office I stand for a while looking at me notes, thinking - London! Well at least I'll be able to put me feet up tonight with a glass of whisky after the Liverpool run.

I lean against the brick wall trying to sort me hours out, deep in concentration and feeling rather tired. I'm suddenly brought back to earth when someone calls out, 'Brian!' It was Colin, one of my mates.

'Wake up! What have you got for tomorrow? Knowing you, I bet you've got a good one!'

'No, I haven't. In fact it's a London for eight o'clock booking.' I gave him his answer short and sweet. 'Anyway, what have you got, Colin? It must be a good one, otherwise you wouldn't pipe up.'

He just smiled at me and said, 'I don't know. I haven't been to the office yet. Brian, do you want a bit to eat after you've tipped your load, or will it be too late after you've been on the docks?'

I know what he's referring to. He thinks if I get on the docks this time of the day I won't be off till late. Little does he know I'm not going on the docks. I was told to leave me load in the yard, because the London load is ready for me just to pull out of the yard, and this would enable me to get home nice and early.

'No thanks, Colin. I've got me load. It's right here. Shane has been in and got it off the docks for me. I think I'll just go home and have a nice bit of dinner with me good woman. I can put me feet up with a nice glass of whisky and think of you running up to Scotland.'

'How did you know I was going to Scotland, Brian?' he asked.

I just looked and smiled!

He smiled back at me, put his cigarette between his lips and tried to puff at it. I'm just about to say something about his cigarette when one of the other drivers walked by and said, 'You'd get more satisfaction out of that fag paper if you were to put more tobacco on.' I just looked at Colin and started to laugh. It's only Monday and he's getting his leg pulled already. We both started to walk back to our lorries.

'Cheerio then, Colin! See you sometime in the week.'

'Yeah! Alright then, mate,' he said and we both go on our ways. Although Colin didn't bite back today, I knew that sometime in the week he'd get back at us.

It's six o'clock. I'd better ring me wife and tell her that I'm coming home. Having a phone in me cab has its good points and its bad points. I can never make an excuse that I wasn't near a phone.

Well, it's ringing. Is she there?

'Hello!'

'Hello, darling. I'm coming home. Can you pick me up at the yard, please?'

'That's good. What time do you want picking up?'

'I'll be there in about an hour.'

'Ok then. I'll meet you there,' she said and with that she put the phone down. This leaves me quite flat because, by the way she was short on the phone, it doesn't sound as if she's had a good day at work.

Holiday to France

We left home at 6 a.m. It was a really nice morning and the birds were singing. We were so excited, just like kids. Brian packed the car so quickly.

'I do hope I'll be able to find things,' I said.

'You will. Everything's neat and tidy,' Brian replied.

One thing I could rely on with Brian was to be neat and tidy. We chatted about everything and anything on the way down to Dover. When we eventually arrived, it was packed with cars.

'What lane have we got to get into Maria? Can you check the paperwork again?'

'I've checked it twice, and nowhere can I see where it says what lane we should be in.'

'I'm going to telephone Shane. He might know what to do.'

I was sitting in the car still looking at this document to see if I could find where we were to go. I could hear Brian talking to Shane. Then I heard him ask, 'Do you know where to go, Shane? There are so many cars here, I just don't know what lane I have to go into. It doesn't say anything on the paperwork which I have here.'

Suddenly I heard this roar of laughter, which came from Brian's phone.

'You're joking, Shane. Where the hell am I going to find a milkman or a paper man?'

'Well that's what I do when I'm lost,' Shane said. With that I noticed Brian had switched his phone off.

'Do you know where to go then, Brian?' I asked very gingerly.

'Yes, I think all these lanes go to the boat.'

'That's good. It means we'll be having breakfast quite soon.'

'It will be quite some time before we have breakfast with all these cars in front of us,' Brian replied.

'Did Shane explain things to you?' I asked.

'No. He told me to ask a milkman or ask a paper man down here.' By the look on Brian's face he wasn't too pleased.

However, eventually we were on the boat, our car was parked up and we were sitting at our table enjoying our breakfast.

The crossing was really good. Nice and calm, thank goodness. It was that calm I fell asleep. When I awoke, I had this rather painful neck.

'Are we nearly there?' I asked Brian with my eyes half open. 'We've only got about half an hour to go until we dock,' Brian said.

Brilliant, I thought. Off this boat, thank goodness. Me and boats don't go together.

The next thing I heard was this rather squeaky voice coming over on the loudspeaker. 'Passengers may start to make their way to their cars.'

When we reached our car we had to wait our turn before we could move. Eventually a man waved us on.

'This is it, Maria. We're in France, and we're on our way to La Mole, wherever that is. At least we have Shane's TomTom with us to help us to find the place!'

'Brilliant,' I said under my breath. Shane had planned our route out. It should take three days for us to get there. Well, that's what Shane had estimated. With Brian's driving we could well be there a lot earlier! Not that Brian's a fast driver. It just means that we won't be stopping that often. Brian was naughty at this.

He always used to say we'll pull in at the next stop, but it was never the next one. It was always about the third or the fourth one.

Still, I shouldn't moan. We got there and it only took us two days. The drive down was good apart from the tolls that we had to keep stopping for. We got ourselves in a right pickle at the beginning. After help from two very nice French people, we actually got the hang of it. I had this plastic bag with small change just for the tolls. I'm OK with our English money, but when it comes to the foreign money I really have to think about it. I suppose I should have sorted out the small change a few days before we set off. I did try and get what I thought might be the right money before we got to the next toll. I must say by the time we had got to our destination I had got the hang of it.

On one particular time when we were at the tolls, Brian had stopped too far away from the bucket into which we had to throw the money. So it meant that I had to get out of the car to put the money into the bucket. I was fumbling around with all this loose change in my hand. I had noticed a very long queue out of the corner of my eye, and this wasn't making me feel that good. Then all of a sudden I heard Brian. 'Oh for goodness sake, Maria, give it to me. You're holding everyone up.'

With that I passed him all the money and immediately got back into the car. Looking through the window at him, I saw that he was turning the money over in his hand. Then suddenly this couple came up to him and helped Brian out. The look on Brian's face was one of relief. He shook the man's hand and said thank you.

'All done, Maria,' he said. 'That didn't take too long, did it?'

'No, not when you have help, Brian,' I said smiling at him.

As we drove off slowly, we heard money dropping down into the change department of the toll machine.

'Brian, you've left our change behind!'

'Oh, never mind. The next person will be lucky. It won't be that much anyway.'

I just looked at him and laughed. Brian turned his head and started to laugh with me. I must say we were both enjoying ourselves.

We tried to get into a hotel the first evening, but the receptionist said that all her rooms were booked and no way would we get a room for miles around as there was a conference on. That night we slept in our car. The lay-by we pulled into was really large, with toilets as well. It was a small piece of land really. We weren't the only ones who were sleeping in their cars. It wasn't a very good arrangement, but at least we had somewhere to sleep. Thank goodness I took our quilt and blankets with us.

Only a few yards from where we were parked there was a small restaurant which pleased us no end. After we had our breakfast it was back to map reading as we set off again. Well it wasn't really map reading. Shane had written everything down, plus we had his TomTom, which was a great help to us.

We had to sleep in the car another night as the hotels were again full. Anyway, we were enjoying ourselves. The weather was nice, and it was a lovely smooth ride.

Brian had only bought the car a few days before our holiday. He always wanted to have a Jaguar. He saw it, he liked it and then decided to buy it. He was with Shane, so I think there was a little bit of influence.

The pair of them came home with the biggest smiles on their faces. At the time I was leaving some holiday information on my computer for Shane. Brian leant over me, and said he had just seen a car he liked and he had bought it.

'Steady on, Dad,' Shane said. 'You ought to take Mum to see it first before you do anything.'

'Come on, Maria. Let's go and I'll show you the car which I like,' said Brian.

When we got to the garage, Brian showed me the car. It was lovely.

'Well, what do you think, Maria?'

'It's a very nice car, Brian. If you like it, then have it. We're only on this earth once.' Little did I know that we would only have one week's holiday in France, before Brian was taken seriously ill.

Eventually, we arrived at La Mole.

The caravan park where we were staying was really nice. It was set in a forest, a very quiet place where all we could hear were birds. We went out most days. Then in the evenings we would sit outside, Brian with his glass of wine and me with my cup of tea. It was so relaxing where we were.

On the Saturday afternoon, Brian was sitting outside and I was preparing lunch. When I called him in to eat I noticed that his leg was very red from his knee down to his ankle.

'What have you done to your leg, Brian?' I asked.

'Nothing,' he said, rubbing it.

'Don't rub or scratch your leg, as it looks as though your skin could tear very easily.'

'It doesn't hurt me.' With that Brian sat down and we had our lunch. After lunch Brian got up from the table.

'Ouch! That hurt.' He started to walk to the bathroom and I noticed he was limping quite a bit.

'Does your leg hurt badly, Brian?'

'No, not too bad. It was when I got up it hurt me.'

'I wonder what you've done to it.'

'Nothing. It just appeared while I was outside I suppose.'

'Shall we go to the doctor's with it, Brian?'

'It could be our beds,' Brian replied. 'They're really low, especially with my knees.'

'We're going to rest up for a few days, Brian, and if your leg is still hurting you tomorrow you must go and see a doctor.'

That night Brian's leg was really hurting him, and he was in quite a lot of pain. Without hesitation, he agreed to see a doctor, which was unlike Brian. He always shied away from doctors. I walked down to the site office and asked if they could get a doctor for me, which they did straight away.

I went back to our caravan thinking, I do hope Brian's going to be alright. I can't drive the car home. We'll have to get Shane to come over to drive us home. Shane had said he would like to come down for a few days and it looked as though he might well have to.

Once I got to the caravan I opened the door and called out, 'The doctor won't be long.' Brian was lying on the bed looking so sad.

'Would you like a cup of tea, Brian?'

'Yes please. That will be nice.'

I had no sooner put the kettle on then there was a knock on the door. I opened the door and there stood the doctor with his bag in his hand.

'Good morning, Madame.'

'Good morning,' I replied. 'Come in please. My husband is in the bedroom through there.'

The doctor turned and walked through into the bedroom, sat down on the bed, and started to look at Brian's leg. Every so often I could hear Brian shouting out in pain. The doctor spoke beautiful English, but I can't speak a word of French.

I could hear the doctor talking to Brian. Then I noticed that he shook Brian's hand and turned and came out of the bedroom.

He sat down at the table and started writing. Then he passed me a piece of paper.

'Fifty Euros please, Madame. I think your husband has phlebitis and should go into hospital.'

No sooner had he told me than he was on his telephone, calling for the ambulance.

The doctor shook my hand and said the ambulance shouldn't be that long. He then turned and went out the door.

I walked into the bedroom and sat on the bed. 'Oh, Brian!'

'Don't worry,' he said. 'Once they've sorted me out I'll be back here in no time.'

'I think I can hear the ambulance.' I walked back into the other room and noticed that the ambulance was outside. My goodness, that was quick coming.

Eventually, they managed to get Brian into the ambulance. He just couldn't bear his leg to be touched, neither could he put his leg to the floor. He was in so much pain.

Once we were in the ambulance we were on our way. The sirens were going and this was quite frightening really.

Brian was chatting away to the ambulance men who were with us in the back. They were laughing as they weren't able to understand each other.

When we arrived at the hospital, they took Brian off to be examined. I started to walk through with him, but I was told to go and sit down and wait to be called to come in. I waited for an hour and no one came, so I decided to go and ask if I could go and see Brian.

'Come through,' the nurse said, 'but only for ten minutes.' I asked Brian everything I could in that time.

'I've had a blood test done, and now I'm waiting for a scan on my leg,' Brian told me.

The next thing I knew that nurse had come back. 'Sorry. Your ten minutes are up. You have to go now.'

I was beginning to feel quite sick at this point. I said goodbye, and told Brian that I was only outside in the waiting room if he should need me. Every half hour I asked if I could see my husband, but the answer was, 'No, you will have to wait. He is having tests.'

Once I was allowed to see him, they had settled Brian in his own room. The doctor came and said that he would have to stay in hospital overnight until they had found out what was wrong.

Brian was very cheerful and he was laughing with the nurses. In himself he seemed fine. I asked the doctor if he was OK. He said yes and that once they had found out what was wrong he could go home.

I told Brian that I was going to telephone Shane and Katy, but he said I shouldn't give them the worry. He said he'd telephone them when he got out which would probably be the next day. I gave him a kiss, and said, 'I'll see you back end of hoping time.' We always said that when one of was going anywhere.

I telephoned Shane and explained what had happened. Shane told Katy and the next thing that happened was that they were on their way to us.

I telephoned Brian the next day and he was very cheerful. He was laughing with the nurses. I asked Brian if he had been on his leg and he said that he hadn't. He said he didn't really fancy the idea anyway, as it was still very painful to touch. I told him that I had telephoned the children, and that they were on their way to see him. I won't tell you what he said to me!

The following morning I telephoned the hospital and they said that he was in a deep sleep. My poor Brian had slipped into a coma, and never really came out of it. When he did it was only for a short time. He never spoke. He only opened his eyes for us.

Myself, Shane and Katy kept talking to him over and over again about everything and anything.

Katy stayed for two weeks. She has her own hairdressing business, which she really had to go back for. Shane stayed on another week. Shane also has his own business as well, in haulage.

Shane drove Brian's car home. It didn't take him that long either! Then I was left on my own. Thankfully, the hospital was opposite a hotel which Shane had booked for me. It wasn't too far for me to walk, thank goodness.

I stayed for three weeks. The hotel staff were very kind to me, and used to look out for me when I came back in the evening. There was always a pot of tea on my table in the restaurant every night. By the end of the three weeks on my own I was beginning to feel really tired. I used to sit by Brian's bed every day and pray that he would come round fully. Although his eyes would open he only responded a little. The he used to drop back into the coma again. The doctors said I should really go home as I was looking very tired. But I said I didn't want to leave him like that.

The following day when I went to see Brian, I asked him about me going home. I explained what the doctors had said, and Brian tried to nod his head, and also managed a smile. I asked him twice, and got the same reaction. I told him that I would come straight back if he were to need me. Unbeknown to me, that evening the hospital were arranging for Brian to come home. Meanwhile, Shane had made arrangements with the insurance company to get me home.

The next day I went to say goodbye to Brian, but he was in theatre having his dressing done. I had to go as a car was coming to pick me up. Just as I was leaving I heard the chief doctor call out to me. I turned around to see what he was going to say to me, and was thinking it was more bad news. But no, it wasn't. He said that my husband was flying home tomorrow to Ipswich hospital. I just hugged him, and the doctor held me tight.

I couldn't believe what he was saying. My stomach was going over and over, and my heart was pounding fast. I had to sit down as by this time I was feeling sick. The doctor sat with me quite some time, just reassuring me that Brian would be home the next day. I telephoned the children straight away. They were so pleased that their father was coming home, and so were the grandchildren.

What should have been a wonderful holiday turned out to be a nightmare. Brian arrived at Ipswich Hospital the day after I got home. He was in intensive care for two weeks. There wasn't that much change. He was never awake that long, before he drifted back into a deep sleep. But we had him home with us.

Sadly, Brian died on the 9th. November 2008. Shane and Katy and the grandchildren were crying every time I looked at them. They were hurting so much each and every one of them. I felt empty and I know they did.

All I can say is we did have a truly wonderful first week. We went to really nice places, and we laughed all the time. Brian even went down a one-way street, which wasn't funny at the time but we did laugh about it in the evening.

At least we had that week together, and that's the week I will always remember.

Night in Ireland

'Whatever has the size of the lemonade bottle got to do with having a wee?'

'If I keep weeing into my small bottle, I'll have to keep getting in and out of my lorry, and I could fall out and crack my ribs, like somebody I know did.'

'Ha, ha. Very funny, Brian.'

'Well, you were drunk at the time, Mac.'

Ignoring the jibe, Mac said, 'The sea tomorrow is going to be like a millpond, Brian.'

'It needs to be because after two nights drinking I shall be needing stabilizers like the boat has got. Come on, Mac. I think it's about time we started to make our way back to our lorries. It's getting late.'

'Dear God, Brian. It's only ten o'clock. It's early yet!'

'I don't care, Mac. By the time we walk back it'll be near eleven o'clock and we shall have to get up at seven. I'd better rephrase that, hadn't I? I'll be getting up first to make a cup of tea. Then I'll have to wake you nice and gently by banging on your cab door!'

'Don't forget I have two sugars in my tea please!'

'By the look of you now you'll be needing half a dozen sugars in your tea to get you going in the morning!'

'Can we have one more drink, Brian? Then I'll say good night to all me friends.'

'Your friends, Mac? You've never seen them before!'

'I know, but they're still Irish like myself.'

My God, whatever does he look like? Well I can see what he's going to be like in a few years' time. He's going to be short and fat with a red face and nose. Mind you, he hasn't got much of a nose now. It looks like a small nodule on the end of a pea pod.

'Come on, Mac. I'm ready.'

'Good night everybody. See you sometime. It's been nice meeting you,' Mac shouted out. 'Here we go, here we go! Good night all.'

'Mac, shut up. You'll wake all those asleep.'

'No one's asleep around here. There's too many pubs.'

'Thank God we are in the south of Ireland, and not in the north. Otherwise I'd have to put a muzzle on him.'

'Did you say something, Brian?'

'No, I didn't say anything. Just hurry up, so we can get back to our lorries.'

'How long did it take us to walk to the pub?'

'Ten minutes, I think.'

'Well I think it's going to take us about an hour to get back to the lorries!'

'That's what you think.' Brian grabbed hold of Mac's arm.

'Oh, Brian, you're hurting me. You could break my arm doing that. I thought I was your friend.'

'Oh, I am your friend, Mac. I keep getting you all these jobs.'

'Not all of them. I got you this one! Brian, you're not walking in a straight line.'

'Just keep walking and shut up.'

'Yes sir.'

'You'll get "sir" in a minute, Mac.'

Finally, Brian and Mac arrived back at the lorries.

'Come on, Mac,' said Brian. 'Get yourself into bed because it won't be long before it's morning.'

'I must do a wee first, Brian. Otherwise I might have to get up in the night. If I leave my clothes on, I won't have to get up so early in the morning will I!'

'Sleep how you want to, Mac. I'll give you a call in the morning, with a nice cup of tea.'

'That sounds good'

Mind you, I'm not feeling so great myself. But I'm not going to let Mac know that. I bet when I lay down it will feel like I'm on the boat already.

'Oh, well. Goodnight, Mac. See you in the morning.'

By the looks of it, this place that Mac has found us to park up for the night is going to be nice and quiet. Just what I need after all that drink I've had. I've set my alarm, so it's good night everyone. I don't think I'll move much tonight.

No sooner had I shut my eyes than the blessed alarm went off. I hope the day will go as quickly as the night has. I'd better wake Mac up. Well, try to!

'Come on, Mac. It's time to make a move or we could miss the ferry.'

'Where the devil do you get your energy from, Brian? You're full of beans. I'm feeling half bloody dead this morning. I'd also appreciate you being very quiet. My head's feeling sore this morning.'

'That's the trouble with you youngsters. You haven't got the experience. Come on, drink this cup of tea I've made you. There's loads of sugar and that'll get your sugar levels up.'

'Brian, my mouth feels like the bottom of a bird cage!'

'Come on, Mac. Let's get rolling, otherwise we won't catch the ferry.'

'Don't rush me, Brian. I feel delicate.'

'Get your arse in that lorry, and forget about your mouth and your sugar levels. We have to head back to the ferry.'

Brian watched Mac as he struggled back into his lorry.

'Mac, straighten your back up and get behind that wheel properly. Start singing. That'll make you feel better.'

'Give me an hour and I'll see what I can do for you. It won't be much, but I'll certainly try for you.'

'On the other hand, forget about singing. I'll tell you when you can sing again. What do those signposts mean, Mac? Slow slower. Well that's made me laugh.'

Still, it's nice and quiet. The roads out here are weird. Or should I say the wording on the signposts. Everything is beautifully green. I wish my back lawn looked like this. Mac's voice interrupted my thoughts.

'Oh, I forgot about the CB. Yes, what do you want, Mac?'

'I've got a hangover, Brian.'

'Oh, have you, Mac. Just concentrate on the road. We're in Ireland and I don't know the roads over here.'

'You've got a rather short fuse this morning!'

'Come on, Mac. Get up front where I can see you.'

'I forgot you don't know your way over here. That's why you put me in front last night to walk back to our lorries!'

'Turn your CB down so it's just loud enough to hear me if I call you, and shut up!' Suddenly, there was peace and quiet. I needed that to be able to concentrate with these roads. I'm all over the road. I hope we don't meet a lorry coming towards us, otherwise I could end up scraping the side of my lorry. Well, at least Mac has shut up, and he's driving nice and straight. Let's turn my radio on. I probably won't be able to understand it, but never mind, it's something to listen to.

Ah, that music sounds nice.

'All roads are clear for those people heading towards the ferry. No windy roads with lumps and bumps in them and certainly no low bridges.'

That just what I wanted to hear. No hold ups. Wait a minute. That sounds like Mac talking.

'Mac, was that you?'

'Yeah. I thought I'd just tell you the roads are clear up front.'

'How do you know it's clear to the ferry? Have you heard it on the radio?'

'I don't know if it's clear all the way to the ferry, but I do know it's clear up front. Well as far as my eyes can see!'

'Mac, that's not funny,' I said with a smile on my face. 'When I get on the ferry I'm going to sit on the top deck and relax. What are you going to do Mac?'

'I've booked a cabin and I'm going to sleep until we get to England,' replied Mac.

Eventually they reached the ferry.

'Come on, Brian. Let's book in and get rid of these lorries. Then we can go and have something to eat and drink.'

'Do lovely, Mac. I'm starving.'

When we got to our table, Mac said, 'Well, Brian, you had good meals in Ireland and you're having another good meal here. And all on hot plates. You're doing well.'

'I hope we're getting well paid for this job, Mac. It's not a sightseeing trip, you know. And don't forget I want to see the rates before you agree to them.'

After the meal Brian wanted to go on deck, while Mac preferred to go to his cabin.

'I'm going to sit in the sun now,' said Brian. 'See you, Mac. And no drinking. We've got some driving to do when we get off the ferry.'

'Now would I, Brian!'

Ah. This is nice up here. I think I'll put my feet up and have a snooze and let the world go by for the rest of the crossing.

Waiting to unload

While Brian was having his mug of tea, there was an almighty bang on his cab door, and then it opened.

'Bloody hell, mate! You could have killed me,' said Brian.

'Sorry, driver. I didn't know you were leaning against the door.'

'I could have broken my bloody neck. Anyway what do you want?'

'I've come to ask if you'd like a brew.'

'Actually, I've just made one. Thanks all the same, mate. They're taking a long time to unload me. There were only a few pallets on my trailer.'

'That's true, but they've found a cat in your trailer.'

'What do you mean, a cat in my trailer?'

With that Brian jumped out of his lorry to see what was going on. There were so many people at the back of the trailer it was like bees around a honey pot.

'Are you sure it's a cat?' Brian asked.

'Oh, it's a cat alright. Poor thing. One of the chaps said it's probably been in there for a couple of weeks,' said one of the men who were unloading.

'Here comes the vet. Perhaps he'll take it and then I can be on my way.'

'Is this your lorry, driver?' said the vet.

'Yes,' replied Brian.

'Well it looks as if you're going to be here for some time. I'm so sorry.'

'You're joking, aren't you? Can't you just get the cat and take it back to the vet's and sort it out there? I want to get back to Felixstowe tonight.'

Suddenly there was this woman's voice. 'If no one claims the cat, do you think I could have it?'

'I don't see why not, but it has to stay in quarantine for at least six weeks.' With that the vet caught the cat and put it into a basket. Then away he went.

Well, thought Brian, I might as well stay here for the night and leave in the morning as there's nowhere I can park up for my other drops.

'There's a good pub down the road where you can get a nice piece of fish and chips,' said the night watchman, who had just appeared.

'That sounds good. I'll have a wash and then I'll go.'

With that Brian got back into his cab to get his washing things and then went to find where he could have a wash to freshen himself up.

'Driver, what time are you going down the pub?'

'Not too early because it will be a long night and there isn't much on television. So I might as well drag the night out.'

'I suppose it must be a boring old life at times, especially when you have times like this, waiting to unload.'

'It's the first time I've ever had a cat in my container, and I don't want it to sodding happen again, thank you very much!'

'Still it's gone to a good home.'

'I wish I was at home. This was supposed to be a short one, up and back. I was hoping to be sitting in my garden tonight with a nice glass of drink and my cat on my lap.'

'Oh, you have a cat then?'

'Yes. Damn thing.'

'Don't you like cats then?'

'Yes I do, but this one gets all the fuss. I'm sure it's bloody human.'

'You ought to kick the cat off, and put your wife of your lap and give her a cuddle.'

'You're joking, aren't you?'

'Why? Does she have those damned headaches?'

'No, mate. She's gone past that stage. Everything now is put down to her age, because the last time she went to the doctor's for something or other he told her not to worry as it was only her age!'

'Never mind, driver. You go and enjoy your fish and chips, and I'll wake you up in the morning with a nice mug of tea. Around 5:30 if that's all right with you. I'll let you get on otherwise the pub will be closed. Give the gate a good rattle when you get back. That way I'll hear you.'

'I hope you do hear me. I certainly don't want to be out there all night.'

'You won't be out there all night. There's no fear of that because there isn't much I don't hear.'

Brian turned and said cheerio. I hope he does hear me, he thought to himself. I don't want to be having to cock my leg over the gate. I've heard about these night watchmen.

I certainly feel nice and clean, I must smell better. With the heat today I must have pen and inked! Well, I might as well take a steady walk down to the pub to see what they have on the menu. I think I'll have a nice glass of Guinness. Now where did he say this pub was? Turn right outside the gate and about a hundred yards down the road. I hope it's only a hundred yards because I don't feel like walking too bloody far.

Ah! What's that? Is it the pub? Looks quite nice from the outside and there's also a lot of people standing around. That's always a good sign. Let's hope it's not one of those push and shove pubs as I call them. Oh it doesn't look bad. Nice and clean, and not too many people inside. They seem to be all outside. Still, I can't blame them as it's certainly a nice evening.

'Yes, sir? What would you like to drink?' asked the barman.

'I'll have a Guinness, please, and a menu as well, please,' said Brian.

'I can recommend the steak, and I've also got some nice pieces of rock eel.'

'I'll have the rock eel with chips, please.'

I could see the old chap beside me was dying to talk to me. I bet in his days he was a lorry driver. Still, never mind. I'll probably be like that. Who knows!

'Are you a lorry driver, mate?'

I knew he was going to say that. The old boy's probably lonely. 'Yes. That's right, mate. I'm parked just down the road. I thought I was going to get away today but unfortunately, when they opened my container, they found a cat in it.'

'A cat in your container? How long had it been there, poor thing?'

'I've no idea. All I know is that it's been taken away by the vet for inspection. I don't know what they're going to do after that. Maybe they'll try and find its owners.'

'Where did your container come from?'

'Probably abroad. All I have on my ticket is today's job. I don't know whether they'll try and trace it back to where it came from, or just leave it here until they find a new home for it. Well that's what I call a nice piece of fish and chips. I think I'm going to enjoy this meal.'

'Well, mate, I'll leave you to your meal. Maybe I'll see you another time. I hope you get on alright with the cat!'

'No doubt it will sort itself out. Good night, mate,' I said to the old chap. With that I started eating.

After I had my meal I walked back to my lorry, hoping that the night watchman had left the gate open for me. There's the yard. Thank goodness for that. I'm feeling quite tired now. Well he said push the gate and it'll open, but it won't. I don't feel like climbing over the gate. It's a bloody high gate anyway. Oh well, here goes. I suppose it's the only way into the yard.

When I was just about to cock my leg over the gate, there was this almighty shout.

'Hoy! What do you think you're doing?'

'It's me! The lorry driver. The one with the bloody cat!'

'Oh, sorry mate. I'll open the gate for you.' It was the night watchman.

'Hold on, mate. I'm still up here,' yelled Brian.

'Hang on. If I pull the gate over to the side where the other wall is you can climb down, while you hold on to the gate.'

As I was climbing down I was thinking to myself, I do hope he doesn't want to talk about the cat. I know what these night watchmen can be like! The vet said he would let us know about the cat tomorrow, and that's enough for me.

'Do you fancy a night drink before you go to bed?' asked the night watchman.

'Yes. That'll be nice, thank you. First, can you give me a hand down, as this bloody gate doesn't seem very sturdy and I don't really like heights. Wonderful, mate. Thank you.'

'I'm sorry, driver. I should have been waiting for you. I usually walk around about this time of night, just to check to see everything is OK.'

His room was really cosy, with two armchairs, a table and a cooker. What more could he need? (He didn't do that many walks around the yard, I know, I thought to myself.)

'Sugar and milk, mate?' he asked.

'You've a real nice room here, mate. How many nights do you do?'

'Four nights a week and there is another chap who does the other three.'

'Thanks for the tea, mate. I'll have to be getting back to my lorry. It'll be morning before I know it. Can you give me a knock on my cab door in the morning about six to wake me up?'

'Of course I can. No problem mate. Good night.'

As I was snuggling down in my bed, well trying to, there was this rather loud bang on my cab door. It can't be the police can it? I'm in a lock up place. I drew the curtains back, and there stood the night watchman with a smile on his face. I wound down my window and put my head outside, thinking to myself, 'Hurry up, mate, I want my bed.'

'I forgot to tell you that when the cat is clear of whatever it has to go through, one of the ladies in the factory is having him. Great, isn't it?'

'Great,' I said, winding my window up and drawing my curtains. All I wanted to do was sleep, and that's just what I was going to do. I turned on my side, shut my eyes and said good night all, just like I always did at nighttimes.

Christmas was such a lovely time

One Christmas we bought Katy a large rubber ball that she could bounce up and down on. It was Christmas Eve and we had to get it pumped up, so Brian went to the garage. It wasn't long before he was back. It was quite late and the children were fast asleep. I was preparing the vegetables for next day. It was only us and the children for dinner, but by the amount of vegetables one would think I was feeding four thousand.

The next thing I knew Brian was behind me, bouncing about on the rubber ball.

'Get off it, Brian, before you burst it.'

'You won't burst it. It's made of toughened leather.'

'Get off then and let me have a go.'

There we were sitting on Katy's rubber ball, laughing away to ourselves.

'We'd better be quiet before we wake the children up,' I said. We then started to put the children's toys into their Father Christmas sacks. After that we had some freshly cooked ham and bread and butter, with pickles. Once we had finished eating it was eleven o'clock, so we thought we had better put Shane's and Katy's sacks beside their beds.

When all that was done it was time for us to get to bed. We both knew we would have an early morning as no way were the children going to lie in bed. Once my head hit my pillow I was gone from the exhaustion of getting everything nice for our Christmas Day.

The next thing we knew, the children were jumping all over us. It was five a.m. Brian got up to make tea and bring our shortbread biscuits up to us. We were in a sea of Christmas paper. Even Tops, our poodle, was jumping around waiting for his present. Once he had opened it, he was straight on to his bone.

Katy was bouncing around on her ball and Shane was playing with his cars and lorries. All the other things which they had were left on our bed. They were really enjoying themselves, and so were we with our cup of tea and biscuits. Brian and I said that we were so lucky to be blessed with two beautiful healthy children and what more could we wish for in life really. We looked at each other and said, 'A bit more quietness!'

'Another half an hour in bed wouldn't have gone amiss,' I said, laughing.

'I can see people's lights on,' Shane shouted out as he was looking out the bedroom window. 'I wonder what presents they've got.'

Eventually it was time to go downstairs.

'Come on, Katy. You'd better come with me, otherwise you'll be bouncing down the stairs,' I heard Brian say.

Away she went following Brian, her eyes on her big orange bouncy toy. Shane stayed upstairs, lining all his cars up along the landing and making all these wonderful sounds like boys do when they have their cars out.

Our day went really smoothly, Shane with his cars and his other toys and Katy bouncing around with her dolly under her arm. She had that bouncy ball for many years and Shane has still got some of his cars today. It's lovely to know that they still have them. Katy doesn't have her orange bouncy toy but she has still got her first doll, which my dad bought her.

I just don't know how families cope these days as toys are so expensive. Even so, they seem to have everything. What I don't like to see is when parents go shopping with the children for Christmas toys. Their shopping trolleys are full to the brim with lots of toys. It doesn't seem to be right in my eyes. I expect most of my generation will say the same thing.

Family standards

Being a lady or gentleman doesn't mean that you have your little finger up in the air when holding a cup of tea, or eating the occasional cucumber sandwich. It depends more on good breeding, as within the family we all learn from one another.

Anne, my sister, was also a firm believer in high standards of behaviour, and I can tell you I wouldn't have dared to let the side down. In the evenings, Anne would teach me the right way to speak and walk, and of course how to sit - which was quite awkward when wearing those tight skirts!

Mind you, I never did wear the really tight ones at home. They were for Saturdays and Sunday afternoon at the pictures, or perhaps the odd evening out with the boys.

I had to look good and thanks to Celia, and the loan of her bedroom, I was able to tart myself up! Quite often I would not be the only one in Celia's bedroom. Very often there would be Dean and Carol Smith sorting through the famous shoebox, which Celia used to have in her bedroom behind her door. We would rummage around for a pair of high-heels. Poor Celia. The odour that must have come from these shoes, with all that smell of leather!

We also had to make a cut in the leather, halfway up the heel. This was all the fashion! Sitting here thinking about it makes me wonder whatever I used to look like - or should I say what any of us used to look like!

Poor Anne. For all her teaching, I could not walk properly in high heels. They were pushing me forward like a duck. I was only thirteen, but I tried so hard and at times I thought I looked and walked really well.

One thing I know I had to be careful about was my manners. If I hadn't, my parents would have heard about it before I got home. Then, Lord help me!

My cultural side has always made me feel proud. I love just sitting and thinking of the old times. When things come into my head, I get pen and paper and write it down in my notebook for later. Then, when I am ready for writing again, I pick up my notebook, read through it and off I go again.

My flair for writing allows me to detach myself, and this is where I very often find peace.

Coming back from Ireland (Brian)

I can't say I don't feel tired - knackered is more the word! I suppose I should ring to find out what I've got for Monday. These mobile phones are great. Just press a button and you're through. Ah. It's ringing.

'Hello. It's me, Brian. Just ringing to see what I've got for Monday.'

'I don't know yet, but there's Barking in Essex for Saturday if you'd like it,' was the reply.

'You're joking,' Brian said. 'Tomorrow morning? I'm on my way from Ireland and I'm exhausted. You know damn well that I have to have a certain amount of hours off. So you know what you can do with that one, don't you. I'll telephone you on Saturday morning to see what I have for Monday.' Bloody cheek. What do they think I've got? A helicopter?

'Brian, come on mate. Are you asleep? Talk to me. It's your old mate, Mac.' These CBs are good things, but you try getting Brian on his. It's like trying to catch fish on a hot day!

'Sleep!' said Brian. 'How can anyone go to sleep with someone like you about! Anyway I was on the phone to find out what I've got for Monday?'

'Monday? You're joking, Brian. All I want to do is park my lorry up for the weekend and unwind with a few beers.'

'Yes I know, Mac. That's all I want to do, but money is money and none of us can live without it, can we?'

'You're probably right. So what have you got for Monday? Knowing you, it's probably a good one!'

'They asked if I wanted Barking in Essex for Saturday,' replied Brian.

'Surely you're not going to do it are you?' said Mac.

'No, I'm going to put my feet up this weekend.'

'That'll be a first, Brian. You refusing Saturday work. Brian, why do you keep touching your brakes! Have you got a dithering Dan in front of you or what?'

'No. I'm just keeping you on your toes. Just making sure you're keeping up with me.'

'You only have to look in your mirror to see if I'm still behind you,' said Mac.

'Yes, I know, but it also keeps you from talking me to death on the CB,' said Brian. 'Ah! Look at that, Mac. Now that is what I call a lovely sight.'

'What are you looking at, because all I can see at the moment is the back of your container?'

'It's a signpost marked Felixstowe. That means I'm nearly home.'

'Go on, Brian. Keep rubbing it in. You know that after I've tipped and got my load off I've still got another good four hours drive before I get home to Hinckley. And I'm knackered already. I'll park up tonight at Felixstowe, because I've run out of hours anyway. Then, in the morning I'll drive home.'

'Come on Mac, you're not getting old are you? Still, I've noticed you're going grey. It'll be the Grecian 2000 out, or are you using it already?'

'Very funny!'

'Mac, where are you going?' Brian could see in his mirror that Mac was trying to overtake him.

'I'm now going to show you how to drive a lorry, and that's without putting me foot on and off the brake. Come on. Catch me, catch me! Now just listen to me, Brian, and that way you'll be able to become a good driver, just like me!'

'Look here, Mac. You couldn't show me anything that I don't already know.'

'I suppose you're right, Brian.' said Mac. 'You've many years start on me. There's one thing I really would like to know. How come I can set off quite a while before you, and you end up there before me?'

'That's called experience, Mac.'

'Well, Brian, I'd better shut up as I think I've lost the argument. That's if there was one. So on that note I'll switch my CB off and I'll see you down at the docks. Bye.'

'Bye, Mac. Talk to you later.'

Me with Shane and Katy on holiday down in Wales.
That was a lovely holiday - the sun shone all the time.

Katy. This photo was taken on our way down to Wales, she is such a happy little child, bless her.

Shane calling out, 'look at me I am Tarzan'.

Shane and Katy with Tops, our little dog.

Betsy, our little dog. She was so cute and loved the grandchildren coming around so she could play with them.

Kieralea, my granddaughter, twenty-seven now - how time flies.

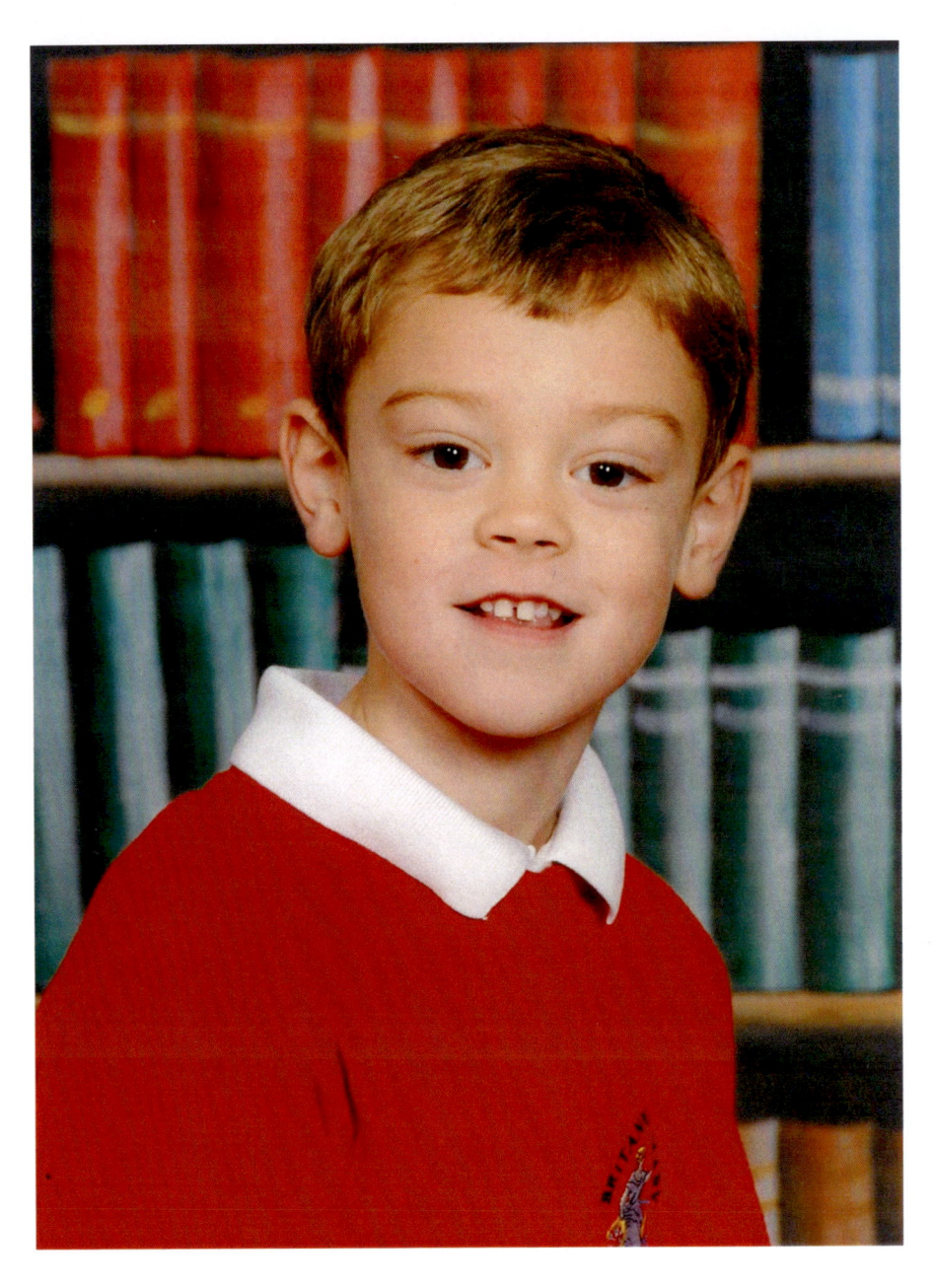

Shaun, my grandson, such a lovely boy.
He's now all grown up at twenty-six, bless him.

Shaun in his army uniform. It was August, such a hot day as well. He's only about eight. He said he was joining the army.

We were down Walton-on-the-Naze on holiday,
Shane and Katy on the steps outside the pub with their drinks.

My four grandchildren ready to go to judo.

Saturday afternoon with my mum and dad standing outside their caravan. Shane and Katy loved their Saturday afternoons with them.

On holiday down Walton-on-the-Naze. Shane and Katy sitting on the steps outside our caravan, with Tops, our little dog, wearing sunglasses. He went everywhere with them on - it was so funny, people thought he had bad eyes.

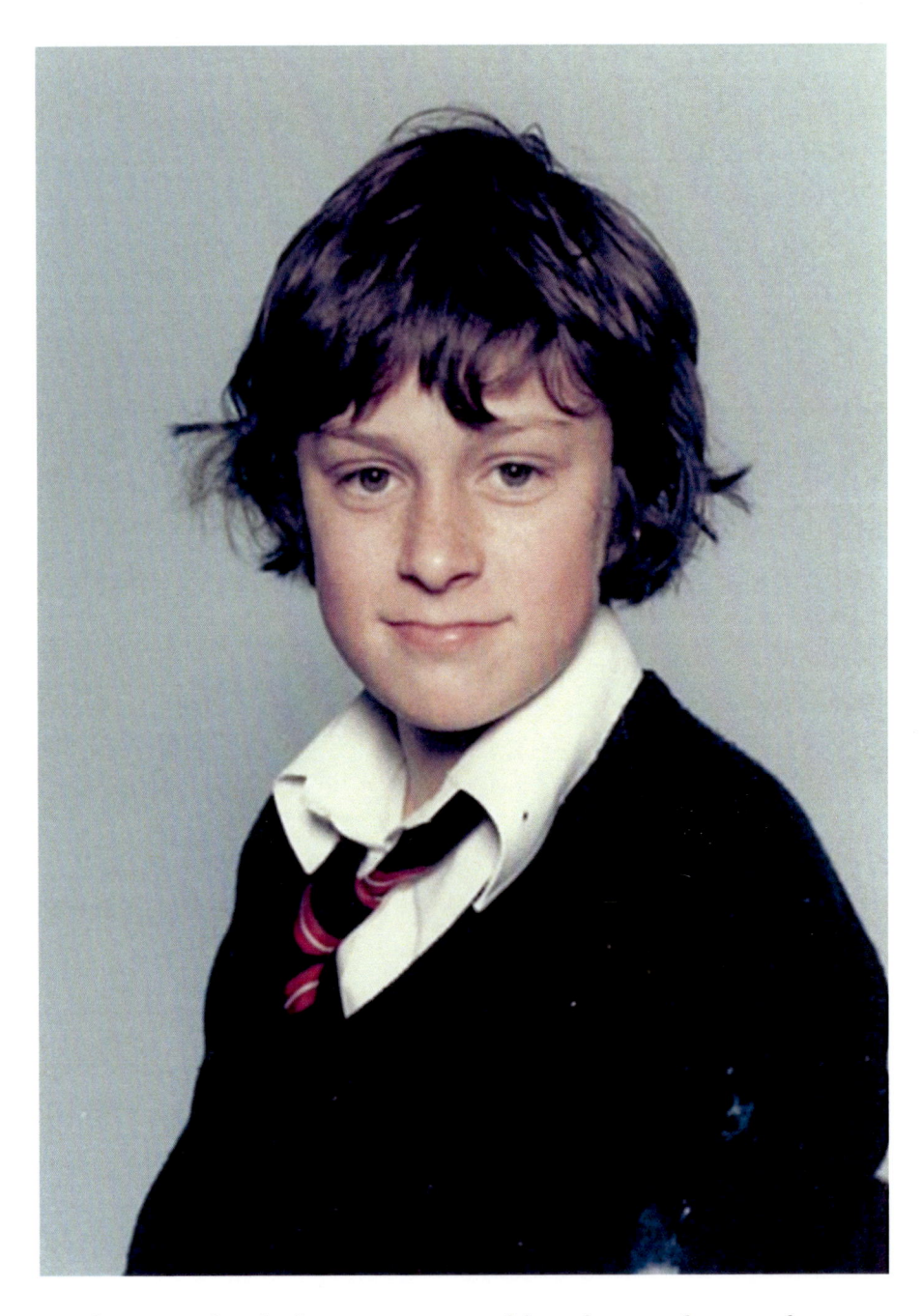

Shane's school photo. He wanted his shirt and tie undone;
we loved it when we saw the photo.

My grandson Charlie Jo in the washing up bowl, bless him.

Daniella, my granddaughter, looking beautiful in her prom dress.

Brian, my husband, with Charlie and Betsy.

Brian on one of our lovely holidays.

Shane and my three beautiful grandchildren with Ceaser
the little dog having a lovely day out.

Granddaughter Chantelle with an owl on her shoulder looking very proud.

Shaun with a drink of shandy, which was a very weak one, saying 'Cheers'.

Shane in his army uniform when he was in the TA.

Shane shaking hands with his dad,
with the lorry that his dad bought him.

My nephew Matthew with Shane going out for a ride.

My beautiful garden.

Brian and Peter Brown's totting days.

Last photo taken before Brian became seriously ill.

Grandson Charlie - Joe.

The Last Supper.

Granddaughter Kieralea School Photo.

Mum and Dad with Aunt Emily, on left.

After the honeymoon

After the honeymoon, I had to get down to real life. That, I tell you, didn't come easy! I couldn't cook. Well I didn't have to while I was at home. I was spoilt rotten - everything was done for me. Having to manage a home, that was just a right laugh.

However, when it came to having to clean the house, this was easy to me. I really enjoyed this part. When I think about it, I had plenty of time to get it right, because as a child I only sat and watched as my mother or sister Anne did all the housework. I would say I was a well-kept spoilt child, and loved every minute of it. I had respect for my parents, and that is where the children of today go wrong.

With help from my mother and from Brian's family, I did make progress. It wasn't long before I got the hang of the money side of things.

However, the very first time I went shopping I can remember sitting in the kitchen thinking, 'How the hell do I make the money last a week!'

'Maria, come on,' said Brian. 'This lot won't unpack itself, you know!'

No. I don't suppose it will, I thought, shaking my head. I didn't dare tell Brian what I was thinking and start another row. As it was, we were having plenty of those!

After we had unpacked the shopping and had a cup of tea, Brian looked at me and said, 'What's for dinner then?'

I sat back in my chair and sighed. All I wanted to do was rest. If this is married life, I was thinking, they could keep it. Now I know what my mother meant when she spoke about married life. It would take me some time before I really adjusted to married life!

Still, I managed in the end.

Honeymoon times

There was one particular time while we were on our honeymoon and staying with Brian's sister Janet and her husband Mick. The men decided to go to the launderette, leaving the women to do the housework.

Janet and I got all our work done and more besides. The boys had been gone nearly three hours. It shouldn't have taken that long as the launderette was just down the road from where they lived.

Janet and I were sitting having a cup of tea when all of a sudden there was a knock on the door. When Janet opened the door, there stood Brian and Mick with big smiles on their faces and clutching their launderette bag.

'Where have you two been?' said Janet.

'We went to the harbour to have a look at the boats while the washing was doing,' said Brian.

'You went to the harbour and left our wash?'

'Oh, it was alright. When we got back it had just finished.'

'Come on then, Mick. You can help me fold these sheets. Brian, you can help Maria fold the other pair.'

Janet tipped the sheets out on the settee, and gave out this almighty shout.

'What have you done to my sheets? They're all blue.'

Janet and I looked at each other. We weren't the slightest bit interested in the boats.

'They're not patchy, are they Mick? They're an even blue,' Brian said. 'I think they look quite nice.'

That night I went to bed feeling quite sad. The two weeks were up and our honeymoon was over. No sooner had I shut my eyes when I heard Brian say, 'Cup of tea. Come on, wake up.'

'I don't want any tea. I haven't been in bed that long,' I replied. 'It's seven thirty in the morning. We're going home today,'

I sat up and had my tea, which I drank slowly. I didn't feel like rushing. I don't know if I was pleased or not that we were going back today!

We were going back to live with John and Malcolm, and I kept wondering whether they really wanted us there.

I knew Janet and Mick would be pleased to have their flat back to themselves, but I was going to miss Janet. I felt we got on really well.

Perhaps they would move back to Brentwood one day.

Hedley Walter School

I thought I would go and visit my old secondary school. I arrived at ten thirty and signed the visitors' book. There was this young lad waiting to take me to Mrs. Evans, and she greeted me with great enthusiasm.

After a tour of the school, and a nice cup of tea with the rest of the staff, I decided to walk around the school myself. My memories were flooding back, happy times and sad times.

I went into the main hall where we used to have our assembly, which was always taken by our Head Teacher. I used to stand with all my classmates in about the fourth row from the front, and I can see myself looking up at the stage.

At the side of the hall, facing us, would be our teacher. All the teachers would be standing in a row facing their classes, not like today. They would be waiting for us to do something wrong and then they would pounce on us pretty sharply.

In those days we wouldn't want to do anything wrong, as if we had it would have been a quick clip around the ear.

At the moment I am in the main hall sitting on a chair looking at the stage and thinking where have all the years gone! Then two boys came into the hall. One decided to play drums and the other played the keyboard. They weren't really playing, they were just mucking around.

Suddenly, the side door opened and in walked this tall man in rather casual dress. He shouted at the boys, 'Are you playing, or are you mucking about?'

'We're playing, sir.'

With that, he just nodded his head and went out of the hall. Not without banging the door behind him, I might add!

I got up from my chair and walked over to the boys. 'Was that your teacher?' I asked.

'Yes, miss,' they said.

Well in my days at school all the teachers were smartly dressed. The men wore suits, and so did the ladies.

Don't get me wrong. I'm not knocking anyone's dress, but just stating how things have changed. Even the clip around the ear has gone. It didn't do me any harm!

One of the boys stood up and said, 'No way would I let a teacher clip me around the ear!' With that they got down from the stage, said their goodbyes, and walked out the door.

The corridor down to the main hall hasn't changed inasmuch as children still air their lungs! However, I did hear a teacher shout out, 'Quiet please! Keep to the left!'

Suddenly it went quiet. Well not that quiet!

The Gypsy way of life

If you aren't a Gypsy, the Gypsy way of life is a lot different from your way of life, because of the traditions which we all follow. Although I myself don't observe all the traditions, I still like to think there are some that I can pass on to my grandchildren. Thanks to my teaching, they have already started to pick up a few traditions and are beginning to speak the Gypsy language.

Gypsy people always prefer the open air. They say it's good for their lungs, but I prefer to have the warmth of being indoors!

Gypsies also like their children's ears to be pierced when they are small. They say it's good for their eyesight. (I have only just started to wear glasses, so that's not bad for my age!) However, you never see Gypsy women wearing glasses, and they all have their ears pierced!

The Gypsy boys have to grow up fast, and they are soon subconsciously imitating the attitudes and style of the men folk.

Carriage lamps are so important for Gypsies, especially for travelling when it's dark. However, there were times when they didn't want to move on and would rather stop another night or two. So they would hide the lamps during the day. Then, when at evening time the police came to move them on, they would make the excuse that it would be too dangerous for the horses to travel in the dark.

Another trick was to remove one of the wagon wheels and say it was broken. They would tell the police that they would try to fix it. My father told me it worked most times - well, until the next morning anyway! At least it gave them another night for stopping.

In the mornings, the women would be up and out early, selling their wares and doing a bit of fortune telling. When they arrived back, the men would go out in the afternoon and do a bit of totting. Then when the police called round to move them on, the women would say that they couldn't leave because the men were out trying to get a piece for their broken wagon wheel. Which was not broken!

The traditional farm work gradually disappeared

Most of the traditional farm work gradually disappeared after the end of the Second World War due to increasing mechanisation. Previously, it was the Gypsy travellers who provided much of this workforce, moving from farm to farm through the summer, picking various fruits, peas, beans and potatoes.

In those days, when it was time for the hay to be farmed, it was cut and tied up in bundles by machines. The Gypsies would gather up the bundles and stand them up to dry. Then, when the hay was dry, the farm labourers and the Gypsies would pick up the bundles and throw them onto the tractor trailer. I can remember this very clearly, as in the summer months in my school holidays I would be in the fields with Mother and, usually, my sister-in-law. These days, all the work is done by machines.

In the summer months, the Gypsies renewed old friendships and strengthened family bonds, especially with those whom they had not seen for many years. By the end of the 60's, all hops were picked by machine and herbicides had dispensed with the need for hand weeding. In the winter months the travellers would park up on the side of the roads or in the Gypsy sites. As the farm work dried up, so did the impetus to keep travelling. A few tried to travel to get work, but it became very hard for them to get any. So the small sites became large sites.

The nomadic lifestyle was further hampered by successive legislation aimed at preventing roadside stopping and caravan dwelling. With decreasing work and the increasing harassment, many families gradually stopped pulling their caravans and remained on permanent sites. With all the farm work drying up this meant they had to find other jobs.

Some of the Gypsies gave up their caravans and bought bungalows. I say bungalows because you don't very often see Gypsies in houses. I suppose living in a bungalow was like being in a caravan - on one level!

The Romany culture is historically an oral one, the culture and language being handed down by word of mouth and song. Many children were born on the roadside in Gypsy caravans or the bender tents. The Gypsies these days are now watching their own grandchildren grow up with a radically different way of life, although they still keep Gypsy values.

The Gypsy children I have spoken to want to go to school. To me that is wonderful, because whatever they want to do it all revolves around education. Even passing a driving test partly involves doing an exam on a computer. This is only one thing, and there are many other hurdles they will have to cross. The help they get is wonderful. I tell them it's out there for them, and they should take it with both hands and enjoy doing it.

Dinner at Dedham Vale

Brian and our friends, Martin Matthews and his wife Sue, decided to invite Bob Harvey (one of his finance people) and his wife Sue out for dinner.

Brian asked me to book up at a classy restaurant, which I did. Bob said he would come and pick us up and drive us to the restaurant. When we arrived at the restaurant at eight o'clock we were shown to our table by this very smart waiter. In the background I could hear a piano, which was quite pleasant.

While we were looking at the menus, Bob requested the wine list. 'What type of wine would you like, sir?' the waiter asked.

Sue, Bob's wife, said she preferred a sparkling white wine, and Sue Matthews and I said that we would like the same. Brian, Martin and Bob decided to have a red wine. The next thing I heard was, 'We'll have twelve bottles of each please.'

I looked at Sue Matthews, and she looked at me. I knew what she was thinking. Whatever is this going to cost us? A bomb, I was thinking.

The main course was wonderful and we were getting through the wine quite nicely.

'Dessert, girls?' said Bob.

'Yes please,' we replied.

'There's strawberries on the menu. Would you like them?' asked Martin.

We all said yes, and with that he called over the waiter and ordered a bowl of strawberries and cream.

While us girls were drinking our wine and talking to each other, Brian and Martin were talking to Bob, trying to clinch the deal for their loan. I had one ear open listening to their conversation on road tax for their lorries. Well, that's what we were there for, and by the sounds of it Brian and Martin had got what they wanted, which was very pleasing for us.

'Strawberries,' the waiter said with this wonderful smile on his face.

I looked up and the waiter had brought our strawberries in these small dishes, which were very delicate and pretty.

'No, mate, I asked for strawberries,' said Martin.

The waiter looked at Martin in surprise. 'They are strawberries, sir.'

'I know they're strawberries, but what I'd like is a bowl full of strawberries.'

'Oh you'd like them in a bowl, so you can all help yourselves. No problem, sir.'

I looked at the waiter and I knew what he was thinking, just by looking at his eyes.

'I'd like them in a bowl like the one you wash up in,' said Martin. The waiter just carried on walking. By this time I was beginning to feel quite sick. What are they going to cost, I wondered. I think this was when I had my first hot flush!

I nudged Sue and turned slowly to look at her. I was biting my bottom lip and it had gone numb! Sue turned and whispered to me, 'What on earth is this going to cost us?'

I just looked at her, shaking my head from side to side. When the strawberries came, I think I could have sat in the bowl, that's how large it was. They couldn't have found a bigger jug for the cream either. The strawberries and cream were really nice though. Not one strawberry was left, and neither was any cream.

By this time I was beginning to feel quite nice with all the wine I'd had, and by the look of Sue she was feeling the same. The price of the meal was still lurking about in the back of my brain. We had eaten everything we could possibly eat and drink. Sue had come out of her shell by this time and was quite chatty, whereas when we first met she seemed to be quite a shy person. It was probably the drink, as we all know it can make us come out of ourselves, one way or another!

'Would you like coffee, sir?'

I looked up and there was the same waiter. He was smiling at Martin.

'That would be nice,' Martin replied.

'Will you be wanting your coffee in the lounge, or would you prefer to stay sitting at your table, sir,' the waiter said, still looking at Martin.

'We would like to stay at our table, if that's OK with you.'

All the waiter said was, 'Yes, sir.'

It wasn't long before our coffee was on our table. The waiter laid our cups out, and then he went and got the coffee for us.

He served Martin first by saying, 'Black or white, sir?'

'White, please,' Martin said, and carried on with his conversation with us. I was looking at the waiter. He had this somewhat half smile on his face, and I could guess what he was thinking. He would have loved to have tipped the cream over Martin's head!

As we sat drinking our coffee, Brian and Martin were looking quite pleased with themselves, having clinched the deal. They won't look that pleased when they see the bill, I thought to myself.

Martin asked the waiter if he could have the bill, and his wife leaned over to me and said, 'How much is this going to cost us?'

'A good arm and a leg, I think the saying is,' I replied.

The waiter came wearing pristine white gloves, with our bill laying on a china plate. Well, I thought, Brian did say book a nice restaurant! Brian and Martin both reached out to pick the bill up.

'Thank you, sir,' the waiter said, bowing his head slightly. Then he turned and walked away.

I don't know if it was the wine that was making me feel sick or the thought of the wine. Sue Matthews looked as if she didn't have a care in the world. She probably didn't have a care with the amount of wine she had downed. Mind you, we couldn't talk!

Bob's hand reached out, and then he said, 'I'll pay for this.'

The relief on Brian and Martins' faces was a picture. They had clinched the deal and Bob had also paid for our meal.

'We invited you out for a meal, Bob. We can't expect you to pay for it,' said Brian.

'That's alright,' said Bob. 'It's a pleasure doing business with you both.'

I gave a sigh of relief. I didn't really enjoy my meal as I kept wondering what on earth it was going to cost us. I wished I hadn't worried now, as it was a lovely meal. If I had known that Bob was going to pay, or at least pay part of the meal, I would have enjoyed it.

After we had coffee, we decided to go home. Bob, Brian and Martin shook hands and we started to walk to our cars.

There was a slight slope we had to go down, and Brian and Martin were talking to Bob. Suddenly I noticed that Bob was going faster than the others. In fact he had started to run.

'Mind how you go, Bob,' Sue called out. 'You're on a slope and with that leg of yours you won't be able to stop.'

Sue Matthews looked at me with a blank expression on her face. Then I noticed Bob, going quite fast, looking as though he was trying to stop himself but having great difficulty. I could hear Brian and Martin laughing.

'Stop it, you two. It's not funny,' Sue called out. 'It's not the drink, it's his leg.'

Sue Matthews and I looked at each other in surprise. 'His leg?' said Sue.

'I've a wooden leg,' yelled Bob, 'and when I go down a slope I can't stop.'

'He will,' Sue said. 'There's a ditch in front of him and when he sees that he'll put his brakes on!'

The next thing I noticed was that Bob was laying over the side of the bonnet of his car, with one leg under the car and the other up against the door. He didn't look a good sight, and I don't think he felt it either. Still, never mind. The drink wears off in the end!

Memories

My father and I used to sit and just talk about the days when he was young. Life was not easy being brought up as a Gypsy child. Most Gypsies had large families.

When the children were small they would sleep in the wagon, which provided a very cosy living space. Across the back of the wagon would be a raised double bed with cupboards beneath, which could double up as another bed. There was a small stove for some of the cooking. They also had a mantelpiece with a mirror, and a small cupboard in which they put their china. The wagon would be laden with all the best china.

The interior and exterior decorations were always very personal and the wagon was a status symbol. The wealthier the owner, the more ostentatious it was. The wagon would be carved out in many shapes of their own design, and then painted with gold leaf.

The painted wooden wagon, or vardo, that has come to symbolise the Gypsy way of life only came into use at the beginning of the nineteenth century. Until then, Gypsies were tent dwelling people who travelled with light horse drawn carts.

When the children were older, they would sleep in the bender tent. With a sad smile on his face, Father said that they would be packed into the tent like sardines. This was not healthy as it was damp and cold sometimes. They lived outside in the evenings, the whole family gathering around the fire to discuss their day's events. To take their minds off the cold and the damp, each one would sing, and then the women would dance. There would be some telling the younger children stories, perhaps about things that happened years ago.

The bender tent poles were made of hazel wood. They were pushed into the ground and then covered over with tarpaulin or sailcloth. Some of these tents were quite sophisticated with a central area in which a fire could be lit. A hole was made in the top for the smoke to escape.

In the evenings, the small children would get five small stones with which they would play a game called five stones. This would help them to count. There wasn't much they could do, Father said. Heaven above knows how they escaped pneumonia from the cold and damp.

They had to live under harsh conditions in the wagons, but they didn't really know any better and just got on with life.

Nowadays, the whole family would have been taken into care. As it was, a couple of my father's family were taken into care, and they couldn't do anything about it.

Life as a Gypsy was not some 'romantic fairy story'. It was a struggle just to stay alive. But at least they had healthy food. The only thing was, it had to be cooked in the same pot every time over the fire. (Many, many healthy stews, warm and comforting.)

Uncle Riley's bike

Celia, my cousin, and I were playing outside one afternoon when we spotted her father, Uncle Riley. There he was with this old bike on the front of which was a sort of machine with a rubber piece which sharpened knives and hedge shears. The bike was on a stand, and the faster Uncle Riley peddled the wheel the faster the rubber piece turned until it was going at great speed.

Celia and I were so mesmerised with this bike he had, we just couldn't shut up asking him questions. We could see that he was getting annoyed with us, so we thought it would be better if we were to go and play elsewhere.

'Bye, Dad,' Celia said.

'Uncle Riley, why are you looking at us like that?' I asked

Like what?' he replied.

'You look as though you're going to bite our heads off.'

'Maria, my girl, you have one sharp tongue.'

With that, I looked at Celia, and said, 'Run, otherwise we might get sharpened.'

After we'd left, I said to her, 'Celia, I like your dad really, but I don't like that look that makes us stand still or run for our lives.'

'Your dad's got the same look when he gets mad, hasn't he, Maria?' said Celia.

'Not just my dad. My mum can give us that look as well! It's the Hearne look, Celia.'

More about the lorry driver (Brian)

I'm doing the right thing by going home, I'm thinking to myself. Eventually I arrive at the yard where I usually park my lorry. Bless her heart, she's there to pick me up. I turn into the yard and give her a wave. She waves back and I notice that she smiles at me. I park me lorry up, get me bag, and climb out of me lorry. I go straight to the boot of the car to put my bag in because no way would she have my bag in the front of the car. I often wonder if she really approves of me in the car with my overalls on.

'Hello, darling. Let's go home. I'm really tired,' I said.

With that she starts the engine up, and we're heading for home. All the way she is chattering away, but I'm so tired it's going over the top of my head. Most of the time I find myself just saying, 'Yes dear!'

We turn into our driveway. I get out of the car and put the garage door up so she can put the car away. As I walk in the back door, our cat Jemima greets me with one of her loud meows.

'Hello Jemima!'

She jumps up onto the kitchen side where she is always fed, thinking she is going to get more food. I put my bag on the side, take my flask out and put it in the sink to be washed.

'Dinner smells good, darling. What is it?' I asked.

'A nice piece of haddock,' she replied.

'Lovely! How long will it be?'

'Not that long, but you have time to have a bath first.'

Do I smell that bad, or is she just being nice to me? I go upstairs and have a bath. Then I get into my dressing gown and go back down for my dinner. It sure smells good, and by God it tastes good too. After we had our dinner we sat in the lounge and had our drink, well deserved by both of us.

By this time it is nine o'clock. It isn't early, and it isn't late, but I've started to think about what time I should get up in the morning. I must have deep thoughts written all over my face because I hear her say, 'Ok, what are you thinking? Is it what time you've got to get up in the morning? If it is, I can tell you. Five o'clock, and I've got to take you back down to the yard.'

I look across at her. She's grinning at me, but I know she isn't too pleased about five o'clock.

'How do you know I'll have to get up at five? I didn't say what I've got for tomorrow.'

'Oh! Sorry! I forgot to tell you Colin telephoned. He told me to tell you he's going to Scotland. And all he has to do is drop his trailer and back under the other trailer. Then turn round, and come straight back. Oh, and he did say to tell you that's what one calls a Nice Earner.'

She just looked at me and laughed.

'You'll have to go somewhat, Brian, to beat that one,' she said laughing all over her face.

We watched a bit of television and had a couple more drinks. Then we both went to bed.

As I approached the bedroom door I'm thinking how wonderful it will be to get in my own bed and stretch out. But it's not to be. Little devil, I think she must have heard me say I was going to bed, as there she is - stretched out and taking up most of the bed again - the cat! If she thinks she's staying like that all night she can think again. I quickly pick her up and put her on the chair. She doesn't look too pleased, but nor am I because I really need to stretch out.

'Can you set the alarm, darling, for four fifteen?' I said.

'Four fifteen! I thought you were getting up at five o'clock.'

'No darling I have to leave the yard at five. My booking is for eight o'clock, and that only leaves me three hours to get there.'

She doesn't answer. After setting the alarm she just turns over and says goodnight. I'm just about to say something when the cat decides to jump on the bed and make herself nice and comfortable. That gives me all the more reason to keep my mouth shut, because if I upset the cat I could end up walking to the yard in the morning. No way could I do that as it's about six miles. So I think the best thing to do is to move over a bit, much against my grain, and give the cat more room.

No sooner had I got into my bed and shut my eyes than the blessed alarm goes off. Oh no! Here we go again, and it's only Tuesday. I've got three more days to go yet, and I'm knackered already! Is it the whisky I had last night, or is it that I'm getting old? I'm certainly feeling it these days. Don't lay here. You've got a job to do, and if it all goes well you could be back nice and early. Though I probably won't be home tonight but that don't matter, because too many nights at home means not a very good week.

It isn't long before I'm up and washed and downstairs. I put the kettle on as I have to do my own flask this time, but at least my sandwiches are done. I never moan. She has a lot to do, what with going to work full time nursing, and running a home. Running your own lorries sometimes isn't as sweet as people think it is. Now I've made the tea I can call her. It won't take her long to get up and dressed. I know what she'll put on; it'll be her old track suit. She'll have combed her hair and that's without looking in the mirror. Oh dear! there she is. Whatever does she look like? She looks as if someone has put a key in her back and wound her up. I'd better not tell her that. Her tongue is like vinegar in the mornings.

'Cup of tea, darling? It's all poured out.'

Without replying she sits down on the stool. Even her expression hasn't changed from when she came into the kitchen. I want to laugh, but I know I'd better keep my mouth shut.

'I'm ready now, darling. Shall we get going?'

She just follows me to the car. While I'm driving down the road towards the yard I'm chatting away. I don't think she's taking a blind bit of notice of me.

You might as well shut up, Brian, I say to myself, because she's not with you. I look across at her. She has her head down with her arms folded and I think she's asleep. Then she yawns.

'Darling, put your hand up to your mouth. You'll take all the oxygen out of the car.'

'Ha, ha! Funny!' she replies. I can't help but laugh.

'You wait, Brian. I'll get my own back on you!'

'Here we are, darling. You can go back and get into your bed for a couple of hours.'

She turns her head. 'It's not worth it. I'm going to work at seven.'

'Why didn't you tell me last night? I wouldn't have come home.'

'You know I work every Tuesday morning.'

'I clean forgot. Sorry, darling.'

She doesn't answer. She just looks at me, and I know it's time for me to get a move on. Otherwise, I could be told something. Believe you me, if she starts there is no holding her back. And it could be ten times worse because it's early morning.

She gets out of the car and starts to walk around to the driver's side. She tilts her head towards me and I kiss her and say, 'Bye! Have a nice day, and don't work too hard.'

'Bye,' she says as she gets into the car.

I watch her as she drives away still yawning her head off. What does she look like? In about two hours she'll look totally different. Not a bit tired, and full of life.

It's not a bad morning, thank goodness. It's nice and light. Still, it should be nice - it's June. Right, I've filled my taco in. Now let's get moving and let's hope I can beat the traffic going into London. I should do as it's only five o'clock.

Oh my God! I have only got out of the yard and I've seen my first magpie. Let's hope I see the other one. You know what they say, don't you? 'One for sorrow, two for joy.' If I don't see another one shortly I certainly won't see any more when I reach the A45 or on the A12. Which means I'll probably be stitched up in London, or have a local for tomorrow. That would mean I won't be having a very good week.

You can't beat the country roads. The hedges are all nice and green, and as I look across the fields I can see the mist rising.

To me there is nothing better than the mornings. Oh! What a shame. A little dead rabbit on the side of the road. Why must they come so close? They have got all that lovely open space of fields to go in, and they have to get near the road. It's a good job my wife didn't see it as she gets so upset. She loves the wildlife.

Ah! Here we are. A45, we can make good time now. It's only about five miles before I get onto the A12. Well, the A45 seems to be dead this morning. Where are all the drivers? Perhaps I'm too early.

Oh dear, what have we got coming up behind now? Yes, I might have known it would be the rep who has got a meeting somewhere and thinks that by leaving at five he is going to be on time. Here he comes with his white shirt and his tie and briefcase on the back seat, thinking he owns the road out there in the third lane. He probably got up so quick he didn't wash the sleepy dirts out of his eyes. What most drivers would say, 'All p******g important?' Still, I suppose he thinks he's doing his job well, just like me.

Ah! A12. London, here I come. Now let's put my CB on. There might be somebody out there. Not that I feel in the mood for talking, mind you.

'You've got a smoky on your back door, driver.' Can he mean me? I look in my mirror and see the police car.

'Who's that?' I said, 'and where are you, driver?'

'That don't matter who I am, but I'm on his back door. You'll see if you look. If we work this one right they could live up to their name - jam sandwiches!'

'Don't you talk like that driver. He could be listening in to you.'

'You haven't got no worries. You're running straight, aren't you driver?'

'Yeah.'

'Well then, what are you worrying about? He's only doing his job, just like you and me.'

'Anyway, where are you? Are you far behind me, because I can't see you in my mirror?'

'No, not that far. Hang on, mate. If you take your foot off the throttle I'll be able to catch you up.'

'You cheeky so and so!'

'Eyeball, eyeball, driver! Yes, I was that Ford car that overtook you. I saw the look on your face. You thought, "There he goes, another rep."'

'How did you know what I was thinking! The speed you were going I'd hardly have thought you would have had time to look up from your window, let alone to see the expression on my face. Anyway, Mr. Rep Man, where are you going?'

'Oh, I've got a meeting in London for eleven. I thought I'd leave nice and early to miss the traffic.'

'You've done well! I wish a lot more would think like you.'

'Oh well, driver, I must get on my way. No disrespect to you, but you lorry drivers are a bit slow for me. It's been nice talking to you. Bye.'

'Cheerio, and mind how you go mate. I hope your meeting goes well and thank you.'

I turn off my CB. Well, he wasn't too bad to talk to. It passed a bit of time. I'm in Brentwood now. It'll only be a couple of minutes and I'll be on the M25. Then we'll see some lorries. Let's put my wireless on and see if there's any nice music on. I do hope I get tipped quickly so I can get back to get another nice one for tomorrow. Could do with a long one really, because tomorrow being Wednesday that's half the week gone already. Still, where have I got to go? Let's have a look. Where did I put my paperwork? Ah, there it is. E2, Suttons and Sons. Well, they're not too bad there. My booking is for eight and I've got to have a break. So if I have my break there, with a bit of luck I should be tipped and on my way back by ten thirty.

Ah, here we are. Suttons and Sons. There's only one other lorry in front of me by the looks of it. Lovely. I think once they start to unload me I'll have a brew up. Let's get out and have a walk about so I can stretch my legs.

Hum. It's good to stretch one's legs. Although it's still morning the air isn't as clean and fresh as down in Suffolk where I live. London is too fast for me. All I can smell is car fumes. Oh well. That's enough of talking to myself. Let's go and have that brew up and one of the cakes me little wife has made. I say little, but it's a figure of speech. I mustn't let her know that.

I've had my tea and I can still hear them in the back so they're still unloading me. I expect they'll be quite some time yet, but not too long I hope. Let's see if I can get a little sleep. Right, where's the pillow that my wife has made me?

Ah, there it is so I won't bother getting on my bunk bed. I might as well just put my head back in the driver's seat and have five minutes and let the world go by.

'Come on, driver, wake up! You can go. We've unloaded you. What are you doing down there, driver? How the devil did you get into that position?' It was one of the unloaders.

I can't laugh, let alone talk. I've got one leg stuck in between the bars of the steering wheel and the other on the floor. I'm in such a deep sleep that I can't even think where the hell I am let alone how the devil I got there. I manage to lift myself up and in doing so I have attracted quite an audience. They are all laughing and by this time I have started to laugh too. Eventually I do get up and have come to my senses and start to feel quite silly.

'Are you alright, driver?'

'Yeah. I'm alright, thanks. When you opened the door you made me jump, and then I slipped down.'

'Here you are, mate. Sign this, and you can be on your way.'

I signed his bit of paper and started up my lorry. I can't wait to get out of here. I expect that story will go around there for quite some time. Here we go, back to Felixstowe to see what we have for Wednesday. I hope I don't meet anybody on the road. I don't really feel like talking to anyone. I think I'll just put MW wireless on and listen to that. I'll probably get Jimmy Young. He's very good. I like his chat programmes.

Look at that! Now, that's what I call a lovely sight. Just what I've been looking for all day. My second magpie, right on top of that container.

I'm back at the docks now. I've finished early and wondering if they'll give me a nice short run for the afternoon, and then another for tomorrow. Or will they make me sit down at these bloody docks all afternoon which makes me more tired than driving. Still, I suppose I shouldn't moan. At least my wheels are turning, and so far I'm able to pay my bills! Not always on time, but who does? At least they're getting paid, and that's what matters.

That's my lorry parked. Now let's see what kind of run they're giving me. I feel a bit fed up today and that's not like me at all. I just want to go home and sit in my garden with a nice cold glass of beer.

One thing us lorry drivers can't do is relax on weekdays. Once we've got our load for the next day, we've got to turn around so we are ready to set off for our destination.

Oh, you're feeling sorry for yourself today aren't you, Brian? And you've started to talk to yourself, and that's a bad thing to do.

Mind you, they say if you answer yourself that's really bad for you. If anyone hears me they'll think I've gone mad!

I must be mad to want to be a lorry driver and be away all week and not have the comforts of my own home. Ah, here we are at the office. Now let's see what they're going to give me.

Bert looked out through the hatch in the wall and said, 'Here you are, Brian. This is a nice earner. Bury St. Edmunds, and it's loaded. All you've got to do is back it under your trailer and away you go.'

'Do you mean to say that I have to waste all tomorrow just going to Bury St. Edmunds and back? And I still have this afternoon free. Still, I don't care. I can go and sit in my garden with a nice glass of beer.'

'Oh will you? That's what you think, because if you look at your notes you'll see the Bury run is for today! Lost your tongue?'

I should have kept my mouth shut, I thought, or looked at my notes first. I'd better not say any more now or they might stitch me up for tomorrow, and then I really could be sitting in my garden, with no work at all.

'I'll say cheerio to you all then, and I'll ring you later to see what I've got for tomorrow.'

'Brian!' he called as I turned to go.

'Yeah, what?'

'Don't be too long. I've got something good for you tomorrow.'

'What is it?'

'Never you mind. Just hurry back.'

I go out of the office and look round. Now where's my trailer? What number is it? Ah, there it is. Not even a heavy one, only ten ton in my box. I won't burn much diesel so that'll be nice. What am I carrying? Let's have a look at my notes. Ah! cardboard, and all the way from the States as well. Haven't we got any cardboard in England? Now, what's the time? Two o'clock! With a bit of luck I should be at Bury St. Edmunds by three and all being well, unloaded by four and on my way back.

I'm all set to go. Let's put my CB on to ask if the A45 is clear. 'One nine for a copy. Can anybody tell me what the A45 to Bury St. Edmunds is like?'

'Yes, driver. There's some road works, but you should be alright.'

'Thanks, mate.'

Oh well, I've got a bit of road works. Still, I'm leaving the right time of day, before the office workers knock off, and also before the mums are collecting the kids from school. Mind you, I suppose I'll cop it on my way back.

Bloody music on the radio. I could do with a good play. It would pass the time and I like listening to a good play. Ah, here's the road works. God help us, he didn't tell me that they'd shut one of the lanes of the A45 off! Still, it seems to be going well at the moment. If it stays like this we should be through it in no time.

Ah, here we are at our destination, and by the looks of it I'm going to be the only lorry here.

'Hello mate, where do you want me?'

'Over there'll do well. If you hang on mate, I'll see you back.' Where's he gone? They always stand where we can't see them! Ah there he is. In his uniform and little pointed hat. Shut up, Brian. He's probably very proud of his uniform.'

'Hold up. That'll do yer, mate,' the man shouted.

'Cheers mate,' I said.

Now the rest is up to them. Let's see if I can get a nice cup of tea and a piece of cake here.

'Have you got a canteen where I can get a cup of tea?'

'Yeah. Just through that red door, down to the bottom of the corridor, turn left through the black door, and it's on your right. You can't miss it.'

After following all the instructions, I eventually get to the canteen. I must say this looks a nice clean place.

'Afternoon, love. Have you got a bacon sandwich, please?' I asked the girl behind the counter.

'Yes. One or two?'

'Just the one will do nicely.'

'If you'd like to go and sit down I'll call you when it's ready.'

I hadn't been sitting down long when she called, 'Bacon roll and a mug of tea.'

'Thanks love. Over here,' I called out.

'You didn't ask for a cup of tea, but I brought you one. Is that all right?'

'Yes thanks, love. I thought I did ask for a cuppa. This plate is nice and hot. I love my food on a hot plate.'

'We serve all our food on hot plates. If you should want anything else, just call out.'

'Ta, love.'

Cor. This tastes really nice. Not too fatty and the bread is even cut a nice size. I'm certainly going to enjoy this.

'Hoy, mate! You the driver of that white Volvo out there, registration number E59 FLH?' One of the unloaders poked his head through the door.

I thought this was too good to be true. 'Yeah. Why?'

'Well, I'm sorry to disturb you, but we've opened up your container to unload it and you'll never guess what's in the back.'

'I suppose I've got a bloody tarantula in the back and someone's been bitten. Or have you trod on it, and I'm in for trouble. Is that it?'

'No, it's a lovely white cat.'

'A cat! Christ! I hope you haven't let it out. That must have been in there for three weeks. Is it alright?'

'Yeah. It seems to be. It's walking about.'

'Alright. I'm coming straight away.'

Just as I was starting to enjoy my sandwich. I'd better pay first. 'How much do I owe you, love?'

'Seventy-five pence, please. That was quick. Have they unloaded you already?'

'No, love. I've got a blessed cat in my container!'

'Ah, poor thing. Has it been there long?'

'Yes. Probably about three weeks. See you love, and thanks. The tea and sandwiches were really good.'

Oh well, I thought this was going too well. I can see this turning out to be a long day. And there I was thinking this is a nice short run. Looks like it's going to be a long afternoon.

'Now, you say the cat is still in my container?'

'Yeah.'

'Right. The first thing to do is to call a vet, because it's not from this country.'

'All right. I'll go and phone right away.'

I can't see myself getting back tonight now. It looks as if I could be sleeping here and probably losing out on tomorrow's job!

I shouldn't feel sorry for myself. That poor cat has been in that container for three weeks with nothing to eat or drink. I'm surprised that it's still alive. Ah, here comes the bloke back.

'I've telephoned the vet. He's coming right away. It won't take him long as the vet's is only just around the corner. How long did you say the cat could have been in there?'

'Three weeks at least.'

'Whatever has the poor thing lived on? There's only cardboard in there, but we'll soon find out. Is this the vet now? Looks like his van. Yeah, that's him. Glad you could come so quickly. This is the driver.'

'Good afternoon,' said the vet. 'What have we got on board? A cat did you say? Can I have your name?'

'Everett.'

'Do you know where this load has come from?'

'America.'

'America! Well that means the cat will have to be put down. We won't be finding the owners now, so there's no one to pay for quarantine if it stays here or the cost of sending it back. But I don't like to do it. The poor thing has survived for all this time on a diet of cardboard and water that has condensed on the walls of the container. It's lived through all that. It seems as if it should be given a chance.'

'I think so too. If it goes into quarantine, how much will it cost?' I asked.

'I don't really know. Not that much I suppose.'

'Right,' I said turning to the men who were still hanging about. 'How many staff do you have working here?'

'Over a hundred,' the manager said.

'Do you think they would be prepared to put some money into a kitty to save the cat?'

'You've a good idea there, driver. I'll go and ask them. You don't mind waiting a bit, do you vet?'

The vet and I stood side by side, and I'm sure I know what he's thinking and feeling. It wasn't long before the manager was back with a big smile on his face.

'Any luck? What did they say?' we both asked.

'They are all prepared to put one pound into the kitty, and I have to ask will that be enough?'

'Oh I should think so. That should be plenty,' said the vet.

'Hold on a minute. What's going to happen to the cat when it gets out of quarantine?' I asked.

They both stood there looking at me. No one seemed to have thought that far ahead.

'Does anybody in the factory want a cat?' I asked the vet.

'What about you driver?'

'Sorry. I've already got one, and a dog. Tell you what though, let's go and ask the workers if they would like to put their names into my hat and whoever's name is pulled out is the lucky person.'

'Now that's what I call good thinking, driver. So what are we waiting for? Let's go.'

We go into the factory and explain about the cat and there isn't one person who doesn't put their hand up. After everybody had written their names on a piece of paper, the vet took my hat off my head and passed it around. Then he folded the edges of my hat together, gave it a good shake and passed it to me.

'Please pick a name, driver,' the vet said.

I put my hand into my hat and stirred the names up once more. Then I picked one out.

I looked around and all I could see were blank expressions, and I wondered how many of them really wanted the cat.

'Come on!' one woman shouts out.

I glanced down toward the bits of paper on my hat, and then I picked one out.

'The cat belongs to Mrs. Joan White'.

There was an almighty scream, and a woman appears waving her arms in the air. The next thing I know is that she then puts her arms around my neck and is kissing me. Thank goodness, I'm thinking. It's someone who really wants the cat. I'm not complaining about what I'm getting, although it doesn't last for long because the next minute she is all over the vet.

'Right now,' the vet said, extricating himself. 'Can I use your phone? I must get some help to catch the cat. One of my colleagues will come up and give me a hand.'

It isn't long before help arrives, and soon the cat is safe and secure in the vet's basket. It's a beautiful long-haired Persian with lovely big bright eyes, in spite of what it has lived through these past few weeks.

'Well, everybody, I must take the cat away and give it some food and drink and a good check-up. If anybody needs a drink now I think the cat does!'

Soon that cat is on its way to another destination. It doesn't know where it's going, but we all do, and it will be a better place.

After its quarantine a happy home will be waiting for it. The workers drifted back to work, and as I turned to go for another cup of tea I see the woman who has won the cat. She is crying.

'Whatever are you crying for, love. You should be happy. The cat is going to be well looked after. When it has spent its time in quarantine it will be able to come home to you. Or have you changed your mind about having it?'

'Oh no, I'm looking forward to having him. I'm crying because I'm so happy. My old cat died last month and I was missing her so much. Now I feel as if she has come back to me. This is just what I needed.'

'Well then, wipe your eyes and let's go and have a nice cup of tea.'

Then, turning to the foreman. I ask, 'Is it alright if I take this lady for a cup of tea? She's upset.'

'Yeah. Ok'

'Come on then, love. A cup of tea will do you good.'

As we walked towards the canteen we don't talk. I don't know what to say to her. She is still sniffing and I don't understand why she is still upset.

'There you are, love. Go and sit down and I'll bring you a cup of tea.'

Where's the clock in this place? Ah, there it is in the usual place over the top of the door. Blimey! It's six thirty. If they don't hurry up and unload me I can't see myself getting away from here tonight. What will I tell Bert? He'd better not dare laugh about the cat. I suppose I'll be getting some wisecracks for a few weeks.

Oh well, I might as well make a move back to my lorry and see if they've unloaded her. If they haven't I'll have something to say as there wasn't much on there to unload.

It's certainly nice and warm out here this evening. It's quite a suntrap round here. Ah, here's the bloke.

'Hello, mate. I see you are sitting down. Does that mean that you've unloaded me?'

'No. Sorry, driver. It's time to knock off and the forklift driver has already gone.'

'Gone! Gone where?'

'Home. It's half past six.'

Bloody nice! That means I shall be stuck up here until tomorrow morning.

'What time do you start work in the morning? I suppose it's not till eight o'clock!'

'No. We start at six in the morning, and you'll be the first one we unload.'

'Big deal.'

'Well, that's the best I can do. Your lorry will be alright in the yard, so you won't be disturbed. Just move it there out of sight of the road. There's a nice pub down the road. They do a smashing bit of food and it's not dear. If you turn left outside the yard gate, it's about a hundred yards down on the right. It's called The Lion. Well, I'll say cheerio to you, and I'll see you in the morning about five forty.'

'What time does the forklift driver start?'

'Oh he'll be here about the same time.'

'I didn't ask what time he arrives. I asked what time he's likely to start work.'

'Six, the same time as myself. Don't worry; you'll be unloaded and gone by seven.'

'I want to be.'

If I'm not it will be too late to get one in for tomorrow. As it is, it won't be the good one. That bloody cat!

Just as well my wife didn't hear me say that as she loves her cat! I suppose it will be taking up my side of the bed tonight. I can hear her now. Come on, Jemima. It's bedtime! You sleep that side of the bed. I wouldn't mind but it always does sleep my side of the bed. The damn thing is never on her side even when I'm there.

'Goodnight, driver. See you in the morning,' the bloke calls out.

'Hang on a second. Are there any toilets around here, or a place where I can have a wash?' I called back.

'Yeah. Just around the back of the factory you'll see a small building. It's not locked. Oh and by the way, we've got a security man as well. In fact he should be here already. He'll see that you're alright.'

'Thanks mate.'

Oh well, what shall I do first? Have a wash or make myself another cup of tea? What's the time? Six thirty! I've got a bloody long wait till morning.

I might as well go and get my washing gear. Then after me wash, I'll put my kettle on and have five minutes. After that I suppose I could find that pub and have a bit of dinner.

Who would want to be a lorry driver? I must be mad. Right, now where is my bucket and washing gear? There they are. I didn't think they would be far away. The lorry isn't that big! Right, I'll go and have a nice wash and brush up. I feel as though I need one. Now, where did he say the building was? Ah, that looks like it. The water's certainly nice and hot. Flannel, soap, toothbrush, toothpaste and towel. I've got everything. Now I can set to and have a good old wash.

'Hello! Are you the driver of that lorry?' It was the night watchman.

That made me jump. I didn't know anyone else was here. He must have come in while I was washing my face. It's a good job I didn't have all my clothes off.

'Yeah. Is there a problem?' I asked.

'No, mate. It's just that I've got your lorry number on my note pad. You might hear me walking about throughout the night. I hope I don't disturb you.'

'No, I shouldn't think so. I'm going down the pub tonight. Do you lock the gates?'

'Yeah, but all you have to do is rattle them and I'll hear you.'

'Oh, right. Thanks.'

'See you later then, driver.'

'Yeah, see you.'

That was nice of him. Well that's my wash done. Now I think I'll go and have a nice cup of tea in my cab. After all it's too early yet to go to the pub. A walk later will do me good. It's certainly a nice evening. Right now, let's put my bucket back in its place. Must keep nice and tidy. Now where is my kettle? Oh yeah, it's under my bunk bed, with my cooking stove, my tea bags and my powdered milk. Let's put my kettle on and wait for it to boil. It won't take that long. Ah, lovely. There's today's paper. I haven't read that yet. Mind you, there's not much in the papers. Ah, there she blows. Have I put my tea bag in my mug? Yes, and my sugar, so all I have to do is pour my water into my mug. Two teaspoons of my powdered milk. Now that looks good.

That's what I call bliss, an early finish! The only thing wrong is that I'm not at home. Still at least I'm not chasing up the M45 or sitting down the docks waiting for my load.

'Bloody hell!' The door suddenly opens and I as near as anything overbalance and fall to the ground.

'Sorry, driver. I didn't know you were leaning against the door.' The security man must have crept up like a cat on me. I didn't hear a sound.

'I could have broken my bloody neck,' I grumble. 'Anyway, what do you want?'

I came over to tell you I've made a brew, and do you fancy a cuppa?'

'Actually I've just made one. Thanks all the same,' I said, trying to sound grateful.

'What time are you going to the pub then?' he asked me. 'When I've finished my tea and cleared things up here.' I suppose it must be a boring old life for him, and he's glad of having someone to talk to. He seems to read my mind.

'It must be boring for you, driver. Especially at times like these.'

'It's the first time I've ever had a cat in my container and I don't want it to sodding happen again, thank you very much,' I said. 'This is supposed to be a short run. I should be sitting in my garden tonight with a nice glass of beer and with my cat on my lap.'

'Oh, you have a cat then?'

'Yeah, damn thing!' I said with a half smile.

'Don't you like cats, then?' he asked, seeming surprised.

'Yeah, I do. But this one gets all the fuss. I'm sure it's bloody human.'

'You ought to kick the cat off and put your wife on your lap, and give her a cuddle,' he suggests.

'You're joking, aren't you?' I said. 'Anyway, she works some nights. And this is one of them, so it would have been the cat or nothing.'

'I expect when you do go to cuddle your wife she has one of her headaches. I've never known a woman who doesn't.'

'No mate,' I said. 'She's gone past that stage. Last time she went to the doctor he told her not to worry because it was just her age. So now everything is put down to her age! You could have got up in the cab and had a cup of tea with me, instead of standing there and giving yourself a crick in the neck,' I add, feeling more friendly towards the night watchman.

'Never mind!' he said. 'I'll come over and wake you in the morning, and you can have a cup of tea with me in my office. It will save you brewing up in the morning.'

'Thank you. If you'd like to give me a knock at about 5:30 that will do me nice.'

'Ok then, mate. I'll let you get on otherwise the pub will be shut by the time you get there. When you come back just give the gates a good rattle. I'm sure to hear you.'

Off he goes at last. It looks as if he's going to start on one of his rounds for the night. I certainly feel nice and clean, and I must smell better. With all the heat today I must have pen and inked.

Well, I might as well get off. I'll lock up first. Can't be too careful. I see he's left the gate open for me to get out. What did he say, turn left outside and it's about a hundred yards? Not too far! That's good. I don't feel like a long walk.

Ah, there it is, The Lion. Looks nice from the outside but there's a lot of people sitting outside. Let's hope it not one of those push and shove pubs. I won't go in the public bar. Too much smoke probably. Try the lounge. This doesn't look too bad. Nice and clean, and not too many people inside. They mostly seem to be sitting outside. Don't blame them. It's certainly a nice evening. Oh, the bartender is waiting for me to order.

'Yes, sir. What would you like to drink?' he said politely.

'I'll have a Guinness please, and are you serving food yet?' I ask him.

'Yes, sir. I'll get you the menu. I can recommend the steak, and I've also got some very nice pieces of rock eel.'

'Cor! The rock eel sounds good to me. I'll have some of that. A nice big piece please.'

'Would you like salad with it sir?'

'No. Just rock eel and chips will do nicely, thank you.'

'Ok. It'll be about twenty minutes. I'll give you a shout. Will you be outside?'

'No, I'll sit inside,' I said.

I pass some empty tables near the door, but I don't fancy that position. I look around. Ah, there's a table in the corner with plenty of room. Only one bloke sitting there, but I'd better ask.

'Excuse me, is anybody else sitting here?' I ask him.

'No. Feel free,' he answers.

Now that I come to look at him, I seem to have sat next to the oldest man in Bury. Perhaps I should have sat somewhere else, but it would be rude to move now. He'll probably want to tell me his life story, and all I want is a nice drink.

Serves me right for not taking one of the empty tables, but I hate to sit where people keep passing me to get to the bar. Stop thinking like that, I tell myself. You chose to sit here, and one day you will be old. Probably by then you'll be wanting to tell everybody about lorry driving and how much it has changed.

'Hello mate. How are you? I haven't seen you in here before,' he said.

'No, I haven't been in before. I'm delivering down the road.'

'Yeah, I thought you were one of those lorry drivers. Have you got one of those big lorries or a little one?'

'Big one.'

'I bet that certainly looks a beast of a thing. Not like they were years ago mate?'

Oh dear, I think. He's got to be a flipping lorry driver. Now I'm going to hear about the lorries in his day. 'What did you do then, mate, for a living?' I asked him.

'Me? Oh I was a bricklayer out in all weathers. If I started talking about the past we could be here all night,' he said. 'It's now we should be talking about.'

The cottage

While we were living at the cottage, my nephew Mark often came to stay with us. We enjoyed having him as he was such good fun, and he loved staying with us.

I think the novelty was our bathroom, which was outside. It had a tin bath like the one which used to hang up in our shed. I can remember my poor old mum having to fill up the bathtub, which would be placed in front of the fire. I expect most of you would remember these.

The bath in our outside bathroom was as deep as it was long and Brian thought it was great. He put a heater on the wall so we would have warmth when bathing. This meant I could lay back in comfort, but when I got out I had to venture into the cold to get back into the cottage. In the winter nights, I had this big dressing gown, which was big enough for three people. I can feel the shivers now, trying to dry myself very quickly and running into the cottage just to be by the fire for warmth.

I wouldn't want to go back to those days. Let us hope we never have to!

Brian made the cottage really pretty inside considering it was to be condemned. I can always remember the first time I ever saw it. From the outside it looked really nice.

'It's nice, Brian,' I said.

'You haven't seen inside yet, Maria.'

'Oh come on Brian it can't be so bad that a lick of paint won't put it right,' I said smiling.

Brian pulled the key from his pocket, put it into the lock and gently turned it. The door opened into this very small kitchen.

'It's nice, Brian,' I said without looking at him. I then stepped up onto small steps that led me through to the dining room area. This isn't a bad size, I thought. It had a large window which overlooked the back garden. It also had a rather nice fireplace, and standing there I could smell the fire with logs burning. A good drop of hot soapy water would make it look nice.

'Brian,' I called. 'Where are you?'

'In here.'

I walked through the dining room and into the lounge, which was a bit bigger than the dining room. Again, it had a large window that looked onto the main road.

'It's not that bad, Brian, compared to what you were saying.' Brian was walking around banging on the walls and tapping on the ceilings, as if it should suddenly fall down.

'Brian, what are you doing that for?' I asked.

'You never know what's behind or what's up there,' he said with this stern look on his face.

We definitely wouldn't be going to live here if it did fall down, surely! By the time we had looked all over the cottage, we were quite happy with it.

'Well, Maria. Have you seen enough? Do you like it?'

'Yes, I do. We can make it look quite nice, can't we Brian?' I could see what Brian was thinking - what a lot of grafting.

As we were walking out the door to go home, Brian said in a very sheepish voice, 'Do you want to know where the bathroom is?'

'Oh yes. Where is the bathroom? I didn't see it. Where was it?' I asked. 'You're going to tell me that we haven't got one. You horror, you left that till last!'

'Of course I was going to show you the bathroom,' said Brian.

'Come on then. Where is it?'

'Follow me.' We turned to walk down the garden. After only a few yards we came across this old brick place. Opening the door, I entered this somewhat unusual bathroom.

I turned around and there stood Brian. 'Well at least we have a bathroom!' he said.

With that we swiftly left the cottage and hurried back to the flat to tell John and Malcolm. They were over the moon for us. Truthfully, I think they were glad to see the back of my moods, although John was always so understanding when I was expecting Shane.

John, Brian's brother, used to work nights. So during the day, he would be over at the cottage doing the painting for us. With the state of the cottage, I really wondered where John would start. However, he made a good job of the decorating.

It was July when we moved in and we were both happy. However, I was finding it quite difficult to settle down to married life - having to wait on someone rather than being waited on!

I can remember one time my sister-in-law's brother came to see us. He took one look at the saucepans and said, 'Have you anyone coming to dinner, or are you two just big eaters?'

'No,' Brian said. 'She just hasn't got the measurements right yet!'

'Well, Maria, you certainly make a smashing shepherd's pie, doesn't she Brian?'

'She certainly does, but it's the quantity that bothers me. At this rate I'll be bankrupt within six months, if the portions don't change,' he said laughing.

I just looked up and said, 'Ha ha. Very funny.'

Brian didn't say any more after that. He knew better.

My first days of nursing

I started my nursing in December 1968, at Brentwood District Hospital, two nights a week, which were Friday and Saturday. My shifts were from eight p.m. until eight a.m. I thought my first night would never end.

I was at the nurses' station a quarter of the way down the ward. I felt sick as I sat there, reading the reports of the patients and trying to understand it all!

Suddenly hearing footsteps, I looked up. There stood this very upright lady, wearing a blue uniform and a rather large frilly hat.

'Good evening, Nurse Everett.'

'Good evening, sister,' I replied.

Her expression didn't change. It was stern and very frightening. I remember thinking, I wouldn't want to cross her! By this time I was standing up, and believe you me I was shaking from head to toe.

'Shall we walk around to see if the patients are alright,' she said with this expressionless face.

As I walked, I tried to be as professional as I could be on my first night of nursing. I didn't say a word. Well, I didn't dare in case I said the wrong thing anyway. I don't know why she didn't ask the other nurse to walk around with her, although admittedly the other nurse was busy.

I kept thinking to myself, I hope to God she doesn't ask me anything because I'm lost as it's only my first night!

We walked up both sides of the ward and everything seemed well, thank goodness.

'Thank you, Nurse Everett,' she said. 'You may go on reading the report. Have a nice night. I'll be back later on in the night to see if everything is OK.'

With that she started to walk away. Then she stopped and turned. I just stood there rigid, to be quite honest petrified. I'd never felt so much fear in all my life.

'Nurse?' she said.

'Yes, sister?'

'Has the staff nurse explained to you that she will be having her break from twelve o'clock until two a.m?'

'Yes,' I replied with a squeaky voice. Then she was gone, and bang went the double doors as she went through them.

That's it, I thought. Wake the patients up. That's all I need!

I sat down at the desk, looked up and saw another two nurses standing there.

'Don't be so frightened. You'll be alright. You've done well so far, hasn't she, nurse,' Sue said to Jane as she stood there with such a lovely smile on her face, which made me feel better. I don't know about 'so far.' I looked up at the clock. It was eleven thirty and I had eight and a half hours to go!

All three of us went out to the kitchen to have a cup of tea, and by God I needed it!

'Did sister explain to you that I'll be going on my break at midnight until two a.m?' asked Jane.

'Yes,' I said. 'Will Sue help me, and show me what I have to do?'

'Well,' she replied. 'You'll be going up to the children's ward for two hours, and then you'll go on your break.'

'OK then.'

'Nurse, will you show Nurse Everett to the children's ward, and introduce her to the other nurse, please.'

With that, the two of us went on our way. At this point we bumped into the matron.

'Good evening, Nurse Everett. This is your first time of nursing then?'

'Yes,' I said in a very soft voice.

When we reached the children's ward, the nurse on duty went through the report with me and then showed me round the ward. This is nice, I thought, as it made me feel involved.

After that, she said, 'I'll show you the kitchen. This is most important as that's where we make the tea.'

Oh good, I thought, a nice cup of tea and I'll be able to ask her lots of questions and hopefully the night will go quickly.

'Now, if you should need anything, just ring this number.' She was waving a piece of paper in front of me, and my stomach didn't feel too good at this point.

'Don't worry, you'll be alright,' she said.

'What do you mean, I'll be alright. Where are you going?' I asked.

'Oh, I'm going on my break.'

'Am I staying here on my own? I've never done any nursing before.'

'Don't worry,' she said, and off she went.

As I was sitting at the nurses' desk I was thinking, roll on eight o'clock.

Many things were going through my head, one in particular being the thought that I wasn't really cut out for nursing.

'Nurse!' I heard this little voice call out. I stood up and started to walk towards where the voice was coming from.

'I need a wee, nurse.'

'OK, darling. I won't be a minute,' I said, and off I went to do my first bit of nursing.

After seeing to the little boy, I made my way back to the famous desk yet again.

'Are you OK, nurse?' I heard. I looked up and there she stood, the lady in blue with the frilly hat and she was smiling at me. I couldn't believe it - perhaps she was nicer than I thought!

'Would you like me to stay with you for a while?' she asked.

'Yes please,' I said very quickly. With that we both sat down and she began explaining things to me. I was so grateful to her, not that I understood a lot of what she was telling me. Nevertheless, she was with me. The next thing I heard was the doors opening and in walked Sue.

'It's your break time now, nurse,' said Sue.

'Come on, nurse. I'll show you where to go,' said the matron. 'Jane will be with you from your other ward.'

The matron took me to the staff room.

'Here we are. I hope you have a nice rest,' she said when we arrived.

'Thank you,' I said.

'Hi,' I heard. 'I've put chairs out for you. Is that OK? Also, there's a blanket for your legs if you should feel cold.'

I was in that chair with my feet up, and I tell you I really needed it. Jane just put her head back and said have a good rest, and that was the last I heard from her. I couldn't shut my eyes. My stomach was still going round and round. However, I must have drifted off, as the next thing I heard was the lady in blue standing by the door and saying, 'It's time to make a move, girls.' I was feeling really sick.

'Did you have a good rest, Maria?' Jane asked me.

'Yes thanks, but I'm feeling sick.'

'Oh, don't worry. All nurses on their first night feel like that.'

The next thing, we were back on the ward and I was pouring out teas for the patients. I was quite enjoying this part until I heard, 'Nurse, don't go to the bed where the curtains are pulled round. I'll need your help in a minute.'

I had actually finished doing the teas and was on my way to the kitchen when the lady in blue was standing beside me.

'Come with me.' With that she took me to the bed where the curtains were pulled round. Oh my God, I thought.

The lady is dead, and I've never seen a dead person before. I was beginning to feel really sick at this point.

The nurse was explaining to me what she wanted me to do when the sister arrived. I promptly walked out from behind the curtains and went straight to the bathroom where I was sick!

'Nurse Everett.' I could hear the sister calling me. 'Are you alright, my dear?'

'No, I feel quite sick,' I said. 'I don't think I'm cut out for nursing.'

'Oh you'll be alright. This is your first night and your first death, but it does get easier. You finish washing the cups up.'

'Come on, Maria. It's time we're going home. Have you got a lift?' asked Sue.

'Yes, thanks. My father-in-law is picking me up,' I replied. When I opened the outside door and breathed in the fresh air, that was wonderful. I got into my father-in-law's van.

'Did you have a good night, girl?' my father-in-law asked me. 'Not too bad, but I'm not overly keen on nursing though,' I said.

However, I did carry on nursing for all of thirty-seven years, and I loved every minute of it.

The weekend in Kent

Joe Boy, my cousin, whom I hadn't seen for a long time and who lived in Kent, asked Brian and me down for a weekend. I knew we would have a smashing time. We did as well!

We arrived at Joe's at 4 p.m. on Saturday. I had not been to Kent for many years. Although I had driven through, sadly I had never stopped off. After my Aunt Becky and Uncle Elijah died, I could not find the time. I know I should have kept in touch, but I had a young family, and working as well made it difficult.

As we drove down Joe Boy's road looking for his house, I could not believe my eyes. There was a lad running a horse up and down the road. The horse had obviously been washed and the lad was trying to dry it.

I said to Brian, 'We can't be that far away, can we!'

'No,' said Brian. 'Look! There he is.'

Sure enough, there he was, sitting on his doorstep, phone in hand. Whatever would they do without the mobile telephone! It did nothing but ring all the weekend while we were there.

How on earth did our parents manage years ago? Word of mouth is far cheaper my girl, my father would say!

Joe Boy's wife, Debbie, gave us such a warm welcome that we felt at home straight away. It took me back to when I used to go and see my Aunt Becky and Uncle Elijah.

That afternoon we sat and talked over old times. Every so often, I looked at Joe Boy and wondered how he recognised me at Appleby Fair. The last time he saw me was on my wedding day, and he was only eight years old.

Still, they do say we recognise our own. Nevertheless, Joe recognised me from the back, which was quite flattering really!

That evening we went down to the pub, The Lully, and what a night that was!

There was singing and dancing and the beer was flowing like water. Tiddler was his old self. He was singing and it seemed just like yesterday, when I used to sit on Dad's coat between Mum and Aunt Becky in the pub. It was supposed to make me look older! I don't know about looking older, but I was still only allowed to drink lemonade!

The brussels sprouts

Shane and Aaron were so fed up this particular morning. They kept asking me what could they do to help me. Well I couldn't think what to give them to occupy themselves. I kept saying, 'Go over to the park and play. That way you won't be fed up as there are lots of trees to climb.'

'We went yesterday and we don't want to go over there again today,' said Shane.

These two pitiful faces were looking at me. Then I had a thought. What if they were to pull the weeds up out of the vegetable garden for me? That would be a good help as it did need weeding. Also, when Brian comes home from work he won't have to do it.

'Right then, boys. You can pull the weeds up out of the vegetable garden. But mind not to pull up the brussels sprouts, as they are growing nicely and we will hopefully be having them at Christmas.'

'You had better show us what are brussels, if you don't want us to pull them up,' Shane replied.

I took the boys over to the vegetable garden and showed them what to do. Then I left them to it. An hour must have passed when suddenly I heard, 'We're finished. Can we have a drink?'

'Of course you can. Help yourself,' I called out.

I didn't go to see what they had done. I thought it would be OK as I had shown them what I wanted. Oh well, I thought. I'd better get our dinner, otherwise Brian will be home and it won't be ready.

I was busy in the kitchen preparing our meal when I heard Brian pull up outside. As he walked through the gate he waved and then went into the garage, and came out with a gardening fork. He'll have a surprise as the boys have done the weeding for him. That will please him.

'Maria!' came this rather loud voice. 'What have you done here?'

I went outside wondering whatever all the fuss was about. When I went around to where the noise was coming from, I took one look and my mouth fell open. Oh my God, I thought. Whatever have the boys done to Brian's garden? I'm in for it now.

'What have you been doing here? Where have all my bloody brussels sprouts gone?'

I pointed at the ground where some were laying. Thank goodness some were still in the ground. The boys had, however, made a good job of pulling the weeds out, and they had left them in a pile as well.

'Shane and Aaron were bored, and they asked if they could do something. So I suggested that they could pull the weeds up. I thought you would be pleased. I did show them what to do, and what were weeds and what were brussels sprouts. Then I left them to it.'

'Did you not think of checking on them to see how they were getting on?' asked Brian.

'No, I thought they would be alright. Don't be hard on them. It really wasn't their fault. I should have checked on them like you said.'

I went in and finished cooking the dinner. When it was ready I called Shane and Katy down from upstairs. We all sat down around the table eating our dinner, and I was hoping and praying that Brian wouldn't say anything. I could see by the look on his face that he wanted to say something.

'Nice dinner,' Katy said.

Then Shane piped up with, 'What do you think of the vegetable garden? Do you think Aaron and I made a good job of it?'

'Oh you made a good job of it alright. You pulled half my brussels sprouts up, and I was growing them for Christmas,' said Brian.

I just looked at Shane and shook my head as much as to say, don't say another word. Shane has got these lovely large eyes, and by the look of them and the expression on his face he was thinking of saying something. But he knew that it would be better to keep his mouth shut at this particular time.

'What's happened to your brussels sprouts then?' Katy asked.

'Nothing. Just eat your dinner, Katy,' Brian said.

As she sat at the table she was giggling away, so wanting to get down and investigate. She knew not to get down until we had all finished our dinner. Once we had all finished, Katy asked, 'Can I get down now please?'

'Yes, off you go,' I said.

I knew what direction she was going. Straight for the bloody vegetable garden. Wait for it, I thought. In a minute she'll be back indoors, shouting off about the garden.

'Oh what have you done to Dad's vegetable garden, Shane? It looks a mess,' said Katy as she nearly fell back inside.

'Oh shut up, Katy,' said Shane. 'It wasn't only me. It was Aaron as well. He helped me. Anyway, Mum did tell us what to do, and how to do it. It's just that we got a bit carried away.'

'Never mind, Shane. We can plant some more, can't we Brian,' I said.

'No we can't. It's too late to put any in now,' Brian replied.

I thought it best to keep my mouth shut, and not ask any questions on the matter, otherwise I could get myself in deeper. And I didn't really want that.

I'd rather just forget about the brussels sprouts. Brian never said any more, but every time I walked by the vegetable garden I couldn't help but think about the brussels sprouts that Shane and Aaron pulled up.

As it was we did have a nice few for Christmas, but that was it. We didn't have any left for the New Year.

The petticoats

It was in the late fifties, early sixties that the can-can petticoats came out. I bought mine in the early sixties. It was a very pale blue with layers of beautiful lace. I only wore mine at weekends as I wanted to keep it in a nice condition.

My friend Sue bought hers the same time as me in Marilyn's, a very small shop in the arcade in Brentwood. Hers was pink. I loved pink so heaven knows why I went for the blue.

Sue and I felt like the bees knees when we were out dancing. We used to wear white shoes with small heels. I tell you we used to strut the floor beautifully on Saturday nights. We used to go to Keys Hall or the Meeds Ballroom, where most youngsters used to go and where we used to meet our friends.

Where have all the years gone. It's quite scary really.

I think of life as four stages. We are born, we go to school then we leave school to go to work, then we come to retirement age. Thank goodness we don't think about the last stage when we are dancing on the dance floor showing our petticoats off and tapping our heels to the music. Life is so short to be thinking of the different stages in my mind. Now I take each day as it comes.

Shane's log carrying days

Brian, Katy and I went to see my parents at Wickford in Essex. While we were there, Katy rode her horse and we sat outside having our afternoon tea. The weather was really nice, and we sat and talked about everything and anything.

I went down to see my sister, Anne, while I was there as she lived on the same piece of land. My sister and her father-in-law and mother-in-law live in one large house which is divided up into two. Her in-laws live in one side and my sister in the other.

Anne showed me what she had been sewing. As for me, I can't sew a button on straight. I'm more into computers. We all have our own hobbies which we like doing.

I used to ride horses, and went to one of our local riding schools to learn to ride. I only had three lessons. On the third, the horse which I was on decided to bolt with me on its back. Then it reared up and off I came. I had a broken arm, and was in plaster for ten weeks.

My sister and I were sitting in the garden talking about it. Then we said that we would go up to Mum and Dad's to get another cup of tea.

'Where have you two been?' Father said.

'Drinking tea and just talking, really, Father,' Anne said. Katy had a lovely time with her pony, Prince.

'Come on. We have to go now. We can't leave Shane too long. I know he has been around Granddad and Nanny's, but we must go.'

The next thing we were all saying our goodbyes and away we went. It wasn't long before we were near our house, and as we approached we could see this black smoke in the air.

'Someone's chimney's on fire,' Brian said.

As we got nearer, the smoke was getting thicker. Brian drove into our drive, jumped out of the van and ran inside.

And there was Shane watching television, oblivious to what was happening outside.

'Shane, our chimney's on fire,' yelled Brian.

'What!' Shane said and jumped up and ran outside to look. Brian was inside feeling our chimney breast. It was red hot, and Brian was so afraid that it would crack. Afterwards he went outside to see if the smoke was dying down.

'Brian, is everything OK?' our neighbour, George, called out.

'I think so. It seems to be slowing down now, thank goodness.'

'I saw Shane carrying this enormous piece of wood across the road. I asked him what he was going to do with it, and he said he was going to light a fire for you, Brian. Looks like he has done that!'

Well eventually the fire did go out, thank goodness, and Brian sat down with Shane and thanked him for making a fire. But next time we would rather he put the heating on.

A place to go

Who are we after we give birth? We hope to be the same person, but with a baby. Yet afterwards, everything is so different. We find ourselves struggling with changes in our life.

My writing is a journey inwards. In many ways, it's like mining. We dig down into the earth and bring back moments that are raw. Yet there is a reward that comes from the work itself. When we engage in the practice for a period, our minds come alive with thoughts, images and reflections, and we begin to sense the presence of our own voice.

Like any journey, there is no single road to take, no easy set of directions. We have our whole lives to write about, but the choice can be overwhelming. I usually start by focusing on a particular time or place, even the tiniest moment that comes to my mind.

I may remember a journey or a view from a window, or the colour of lights against a wall. Feelings create energy, and energy creates momentum that will carry me forward, often to a place I have been to.

The coat

Shane had a friend called Harry, who lived in the next street to us. They were great friends and would play most days either at our house or down at his house.

I grew up with his father, Harry. His mother and I used to walk into town to get our shopping sometimes. When it was fine, we would take our prams and off we would go. We used to walk everywhere. Well in those days we couldn't get on a bus. We just had big prams, not like mums have these days.

However, the pushchair could be folded up when our children were walking. Then, if their little legs got tired they would get into the pushchair, which had lovely covers so the children did not get wet if it rained.

When my sister-in-law moved into the village it was really nice because we used to go everywhere together after that. On one particular day we had walked into town to get our shopping. At this time Katy was a baby and Shane was in nursery school, so that was a good time for us to go shopping. We really used to get a move on, having to walk there and back and unpack our shopping and then collect the children from nursery school. So we really couldn't hang around. Still it kept us fit.

I was always having to buy new shoes because of the walking, because there were only so many times I could get them repaired. I must say I did enjoy the walking though.

I had picked up Shane and Janet had picked up Heath. We said our goodbyes at our usual place, and then we both went on our way home. After our dinner that evening, Brian went upstairs to bath the children while I was washing up. Once everything was done and the children were tucked up in their beds we sat down for an evening of watching television.

'Is that our back door? It sounds as if someone is banging hard at it,' I said to Brian.

Brian got up to have a look to see who was there. 'Who is it?' I called out.

'It's Harry,' Brian replied.

With that I got up to see what Harry wanted. There he stood with this rather large coat in his hand. He was just about to hand it to Brian when I shouted out, 'What's that Brian? You don't need a coat. You have plenty.'

'Maria, can you help me. I need you to hold on to my coat for a while,' said Harry.

'Why? Are you in trouble?' I asked. 'Not really, but ...'

'What do you mean, not really? You either are or you're not in trouble. And if you are we don't want anything to do with it. So you can take that damn coat home with you.' With that I turned and walked away. I went into the lounge to watch television and left Brian and Harry talking at the back door.

It wasn't long before Brian came in and asked if I would like a cup of tea.

'What was Harry like when he left? I bet he was in a mood,' I said to Brian.

'No, he was alright. We just had a chat and he went home,' Brian replied.

'I hope he took that coat with him, Brian. I don't want that thing here,' I said.

Brian didn't answer me. He just carried on watching television. 'I'm going to bed. Do you mind, Brian?' I said.

'No. I'll be up later.'

I didn't hear Brian come to bed that night. I was shattered from the walk into town. I was always tired in the evenings, unless it was the night for me to go to work. Then I used to come alive.

A few days later, when the children were playing in the conservatory, Katy wanted her doll's pram out of the cupboard. As I opened the door, I noticed there was a bundle at the back of the cupboard. I knew immediately what it was.

My blood started to boil, and I was none too pleased because Brian had told me that he didn't take the coat off Harry. I got Katy's pram out for her to play with. Then I shut the door and turned the key.

That evening over dinner I said that the children had a lovely day playing in the conservatory, Shane with his little cars and Katy with her doll's pram. I kept my head down just enough for me to notice that the expression on Brian's face had changed.

I lifted my head, and said, 'Are you alright, Brian? Or do you have something to tell me?'

'Later on I'll explain to you,' he said.

'Too right you'll explain,' I said.

That evening after all the chores were done and the children were in bed, I went out to the cupboard where the coat was and took it to our old dustbin to burn.

'What are you doing, Maria?' Brian shouted out.

'I'm going to burn it. That way you'll not save any more coats or anything else before you talk to me first.'

'Wait. Don't burn it. I'll take it to him this evening.'

With that I lifted this coat out of the bin and handed it to Brian. 'Well, don't just stand there. Go on. Take it to him before I burn it. And I assure you, Brian, I will. Also, you can tell Harry he's not to come round to my back door ever again.'

The air was quite raw that evening. Brian and I didn't say too much to each other. We both knew when to keep quiet, and this was the evening to do so.

The coat was never mentioned again. Whenever I saw Harry he would try and speak to me, but I never spoke to him again after that.

Whether he spoke to Brian, I never knew, because Brian never mentioned his name again. His son Harry still came to play with Shane which was nice. He was a nice lad.

Peas in the bucket

In the summer months, my sister-in-law Janet and I would go to Billericay farm to get our peas. Once the peas were ready, the farmer would thresh them with his pea machine (well that's what I called it) and sell them for a pound a bucket. These were really nice peas, especially for freezing. They were lovely and sweet when cooked.

Every year Janet and I would go and get the peas by the bucketful. Father- and mother-in-law would have the hot water ready for us. This was for blanching. Once they were blanched, he would lay them out evenly on a tray. Then he would put them into the freezer. Once they were frozen he would put them into freezer bags, so when we needed any peas for our dinner we could go and get out nice sweet peas from our freezer.

The only thing was, mother-in-law was never satisfied with just a couple of buckets of peas. Oh no, she gave us ten buckets! Janet and I would be laughing all the way to Billericay. It was quite a way from where we lived.

Once the farmer had filled our buckets, we could put them in the car. We only had a Fiat 126 and it wasn't very big, believe you me. We would stick these buckets full of peas into the car and off we would go. I had four in the front - two on the front seat and two on the floor. Poor old Janet. She had six in the back with her.

I used to put Janet in the car first, and then I would pass the buckets to her to place them in the car safely. All I could hear was laughter from Janet in the back. When we went round a bend, I could see Janet in the interior mirror holding on to the buckets.

'Don't go fast, otherwise these peas will be everywhere,' Janet said.

The tears were rolling down my face with laughter. I so wanted to hit a bump (not a big one, just a little one), so a few of the peas would go up in the air! But I knew it would be more than my life was worth. All I kept hearing through Janet's laughter was, 'Go slow. There's another bend just up here and also a bump in the road.'

Once we had arrived home, father-in-law would be waiting for us at the gate. We had hardly got into the driveway before he had opened the car door to get the peas out.

'Come on girl. Grab a bucket. Mother's waiting for you. She has the water ready for blanching the peas.'

It was a two-door car and I had really packed poor old Janet in. I got the buckets of peas out one by one. Janet couldn't get out because she was so wedged in. When she eventually did get out I looked at her and noticed that her eyes and face were red from laughter.

'I don't think I could do another trip like that,' Janet said.

'Of course you could,' I heard from father-in-law.

We went indoors and had a well-deserved cup of tea. Janet sat in the chair with her legs stretched out.

'Do you know, Maria, we got ten buckets in the car. How on earth did we do it?' Janet said.

'With a push and a shove,' I said.

Mother-in-law came in and said, 'Here you are.' She was holding a ten pound note which she was waving about.

'What's the ten pound note for?' Janet said.

'It's for you two to go and get some more peas before he runs out.'

All I could hear in the background was father-in-law saying that they were a good buy, only a pound a bucket, and they were good peas as well.

Janet got up from the chair, rubbed her back and said, 'Oh, well, come on Maria. We might as well go.'

'There's some money on the side, Maria, for you to put petrol in,' father-in-law said.

'Thank you,' I said.

It was such a hot day. I would much rather be sitting in my garden reading a book. Still I'm having a good laugh, and I should be thankful for that. I don't know about Janet. I don't think she feels it's a good laugh. Still, I shouldn't grumble really because father-in-law used to freeze and bag mine and Janet's peas for us to take home.

Every time we got back we heard from mother-in-law, 'Do you girls fancy going to get more peas before they run out?'

Finally, Janet and I looked at each other and said, 'OK then, but we'll go tomorrow if that's all right with you.'

We both knew that this would be the last time of getting the peas because the man had already told us that the peas would be finished by the weekend. I looked at Janet, thinking please don't tell her that the peas will be finished at the weekend, otherwise she will have us going today.

I don't know how many trips we did but we had peas for months, which really was good.

Katy's doll out the window

When the children were on school holiday, they sometimes got quite bored - no different to any other child really. On this particular day Katy was around her nan's cooking, which she really liked doing.

Shane was upstairs in his bedroom. He had got Katy's doll and was putting string around its neck with a handkerchief tied onto the string for a parachute. Unknown to me, he often did this with his action men. Then he would throw them out of his bedroom window, hoping that the parachute would open. With his action men being light, the parachute always opened. But on this occasion he had got Katy's doll and he was hoping that the parachute would open just like when he used his action men.

With nobody looking, as he thought, he threw the doll out of the window. The parachute only opened slightly, and then there was this bang as the doll hit the ground.

I looked up because I had heard a sound and I noticed that Shane was slowly shutting his window. The next minute he was in the kitchen, with a rather sheepish look on his face. I knew that he had done something wrong.

'What have you done, Shane?' I asked.

'Nothing. Why?' he replied with a half smile.

The next thing I heard was Katy coming through the gate shouting out, 'Mum, what has Shane done to my dolly, and why is all this string around it?'

I immediately stopped what I was doing and went to where Katy was standing. 'Shane,' I called out, but Shane had made a hasty retreat.

I knew what he had been doing by the way he had tied the string and the handkerchief for a parachute. Thank goodness her doll wasn't marked in any way. Her granddad bought it for her, and she loved it so much. She would dress it and then in the evening she would put it in the bath with her. But Shane is in for it now, big time.

'Mum, is that Shane?'

I could hear Katy running through the house to find Shane. I could hear noises upstairs, so I went to the bottom of the stairs, just in case I was to become referee. I could hear them talking, and as it didn't sound that bad I went back to the kitchen to get on with dishing up the dinner.

'Come on, you two. Dinner is on the table.'

No sooner had I spoken than they were down and sitting at the table eating.

'What have you two been up to today?' Brian asked them.

'Shane threw my doll out the window,' Katy said.

'No, I didn't throw your doll out of the window. I put a parachute on it, so it would land softly,' Shane replied.

I wasn't going to say a word, because I knew if I were to say anything it would all kick off.

'Come on, eat your dinner up and I'll have a look at your dolly after we've eaten,' Brian said.

'Anyway, Shane, if I find your action men they won't go out the window with a parachute,' Katy said, looking at Shane.

Shane didn't reply. I could see he was trying not to laugh. He was biting his lip so hard I thought he would make it bleed.

'Who would like apple pie and custard?' I asked.

Everyone called out, 'Yes please.' Well, I thought, that's stopped that little bickering. Which it did, and we all ate our desserts in peace. The rest of the evening was also peaceful, which was wonderful.

Brian and Shane watched the television while Katy played happily with her doll in her bedroom.

Patsy's tattoo

It was a Sunday morning and I was sitting on our back doorstep.

I could smell our dinner cooking and there was nothing better than that to me. Also, I waited for the saucepan with the leftover custard. It always tasted creamy and delicious. Mum would hand me the spoon and the saucepan, and I would sit there scraping the saucepan out until there wasn't a scrap of custard left.

This particular Sunday, Patsy came and sat beside me. I used to love sitting next to him, but this time when I leaned close to him he flinched and pulled away. It was very unlike my brother to do this.

'Why did you move away from me like that?' I asked.

'If you promise not to tell Mum or Dad, I'll show you something,' Patsy replied as he turned to see if Mum had gone out of the kitchen. Then he quickly rolled up his sleeve.

I couldn't believe my eyes. On his arm was this mess. Well that's what it looked like to me.

'What is it?' I asked him.

'It's a tattoo. When it heals up it will look nice.'

I didn't say anything. My bottom lip was pulled tight, like when something hurt you. Patsy's arm looked awful. But I never said a word to Mum or Dad.

When his arm was healed and Patsy started to roll his shirt sleeves up, Dad noticed the tattoo.

'Patsy, what have you got on your arm?' Dad shouted out in a very stern voice. He walked over to Patsy to investigate his arm, and I was gone like the wind. I didn't want to be around, because I knew if Dad lost his temper it wasn't wise to be in the same place as him. Although they were only words which came out of Father's mouth, they were strong words. And yet he never lost his temper with me. Mum did, but I think I deserved it though.

In the evening while we were having dinner, I so wanted to ask what all the fuss was about, and yet I knew all along that it was the tattoo.

'Have you seen what's on Patsy's arm, Maria?' Anne said.

'No. What's on his arm?' I said with a very pitiful looking face.

'It's a tattoo. Would you like to see it?' Patsy said.

'Not at the dinner table,' Dad said harshly.

'I'll show you later, Maria,' Patsy replied.

While all this was going on, Anne was trying not to laugh. When Anne got the giggles it was hard for her to control them. Just like my daughter Katy, she's a giggler.

'Eat your dinner, Anne. It will get cold. All the laughing can be done away from the table, not while we're eating.' Dad was very strict about table manners.

After we had eaten, I followed Patsy and Anne outside. Anne was asking Patsy if she could have a look at his arm. He started to roll his sleeve up to show Anne when I heard Dad call out. 'That's enough of that showing your arm off. It's nothing to be proud of.'

With that, Patsy pulled his sleeve down and Anne and Patsy walked away from Dad.

'Wait until Dad isn't around. Then I'll show you,' said Patsy. Anne went back indoors and no one mentioned the tattoo on Patsy's arm. But what I did see in the evening was Anne having a good look at it. By the expression on her face Anne didn't like the look of it.

I didn't mind it though once it had healed over. In fact it looked quite nice. After all the years of knowing about the tattoo, I can't remember what it depicted. But it became part of the Patsy that I knew and loved dearly.

Where we |used to live

We eventually moved out of John's and moved into our very own place. We were so excited. It was a cottage at Bulphan in Essex.

It was a lovely cottage. Brian used to work for the farmer who owned it. He was a real old gentleman, and always tipped his hat when he saw me. I think it's lovely when a man tips his hat to you. Good old politeness, I say.

The cottage was condemned, but the farmer offered it to Brian and he said right away, 'Yes please.' We did not even have to pay the farmer rent. John and Brian worked on the cottage to make it look nice for me. I was so pleased with what they had done. Even my mum, God bless her, helped to clean.

I was not the best person to be around when I was carrying Shane. I was terrible. Looking back on it I was hateful. Poor old John. I used to argue with him, and all he said was, 'That's alright. I understand you're not feeling too well.' He was so kind, and still is a very kind man. I hated myself. Janet, my sister-in-law, and her husband Mick understood. Janet was pregnant at the same time as me. In fact, there were only two days between the babies. My parents were so worried about me as I was only twenty and was very spoilt when I was at home.

The cottage had a kitchen, which was small (but I loved it), a dining room and two bedrooms. Everywhere was decorated and made very nice except the second bedroom. Brian used it to store his pears and apples. When I opened the door of the bedroom it smelt quite pleasant.

I looked in there one day and saw apples and pears piled up in boxes, each one wrapped up in paper. I do hope he doesn't expect me to cook this lot, I thought. I don't suppose he will just in case I muck it up. His mother will be doing it, but then I'll have to offer, won't I. If I knew the day she was going to start on them I'd say they needed me at work as there were two girls off sick. But I mustn't say that in case I get caught out. Anyway, it will do me good to help. That way I would learn something.

I hope she doesn't do the whole lot at once. With my moods I don't think I could last that long, looking at the amount which is laid all over the floor. I will have to Sellotape my mouth up, and it would have to be with good tape! I turned and shut the door. Only three months to go until I have my baby, I thought. To hold my baby in my arms and to feel a mummy for the very first time.

My parents kept saying you must come to live with us when you are seven months. 'Why seven months, Mum?' I asked.

'You're out in the sticks and don't have a telephone, and it's your first baby,' replied Mum. 'What would you do if anything happened to you?'

Suddenly I had all these thoughts flashing through my head. 'Ok, I'll live with you for the last two months.'

When I spoke to Brian about it, he wasn't overly keen but he did think it was wiser. If I was in the cottage on my own, anything could happen. It was quite funny really because Dad used to prop his bike against the wall just in case I went into labour, so he could rush to get help.

Every day I was getting bigger and was quite scared really. I had heard lots of stories.

'Don't do this but do that, love. Then you'll be alright.' In those days no one really told you much, whereas nowadays the nurses are so helpful.

While I was living with my parents the council man came to visit me to tell me that he had a flat for us. Mum asked where it was.

'36 Elizabeth Road, Pilgrims Hatch,' he told her. 'There is someone in there at the moment, but I'm sure they will show you around the flat.'

'That's lovely, Maria. Brian will be so pleased when he comes home.'

That evening when Brian came home we couldn't wait to tell him the news.

'Brian,' I said. 'We have a flat. It's at Pilgrims Hatch, number 36 Elizabeth Road.'

'That's great. When can we move in?' Brian asked.

'I don't know because there are people in the flat at the moment, but we can go and see it this evening, the council man said.'

After we had our dinner we went to see the flat. 'I'm so excited,' I kept saying to Brian.

'You'd better calm down. In your condition things could happen.'

'I can't calm down. Even the baby is moving around in my stomach and knows what's happening.'

We parked our van outside the block of flats.

'I don't like these flats,' Brian said with not a happy face at all.

'Well, Brian, we have to go somewhere, and it looks as though it's going to be here.'

After climbing three flights of stairs, I was out of breath. We found number 36 and knocked on the door. I could hear a baby crying. The door opened slowly.

'Hello,' this young woman said with quite a nice smile.

'We are the couple who hopefully are going to have your flat,' Brian said.

'Oh, come in,' she said, calling out for her husband. It wasn't long before he came downstairs.

'Hello,' he said and shook our hands. 'So you're the couple who might be having our flat, then.'

They showed us round the flat, which was quite large. It had a bathroom and two big bedrooms. Downstairs there was a nice kitchen, with quite a lot of space. The front room was also large with a nice bay window. All in all I liked it, but I couldn't make out what Brian was thinking.

Once we had our good look around, we said our goodbyes. Brian never said a word and neither did I, until we got into the van.

'You don't particularly like it, do you Brian? But we have to move out of the cottage as it's too far from work for both of us.'

'I liked the flat, but I didn't like the stairs. It's the pram I'm worried about. Pulling it up the stairs, then having to take it back down again. Maybe there's a shed in the basement where you can leave the pram.'

'I'm not leaving my pram in a shed down in the basement. Anything could get inside it.'

'Anyway, Maria, you can go to the council tomorrow and find out when we can move in.'

'I'll be up there first thing in the morning to find out everything,' I said, smiling.

Mum and Dad were waiting for us to get in to find out the good news.

'Well, Mum, Brian and I have agreed to have the flat. I'll be going to the council in the morning to tell them.'

'I'll come with you,' Mum said. They were both really pleased for us.

'Good night,' Dad said. 'I'm going to bed now, and I wish you luck for tomorrow.'

'Thank you,' we both said. After that we all decided to retire to our beds.

'Good night, Mum,' I said and kissed her on the cheek.

Once we were in bed Brian said the flat would be nice when it was decorated.

Gypsy culture

Ever wondered where words like 'cushti' and 'wonga' came from? In fact, they are Romany words, and part of an ancient language that originated in the Indus Valley in the Indian subcontinent over 1000 years ago.

No one quite knows why, but tribes of people left in the 9th. century. Written records suggest that they made their way across Europe, first arriving in the UK in the early sixteenth century. It was initially assumed that these dark travellers were from Egypt and today's word 'Gypsies' is a shortened version of 'Egyptian.' There is are large populations of Gypsies in Kent and also in Cambridgeshire, Essex and Surrey. It is no wonder, therefore, that the Romany language should have an impact on everyday speech in the region.

A couple of generations ago most Gypsies were still leading a horse drawn lifestyle. So the way their children lived was very different to the way the gorger-bred children lived - even their language was totally different. It was so hard for the children, and I can talk from experience here. However, nowadays the young travellers are growing up in houses and leading a very different life to that of their parents and grandparents.

These days the majority of Romany Gypsies lead a different lifestyle in houses or on permanent sites and the youngsters are spending a lot more time with non-Gypsy children, so, the use of the Gypsy language is diminishing. However, it will not go completely among Gypsies, as this is their culture, and has been with them for hundreds of years.

The Romany language has been spoken around non-Gypsies, but never been taught to them, as this would cause problems for many Gypsies, particularly the older ones. This is because the language has always been kept a close secret from the non-Gypsy population and producing teaching materials would make it available to anyone to learn. It has always been a spoken language, with little or no tradition in the written form, which means that there is no one versed in Romany literature who would be able to help. To be honest, I don't think they would be willing to help, as it is a very guarded language among Romany Gypsies.

Cousin Becky in Kent

After having a wonderful evening with my cousin Joe Boy, they took us down to see my other cousin, Becky. While we were sitting on the floor in Becky's trailer, we went through all her old photos of her three daughters and grandchildren.

It was fascinating looking at the photos of us when we were small, with our ringlets. These days the girls have either the crunched-up look or the straight look. All they have to do is wash and leave it. My poor old mum used to wash my hair every evening and then put it in rags overnight. Then in the morning, when she took the rags out, she would twist it around her finger to make lovely long ringlets. That was at weekends and holidays. For school days I had to have my hair in plaits.

Then Becky started to tell me a few stories. If only I had put her on tape for my family to listen to. That would have kept them quiet for a few hours.

There was one particular story about when she went to the pub with her husband Billy. Gypsy women never sit with the men. They always sit with the other women, drinking and telling their stories, what they got up to in their working week.

So Becky was with the other travelling women, having a good old laugh and plenty to eat and drink, and the hours were slipping by.

'It's getting late,' she said. 'I think I'll go and find Billy. It's about time we were getting home. The landlord has called, 'Time gentlemen' four times, and if I don't go and get Billy he'll be quite happy to sit there until morning!'

She pushed and shoved her way through, until she got to the bar. 'Where's Billy?' she asked. 'It's time we were heading home.'

'Billy,' someone shouted out. 'Becky's waiting to go home.'

'Becky!' a voice came from the crowd. 'He's gone, my girl. He went home about half an hour ago.'

'Gone home!' exclaimed Becky. 'What's he thinking about? I'm still here. You wait till I get my hands on him. I'll f*****g kill him! Call me a taxi someone will you.'

The taxi arrived and Becky went home. I wouldn't have wanted to be in Billy's boots when she gets home, one of the women said, as she sat drinking with her friends, 'I don't think we'll go around tomorrow to see them.' The others agreed, shaking their heads and laughing.

Eventually Becky arrived home, and after paying the taxi man in she went.

'Billy! Are you there?' There was no answer, so she shouted again and again, louder each time.

'Becky, is that you? I'm in bed,' came the reply.

'I'll give you bloody bed, Billy! What made you come home without me?'

'Becky, I called you, but you never answered. I thought you'd gone home, girl.'

'You only had to walk over to our table, Billy. You knew we were sitting there.'

'I did call you, Becky. I really thought you'd gone home. Don't nag me, love. I'm too tired to listen, and I've had a few too many pints to argue with you. Come to bed, girl. It'll be morning soon.'

'Billy, you haven't heard the last of this.' Becky turned around to say a few choice words. She could see him in bed, mouth open wide, snoring away like a pig. What's the good, she thought. I'm not going to get any sense from him tonight. Might as well go to bed as well.

As Becky stood there looking at him she thought to herself what a good looking man he'd been in his younger days. Now look at him. He'd shrunk and got wider. Then

Becky turned and got a glimpse of herself in the mirror. I don't look too pretty these days either, she thought. That's enough of that. I'm going to bed.

'Good night, Billy,' she said.

He didn't answer. He wouldn't have heard a thing she said anyway, snoring like that!

The five grandchildren

All my five grandchildren were born in Suffolk. Four of them were born in Ipswich Hospital, and the other one was born at Eye Maternity Hospital. They are wonderful children, and are a pleasure to have around. Or should I say sometimes!

My daughter, Katy, and my son-in-law and their two children Kieralea and Charlie Jo now live in Doncaster. I try to visit when I can, but I do find the travelling hard (even by train) as walking is difficult for me these days. Plus I have my little dog to take with me. It's not what you call a short distance. I don't like taking the car. It's far better and safer by train for me!

Kieralea, the elder, is sixteen in February. She can't wait for her birthday. She thinks once she is sixteen she can stay out longer. Her mum keeps on telling her sixteen isn't eighteen, and even if she was she has to abide by Mum's rules while she is under her roof. While they were having their little chat I just sat and listened. It took me back to when Katy was my granddaughter's age. Believe you me, my daughter was very strong minded, but she could never go by me. Well, I didn't think she could, but she probably did at times.

Charlie is only six at the moment, so he is quite happy playing with his toys, plus this Wii game which most children have these days.

Shane's three children are all different. Daniella, who is six, is quite happy playing with her dolls. Chantelle, who is eleven, is very happy if left alone watching television. I think she will be a television critic when she grows up. There isn't much she doesn't know about the programmes on television. The eldest, Shaun, who is thirteen, is as tall as his father with size nine shoes and size fifteen clothes, with the hormones to go with it as well!

He is so funny in the summer when he brings all his tent gear around to ours.

'Granddad,' he would shout out, 'can I put my tent up in the garden?'

'Of course you can,' Brian would say, standing by the back door with his hands tucked in his braces. 'Well, that's the end of that bit of garden for the summer months. That'll be a lovely yellow when he takes the tent down.'

I always wanted a lovely green weed-free lawn. I have never had that with the children running over it with their bikes. Still at least we have a lawn, as Brian used to say.

I shall miss seeing Brian this year mending the children's bikes. If he wasn't pumping the tyres up he would be straightening their handlebars or adjusting their seats. Then, after a drink and a cake, off they would go as fast as their legs would carry them. It's lovely to see the children playing in the garden with their toys and riding their bikes.

There was this time when I decided to buy a swimming pool for the children to play in. I bought it through Argos on the internet.

'Brian,' I called out. 'Would you come and check the sizes for me, as I'm not quite sure how big it will be when it's open.'

Well, it arrived the next day in this rather large box.

'Brian,' I shouted out. 'It's arrived! Come and help me unpack it.'

I looked up and there Brian stood, hands on his hips with an expressionless face. By this time I had undone the box, but couldn't get the pool out without Brian's help.

'That's one big swimming pool, Maria. It's even got a ladder with it.'

I didn't answer or even look up. I just carried on trying to get the blessed thing out of the box with Brian.

Eventually it was out and we were straightening it out.

All I could hear from Brian was, 'Bloody hell! What on earth have you bought here?'

'It's a swimming pool for the grandchildren.'

'You could have bought a smaller one. When they get in this we won't be able to see them.'

'That's alright, Brian. I've sorted that out.'

'What do you mean; you've sorted it out, Maria?'

'Well I thought we could take it in turns to be the lifeguard.' Brian didn't answer. He just looked at me with a deadpan face while we were pulling out the swimming pool.

'Maria, telephone Shane and ask him if he could come and give us a hand getting this pool up.'

'Ok.' With that I went straight away to telephone Shane for help. 'I've telephoned Shane and he said he will come round.'

'That's good,' Brian said, still not looking very happy with what I had bought.

'Bloody hell, Mother! What have you bought?'

I looked up and there was Shane and his little family. Shane was laughing all over his face. The children were so excited, all they kept saying was, 'When can we get in, Granddad?'

'Well you certainly won't be able to get in it today. It will take at least two days to fill up,' said Brian.

'By the size of it, Dad, it will take at least three days to fill up.'

'I'm not filling it to the top, Shane.'

'Why not, Granddad?' the three children shouted out.

I think Danielle thought it would be filled up that day, as I noticed that she had got her life jacket with her and was all ready for a swim. The other two just stood there with big smiles on their faces. Shane and Jo were laughing as they pulled and tugged at the swimming pool, which was getting bigger.

'It's enormous. We'll all be able to get in it,' said Shane.

'Yes,' the grandchildren shouted out. With that I thought it was time for me to escape and make a cup of tea for all of us.

Well, the pool was eventually ready after two days filling up with water, and the children had a wonderful time in it. Brian and I were lifeguards, which was fun. I don't know how many times they got out and climbed the ladder to get back into the pool. Oh! what fun they had that summer of 2006.

Shane's magazine pages

Shane never used the phone and never answered it either. Then, one evening it all changed. All the phone did was ring, and it was always for Shane. This was so unusual it seemed he must have a girlfriend.

Every time the telephone rang, he was out of his chair as if someone had given him a right old shock. We never said anything, but Katy used to sit laughing away, which made me think all the more it was a girl.

One day when I was off work I decided to give the bedrooms a good cleaning. Shane used to have asthma, and once a week I always hoovered his mattress so it was nice and clean. Then I'd clean his wardrobe. He had so many books I liked to take them out and wipe them over, and then wash all inside his wardrobe. Once Shane's bedroom was done I'd target Katy's room.

I was wiping his books over before putting them back into his wardrobe, when all of a sudden these pages from some girlie magazines fell out of one of the books.

Oh my God, that's what the telephone calls in the evenings have been about, I thought, as I sat down on the unmade bed. And there I was believing that Shane was a quiet boy. Well, perhaps a little too quiet! This one is for Brian to deal with, I thought, raising my eyebrows as I sat there holding these somewhat creased up pages.

Brian was usually in by 4 p.m., which gave me a little time to show him the evidence. I finished off Shane's bedroom and made it look very nice. I also placed his magazine pages neatly back into his book.

'Hello,' I heard. It was Brian. If we were quick enough Brian could see the pages and I could leave it all up to him.

'Brian, I have something to show you.' Brian came upstairs and we went into Shane's room.

'What on earth are we doing in Shane's bedroom?' asked Brian. 'If he comes home he'll floor us.'

I showed Brian the pages and his eyes popped out of his head. I didn't know whether it was with the excitement of looking at the girls, or whether he was surprised that Shane had got them in his room.

'You'll have to talk to him this evening about them. I think this is why Shane is having all the telephone calls in the evenings. But what is he doing with them?'

'He's selling them.'

'Selling them?' I said, looking up at Brian with a very blank face. 'What, page by page? How much is he getting for a page?'

'Don't look at me, Maria. I don't know what he's getting for them.'

No sooner did we go downstairs than I heard Shane come through the back door.

'Hello, I'm home,' Shane called.

I made a nice pot of tea and biscuits and away he went into the lounge to watch television.

'It's your chance now, Brian, to have a talk with Shane,' I said.

'Why can't you do it, Maria?' said Brian.

'I'm not a boy, and I wouldn't know where to start.'

'Oh and you think I will, Maria.'

'Yes. You're the man of the house.'

'Oh suddenly I'm the man of the house, am I?'

'Shut up Brian and go and see Shane,' I said, half smiling. Thank goodness I hadn't got to cope with that one. I went back to the kitchen and started to get the dinner on.

It was a while before Shane and Brian came downstairs, and when they did everything seemed normal. That evening after dinner the telephone kept ringing, and Shane was up like a shot to answer it. All I could hear was, 'Oh. I'll see you at school tomorrow.'

'Did you have a word with Shane, Brian?' I asked.
'Yes,' he replied.
'Well what did you say?' I asked
'He's a boy, Maria. It's part of growing up.'
'Where did he get the pages from, Brian?'
'He didn't say.'

I just looked at Brian, shook my head and thought, 'Oh well, this seems like a losing battle.'

'Don't worry, Maria. Your turn will come when Katy does something wrong.'

I knew when to keep my mouth shut, at least sometimes I did. So I didn't say another word.

The telephone carried on ringing in the evenings, but I didn't take any notice. We never did find out where the magazines came from, but apparently Shane was getting ten pence a page!

Who are Gypsies?

It is not only in the highly romanticized versions of popular lore that the Gypsies are shrouded in mystery. The historical account of their origins reflects some degree of uncertainty as well. It appears that the term Gypsy is a corruption of 'Egyptian', reflecting the widespread belief during the middles ages that these people were of Egyptian origin. It is more likely that they originated in northern India, in the Punjab region. It is said that they acquired the name 'Gypsies' from their settlement in a Greek village named 'Gyppe'.

It is thought that they made their way through many countries, and that they arrived in Germany in the late 1400's after a series of migrations which brought them from northern India, through Persia, Asia and Greece. Itinerant lifestyles combined with their non-conventional behaviours and their mystical image brought them under government suspicion from the early Middle Ages on. They were fairly consistently defined as 'stateless' wanderers, a threat to the moral order and a burden on society.

Romany Gypsy customs and traditions are still as strong today as ever they were. There remains a fine cultural thread which holds the Romany people together, no matter where they may be.

The Romany Gypsy people have been known as entertainers in every country they have travelled in. I can remember my father telling me that his mother used to sing while his father would be playing his penny whistle or his violin in and around many pubs for extra money.

Unfortunately, I don't have any photographs of my grandparents on my father's side. However, I do have a good image of them in my head! I can picture my grandfather sitting on a chair, his hair black as coal and his eyes the same colour. My father told me that both his parents had large eyes, which sparkled when they spoke to you. My father rarely spoke about his childhood, and when he did he always had a sad look on his face.

What odd people Gypsies must have seemed in olden days, what with their language and great stock of strange secrets. Study of the language might hold the key to understanding the Gypsy people and help to trace their past wanderings. The language, however, has been preserved mainly through speech rather than writings, which presents an extra challenge.

By the late eighteenth century there were reckoned to be 700,000 Gypsies in Europe. While ordinary people still regard them with fear, aristocrats, intellectuals and scholars came to be fascinated by them, particularly after they had traced their origins back to India. Romantic writers like Walter Scott and Goethe invested them with the splendour of the noble savage. Their talents, particularly in music, came to be appreciated. They had their own rhythms to Magyar music to create a Gypsy style, which inspired sophisticated composers such as Liszt.

Getting old

I have reached the ripe old age of fifty, and believe you me I don't like it! The only good thing about being fifty is that I have actually reached it! I suppose I should be grateful for that, because whatever way I look at it I can't get away from it.

On my birthday, Brian and I went out with friends for an evening meal. All I wanted to do was stay in bed and put a pillow over my head so I could shut the outside world out. The meal and the company were really nice, but being fifty wasn't, I assure you.

I woke up the next day feeling not too good after consuming far more food and drink than I should have done. There I was looking into the mirror and I noticed that my eyes were all puffy. Was it the drink that had given me the puffy eyes or had my aging process started, I was thinking.

Then I noticed one long eyebrow hair. Where are those tweezers? Ah! There you are! Right, let's pull you out then. Ouch! That hurt. It looks like barbed wire. It must be at least an inch long.

This is making me feel worse. I'm going to put on my make-up, and it might make me feel better. Well, if it doesn't make me feel better it should make me look better. I hope so, anyway. I've had enough of looking at the mirror. I could find more flaws in myself.

Katy burning her hand

When Katy left school she wanted to be a hairdresser. She was waiting to get into college, so in the meantime she decided to go to the job centre. They came up with a job at the electrical factory at Harold Hill in Brentwood and she went to see the manager to find out what she would have to do. He told her that she would be putting certain pieces into the back of a television, and would also be using electrical probes. She took the job immediately.

When she came home she told Brian and I that she had got a job. After breaking the news where she would be working, Brian was none too pleased. However, Katy kept saying it was only until she got her place at college.

'You only have to wait a few more weeks before you start your hairdressing course,' Brian said.

But no. Katy wasn't having any of it. She was adamant about starting work and earning money.

Well, she did start the next day and she quite liked it at first. Well that's what she said. I didn't really believe her, but no way was she going to let me change her mind.

Then one morning Katy was up early as normal and after breakfast she was off to catch her bus for another day's work. It was around two o'clock when the telephone rang. There was a man on the other end of the phone with a rather shaky voice.

'Are you Mrs. Everett, Katy's Mum?'

'Yes. Why? Who are you?'

'I'm your daughter's manager. She's had an accident. But don't worry, she's OK.'

With that I automatically said, 'What do you mean, that she's hurt herself?'

Then he explained that she had been burnt with the probes. The probes were faulty and touched her hand, pushing her backwards off her stool.

'What hospital is she in?' I asked him.

'Harold Hill,' he said.

I didn't ask him anything else. I just put the phone down and went straight to the hospital to be with my daughter. When I arrived, Katy was all wired up. It made my legs go all weak. I felt so sick. She looked so ill, laying there. A man came up to me and shook my hand. I thought he was a doctor. He introduced himself as the manager of the factory. He was muttering on, but it was just going through one ear and out the other. All I wanted to do was to speak to a doctor.

It wasn't long before a doctor arrived and explained everything to me - well, as much as I could take in.

The heat from the probes had burnt both Katy's hands badly. Health and Safety were called into the factory straight away. They had found out that the probes that she was using required training, but poor old Katy had been put on the job the very next day. She was straight out of school, and had been very nervous about speaking up for herself.

Anyway, Katy didn't go back there any more, although the manager offered her other work. But no way was she having any of it.

It was a long while before her hands healed. The burns went straight through the centre of her hands, which made life quite difficult for her. She had to attend hospital for quite some time. Our solicitor wanted photos of both her hands. Brian and I were so worried. She so wanted to become a hairdresser, and she would be using her hands all the time with that job.

The pains Katy had were all over her body. She said that she even had a burning sensation inside. It was ages before the pains settled down. All I kept thinking was, I do hope she can manage to hold a pair of scissors and also a dryer. Otherwise, she wouldn't be able to follow her dream.

Well, Katy did become a hairdresser, and still enjoys her hairdressing today. She went to college for four years, three for women's hair and one for men's. She stuck it out for very poor pay. Still in the end it was very rewarding.

Killing rabbits for food

Dad used to breed his own rabbits. On a Saturday, when we went to visit my parents, we could see them hanging on my mother's washing line as we arrived.

I could hear Shane shouting in the back of the car. 'Granddad has got his rabbits hanging up again, and they stink, Mum.'

'Stay away from them, then,' I used to say to Shane.

'I don't like to, Mum, because Granddad shows me how to do lots of things. He also tells me what it was like when he was a child.'

After our cup of tea and piece of cake which we always had, Shane and Katy would go off and do their own thing. Katy would go down to see my sister, and Shane would go outside with Granddad. Shane really enjoyed being outside with Granddad, but he didn't like the smell. Nor did he like the look of the rabbits hanging from the washing line. I didn't like it either, but I was used to it, because when I was a child my dad always hung his rabbits on the line. Then when they were ready he would skin them.

The smell I could put up with. But when he skinned them and put them into a bowl to soak, I couldn't bear the sight of them. It freaked me out.

My dad taught Shane how to use a catapult, which Brian and I didn't really agree with. That was one of many things that my dad used when he was a lad, so he could keep hunger away. I don't know about hunger. The smell would keep me away. Shane used to come in and say, 'I'm not staying out there. The smell is killing me, Nanny.'

I used to watch Shane eat the cake that Nanny had bought for him that morning. He would sit back in his chair with his cup of tea on the table, waiting to be drunk. But I think the cake was more important to Shane.

'Are you coming out, Shane?' my dad called out.

'No, thank you. I'm having a cup of tea.'

'I see it's not only a cup of tea. You have a nice cream cake as well. You stay there, me boy, and enjoy your cup of tea and cake.'

'Do you think he minds, Nanny, if I don't go out with him?' asked Shane.

'No of course he doesn't,' replied Nanny, 'he knows the smell is bad. He often comes in and says those rabbits are smelling. Don't worry. He understands. You're only a small lad.'

With that I noticed that Shane got stuck into his cream cake with no hesitation.

'Luvvie, have you got a bowl and some salt, so I can soak these rabbits?' Dad asked.

With that Mum got up and got a rather large bowl with a drum of salt for Dad to use.

'Shane, you sure you don't want to help me?' said Dad.

'He's alright, Ambrose. He's got his cake and a cup of tea,' said Mum.

I heard Dad say, 'Alright, mate. Enjoy your tea.' I looked through the window and noticed Dad was whistling through his teeth as he washed his rabbits off. Shane was quite happy eating his cake and drinking his tea. I knew he would rather be indoors, as it was quite cold outside, and Shane didn't like the cold.

Suddenly the door opened and in walked Anne. 'Hello, me dears,' she called out.

'Would you like a nice cup of tea, Anne?' asked Mum.

'That will be lovely, Mum, thank you. I see Dad's outside again with his rabbits. I thought you liked helping Granddad with his rabbits, Shane,' said Anne.

'No. They're too smelly for me,' said Shane.

'Do you know, I could easily become a vegetarian,' Anne said as she sat on the settee.

'Cream cake, Anne?' Mum called out.

'Oh, that'll be lovely, Mum, thanks,' she said.

'Anne, how could you say you could become a vegetarian when there is cream in that rather large cake that you're eating?' I asked her.

'Oh don't worry about that, Maria. It's not real cream, it's synthetic.'

'Mum,' I called out. 'Is it true that Anne has got one with synthetic cream in?'

'Yes. Why?' Mum replied.

'I thought we all had real cream in our cakes.'

'Don't you like real cream then, Maria?' Mum asked me.

'Yes, I do,' I replied. 'It's just that Anne said she could easily become a vegetarian. She was looking at Dad's rabbits and it made her feel bad.'

I walked into the kitchen and asked Mum if there was any way that she could have got those cakes muddled up.

'No,' she said. She was sitting on the dining room chair, drinking her cup of tea and looking out the kitchen window at Dad cleaning his rabbits. 'Anyway, why would you prefer the same cream as Anne?'

'I don't. I like the real cream, thank you very much. The reason why I asked was that Anne said she could become a vegetarian. I thought she was eating real cream and I was going to have a good old laugh. Still, never mind.'

'She would have known, anyway, my girl. It tastes totally different.'

'I wouldn't know what it tastes like. I always have real cream.'

'That's you, Maria. You've always been spoilt,' Anne said, sitting the other side of the table. She was laughing all over her face and licking her lips. 'This is lovely, Maria.'

'I know. It was real cream as well, thanks to Mum,' I said.

'Anne! Maria! Pack it up you two. You're just like two spoilt children.'

'I was never spoilt, Mum,' Anne shouted out with cream all over her face. 'I had to do lots of things, and Maria didn't have to do anything.'

It was taking me a lot of effort not to laugh. The next thing I heard was, 'Mum, she's laughing at me again.'

'Shut up you two, otherwise I'll send you out with your father and you can help him clean the rabbits.'

We no sooner heard the word rabbits than we were up from our chairs and into the front room we ran, just like rabbits down their burrows.

'Why are you running,' Shane asked.

'Nanny mentioned rabbits so we came in here to torment you,' Anne said still laughing.

It was lovely to have a good old laugh with Anne. We still do even these days.

The roughs and Romanies

It was eleven thirty in the morning and I had been shopping. On my way home I decided to call into our local Gypsy site, not far from where I lived. I wanted new information on the way the travelling families live today for my second book. As I looked around the site, I saw that things hadn't changed that much from what my parents had told me about their way of life.

There were some smart trailers and these belonged to the families with the money. They were parked at one end of the site, whereas the others, not so smart, were at the other end of the yard. These were called scamps, as my mother would say. I noticed a group of men, who were real Romany Gypsies. Most of them had the silk patterned neckerchief with the travellers' knot tied around their necks. I never did see my father without his neckerchief on, nor without his dealer's boots. These had to be the tan ones, and not any other colour.

There were one or two Jack Russell dogs running around. You don't very often see Gypsies with big dogs - perhaps less to feed! More likely it's because Jack Russells are used for the odd rabbiting.

There were two men trying to put a gas bottle on. I could sense that the Gypsies here didn't really want me on their site, probably because they didn't know me. Every so often they would look up as I was walking towards them. I showed one couple my book which I had written. As I was doing so I noticed a young woman from another caravan quickly getting her young child in. She probably thought I was from the school board!

I explained that I was looking for more information on the Gypsies of today, and that I too came from a Gypsy family. After they had given me the once over, and realised that I was also a Gypsy woman, they became relaxed towards me. They told me to go to the other end of the yard and through the gate where there was an old Gypsy lady who would be able to help me. I shook their hands, thanked them, and went on my way.

The caravans were spotlessly clean. Not only did they sparkle on the outside, but on the inside as well. Passing through the gate, I arrived at the old Gypsy lady's trailer. Outside was this milk churn, which was for their water. I noticed the lady looking through the window at me, and eyeing me up and down, probably wondering who the hell I was! I walked over and knocked on her door, trying not to leave any finger marks. It was that clean you could see your face in it and the mat that I was standing on looked as if it had been bought that day. I took three paces back so as not to appear too rude.

'Come in love,' she said in this rather deep voice.

I had already wiped my feet, but I still banged them on to the ground, just to make sure there was no dirt on them. I opened the door slowly, and stepped inside the trailer. It had been a long time since I had been into a trailer. In fact the last one I had been in was my parents', and that was in 1983, the year they both died. Old memories were coming back and it felt like yesterday, not twenty years ago.

By this time I was beginning to feel quite sad because the Gypsy lady who owned the trailer didn't look much younger than my own mother would have been. Oh how I wished my parents were still around. But, who knows, probably they were looking down on me!

The Gypsy lady offered me a cup of tea and I gratefully accepted. 'How can I help you love?' she said while she was getting the cups out, which I noticed were bone china.

'I've written this book about my childhood.' I could see by the look on her face that she was wondering what it had to do with her.

She looked at me and said, 'I knew you were a travelling girl when you came through the gate.'

As she turned over the pages, I noticed that she was just looking at the pictures without any real change of expression on her face.

'This is lovely, my girl. Did you write this yourself?' she asked. 'Yes,' I replied.

'I can't read, my love. The war broke out and Father took us out from school, and that was the end of my schooling days. I wish I could read. But never mind, I get by, and so did a lot of others in your parents' day. Who are your parents, love?'

'They were the Hearnes, Luvvie and Ambrose. They came from Brentwood.'

'I've heard of the name,' she replied.

'It was a hard old life, wasn't it,' I said looking at her.

She had this real Gypsy appearance, with lovely dark eyes and wavy hair. She was wearing an old fashioned pair of Gypsy gold earrings, and although it was winter her skin, like most Gypsies, was rather tanned.

I was discretely looking around her trailer. Everything was clean, as I said before. Not that they needed it, but she was washing her cupboards out when I arrived. There was beautiful bone china, which was used every day and wasn't just for show; also crystal vases which held artificial flowers - not the cheap ones but the real McCoy. They must have cost her a fortune. Still I have yet to see a real Gypsy who didn't have the best! She even had this plastic bucket sitting on the kitchen side with pretty wallpaper around it.

We sat for quite some time just talking about the old days, and what it was like being brought up in a large family, sleeping either in the trailer or the tan, which is another name for the caravan. Or they might sleep in a separate tent, called a bender.

'We were all packed like sardines,' she told me with a half smile on her face, probably wondering how the hell they managed!

The stories the Gypsy woman told me weren't that different from the stories my mother and father used to tell me. When they did their washing they had to do it outside. They had this old tub with a rubbing board on which they used to rub their clothes up and down. They couldn't afford much washing powder so they had to be very careful using it.

'How on earth did you dry them and get them aired in the winter months?' I asked her.

'We had to look after our clothes, and only wash on the good days,' she said. 'Sometimes the clothes were not aired properly. There wasn't much we could do about it. Heavens above knows how we escaped pneumonia. We used to sit around the fire at night telling each other about our day's work. We would say how well we had done selling our flowers or pegs, or the odd bit of fortune telling with the lucky heather, when it was in season.'

She went on to say that they didn't always have good days. 'But,' she continued, 'we never went without our food. My mother could make a good drop of soup from anything she had. It was usually rabbit or chicken with loads of vegetables. This was cooked all together in one pot on a fire which would be outside. This would go down very nicely at the end of the day.'

'I can remember my mother telling me about the cooking outside,' I replied to her.

Suddenly I heard a ringing noise. Looking up I spotted one of the travelling men in the yard using a mobile phone.

'How times have changed, my love,' she said peering out of her window. 'We never used to need a phone to make arrangements. Everyone always turned up on time for important events like weddings and funerals.'

My garden

Well, it's autumn now and my garden has started to die down. It's wonderful really how things die down, and then in the spring they come up again, showing their faces.

I have a beautiful grapevine by my back door. It's laden with grapes and the birds love them. Brian used to enjoy sitting on a chair by the back door and watching the birds take the grapes, narrowly missing his head.

Myself, I like to sit and eat the grapes. They are big and black, and ever so sweet. The pear tree is also full of lovely fruit, and each day I go and pick a pear for eating. What with the grapes and the pears, I really do well this time of year for fruit. I'm lucky this year as there's hardly any wasps around.

Some people say that once autumn comes there is no more to do. But to me, gardening never stops. There is always something to do to keep the garden tidy, and I try to keep mine so it looks nice all year round.

The apple trees have just been pruned as well as the pear tree. Although they still have plenty of fruit on them, I was told to start pruning. This is so the light can get to the fruit, enabling them to get bigger. Mind you, it could be the watering as well which I'm doing that makes the fruit swell out nicely. To see on your table a bowl of fruit picked from your own garden is rather nice.

I have this quite large conker tree at the bottom of my garden, and this time of year it sheds its leaves. No sooner have one lot of leaves been cleared away than another lot falls.

I don't like the autumn. It's spring that I enjoy most, when everything is on the move and the hedgerows are changing colour. All the plants are opening up to show their little faces. Not like the autumn when they are all shutting down and putting themselves to bed for the winter. Even the garden furniture has to be put away. I do like to be out in the garden though, breathing the fresh air.

From my office window, I look out on part of my garden - my summerhouse and a border of many flowers which are getting ready to die down for the winter. I have a wonderful bay tree which I have trimmed up every year, otherwise it would get enormous and out of control, which I don't want.

My grandson Shaun helps me a great deal. He cuts down the shrubs and then he edges up for me, as well as many other things.

My little birds in the garden are eating all their food from their containers which I hang up all over the place. As soon as I hang them up, they are after the food. They have even started to eat my grapes. I don't mind though, as they are so tiny they need all the food they can get for the winter months.

That's the reason why I won't have a cat. I'd lose all my birds and I don't want to do that. Betsy and the birds in the garden get on very well. They hop right up to her. I think she quite likes it, and they certainly don't mind her. They don't fly away when I walk out the door. They just sit on my garden table looking at me, much as to say, 'Come on. Where's our food?'

Night work

The hours of night work haven't changed. It's still a twelve-hour shift. The only thing to change is that the government is cutting back on the number of nurses, so there are far fewer nurses on the wards than there used to be.

When I was working at Little Highwood in Brentwood I used to feel so tired the next day after going without sleep at night. I think the only thing that kept me going was the laughs we used to have. School holidays were the worst, because having the children at home meant that I couldn't get much sleep during the day. My mother-in-law, who lived a few doors away, was really good because she would have the children for a few hours so I could get some sleep.

Once I'd had a good sleep, the only way to take my mind off sleep was to keep busy doing housework. After I'd done my housework, I used to try to find extra jobs to do during the day.

If it was nice weather, I'd take the children out for the day. I don't know if this was a good idea or not! By evening my eyes were sunken, and to be honest I don't think my make-up made any difference, although I thought it did at the time. I think we all did!

Our ward was so cold at night we used to have to put a blanket around our legs just so we could keep warm. Then came the day we were not allowed to have anything around our legs. We didn't wear uniform, which was a good thing as this meant we could wear trousers, one way of keeping our legs warm.

Once the patients were asleep and we had done our chores, we would get our supper and hopefully have a quiet night. I can honestly say we never had many of those. We were all glad of busy nights just to keep warm. Every hour on the hour we had to go and check our patients, and our night sister would come in to see us and check the patients.

My worst time was four o'clock in the morning. I used to feel so sick and tired, but by four thirty I would pick up. That's when I would have a piece of toast. Then it would be head down for the morning rush. Sometimes this would go smoothly, other times it would go what I call pear-shaped! If you've been a nurse you know what I mean, and if you haven't I don't think I should explain. I'll leave it up to you to think about it!

The days when I could go to sleep after putting the children into school were bliss. You could bet your bottom dollar, once in bed I would start to think about the previous night shift. If anything had happened which was funny that evening I would get the giggles. If anyone had heard me, they would have thought that I had gone mad, knowing that I was laughing to myself in bed. I couldn't help it. I always got the giggles after a night shift. A couple of my friends used to have the same problem. I used to have a hell of a job to get to sleep if I got the giggles.

Mind you, with some of the things that happen in the night I am not surprised I couldn't sleep the next day.

I can remember one particular evening when I was having a well-deserved cup of tea with another member of staff. All of a sudden, we heard a rattling noise in the kitchen which sounded like someone getting out the morning cups. We looked at each other and, getting up, we slowly walked towards the kitchen. Now bearing in mind that the kitchen was only about ten feet away from where we were sitting, if anyone had come into the ward we would have heard them open the door. You could never open the door quietly as it always made a noise.

However, as we were very sheepishly making our way towards the kitchen, two pictures fell off the wall right in front of our eyes. Without a word, we looked at each other. There wasn't a sound coming from the kitchen.

'Is anyone there?' said Yvonne. The picture frames were on the floor and there was glass everywhere.

'Ok,' I said. 'Come out, whoever you are. It's not funny.' Nobody answered. I turned the door handle and we both walked into the kitchen. There was not a soul there, not even us because we didn't stay around! We never did find out why this happened. All I do know is that it was bloody scary!

When I think about it, us women do really have a hard time of it, don't we? Whatever the job, we women do work hard. I know the men also work hard, but we do three jobs, don't we girls? Think about it!

Maybe I'd better close there!

Must move on

When people read about Gypsy travellers, many of the headlines portray contentious issues such as unauthorised camping by the roadside. Also, pressure of life means that they seldom have time to try and make a living. I feel the public is being made to feel uncomfortable about who these people really are.

The Gypsy communities have always maintained an identity which has been markedly different from the rest of the population.

Gypsy travellers have a strong sense of pride and independence. They have this great strength of community, which is confirmed and reinforced by the importance of bonds with family and friends. This they prize very highly.

Changes over time have had a serious impact on the Gypsy way of life. As a child in the fifties I can remember a few Gypsies who used to come and stop down the lane where we lived. My father and mother always visited them and so did I and my cousin Celia. The young children would push a pram with water urns from where they lived up to our bungalow. We used to fill up the urns for them and one of my parents would put them back into the pram. Then off they would go to their campsite.

I must have been about ten at this time. I used to think to myself that when we wanted water all we had to do was turn a tap on!

It's so nice to know that the schools want to help these days. Also, there is other help out there for Gypsies, like adult education. I know this is very difficult for the Gypsies who travel around, but in every area there is an adult centre.

If they were to call in I'm sure they would be able to get help. They do need the help these days to get on in life.

VAT due (Brian)

Now if I'm thinking on the right lines my VAT is due soon. I must go through my paperwork to see if everything is OK, although the wife will probably have seen to it all. I still like to check if it's alright before it goes off to the accountant. VAT and income tax are two payments I hate having to make. I think I'll give the wife a ring. On the other hand, I don't think. She'll probably say it's all done and ready for me to look at.

I hope it won't be too hefty a bill. I have my lorry tax to get as well this month. This could make things rather tight, with so many expenses coming up. I do hope the wife has booked my lorry in for its MOT as that's also due this month. As a rule, she books it in for a year at a time, and then they send her a reminder when it's due. Even so, I'll have to ask her if she has done everything for me. She'll probably say, 'I've done that. You know I always check on the MOT.'

I don't think there's anything else to think about. Mind you, I don't think I want to think about anything else. It could get worse!

People look at me and I know what they're thinking. Look at him with a fifty- thousand-pound truck. He must be well off. I wish I were!

I think that's enough for my old brain box for one day, otherwise I could make myself feel bad. I don't want to bring on one of my headaches this early as I'm bound to get one when I look at the paperwork at the weekend. Odds on I'll get a real beauty, and women are supposed to be the only ones to get them, aren't they?

Now then Brian, don't start getting nasty. You know she has a lot to put up with. She still works full time with her nursing and no way can I get her to give it up. Come on Brian, shut up. You're not only making your brain go nineteen to the dozen. You're even talking to yourself. That can't be good! I did hear they put people away for that years ago. I wonder if they still do. Perhaps I would be exempted from paying my VAT and tax bill this month if I were to be put away. With my luck, I would have to pay the bill when I came out. They would hand it to me as they opened the door to let me out! They would probably say, 'Here, sir, I think this is yours.'

Still, mustn't look on the black side. What is that song Mac is always singing? 'Always look on the bright side of life,' and there's more, followed by his famous words. I don't think he will be singing those words tomorrow. He would have found himself a new song to sing. What with the singing in the pub with his Irish mates. Still, at least I got him back to his lorry early. I'm such a worry guts. I just don't want to miss the boat. If Mac doesn't get a good rate for this job. I'll kill him!

I reckon it's about time I went to sleep. Otherwise, come tomorrow, I'll be shattered. And when you have Mac around you, you don't want to feel like that. I don't know where he gets all his energy. Still, he is twenty years younger than me isn't he?

Right, that's it. I'm going to bed, otherwise I won't be getting any sleep.

Ah. It feels good to stretch out, but it's certainly not like my bed at home. But I mustn't grumble. I'm earning money. Thinking about home, I wonder what my wife is doing. It's eleven o'clock. Thursday. I forgot she's at work tonight, probably drinking her cuppa soup, which she loves, and laughing with her friends. Still as long as she's happy, that's all that matters.

Driving test

It has been many years since I lived in Gloucester Road. Things have certainly changed, or is it me!

From the outside, though, the house where we lived looks as nice as ever, and the people who moved in when we left are still there. I knocked on the door and said who I was. I explained I was writing a book, and they kindly let me in.

They still had the conservatory up that Brian had built in 1969. They did not have the original garage gates, but I suppose they couldn't last that long, especially after the hammering I gave them. I can remember hitting them on one of my driving lessons! It made Mick, my brother-in-law, feel a bit sick as he was in the car at the time! Mind you, I think the worst time was the day I passed my driving test.

Brian was in Harold Wood Hospital undergoing tests. I had my driving lesson at nine o'clock for an hour; I suppose to see if I had remembered everything. Too late if I hadn't as I was having my test immediately after. The hour before my test went so quickly, and I was feeling quite sick. Janet, my sister-in-law, was at home looking after my daughter plus her own daughter. If I pass, I'll take them out I thought. That's if Janet will come with me!

In those days, we had to use hand signals when driving, so the window had to go down in all weathers. Instead of electric windows, we had the old fashioned handle, which you had to wind down to open the window. Up and down, we had to wave our arm out of the window to indicate that we were slowing down. We had to make sure our arm was straight, not just hanging out the window like a wet piece of rag, as my driving instructor used to say. We had another signal where our arm had to be straight out to turn right and it had to go round and round to indicate that we wanted to turn left. Thank goodness, that has stopped now.

One thing that used to be easier was learning the Highway Code. Our codebook had about fifty pages whereas today's has hundreds. At least I think it has - I've never looked at it!

The hardest part of all was when I had to wave my arm up and down and around and around at the same time, as we approached a corner. This was to let the person behind know that I was going round the corner. All this had to be done at the same time as changing gears!

Those who took their test many years ago would probably sit back and have a good laugh about it now!

I can even remember the route I went on for my test. The examiner was very nice with a pleasant looking face. As we walked out of the test centre to go to our car, he stopped and asked me to read the number plate on the vehicle which was parked about fifty yards down the road. I could read it quite clearly, as in those days I didn't need glasses!

We eventually got into our car. 'You can go when you are ready,' he said.

Ready, I thought to myself. I don't think I'll ever be ready. I turned the ignition key and it started up first time. Thank God for that, I thought. I looked across at him. All he did was nod his head, my cue to go! My thoughts of him earlier on went straight out the window.

I drove down Warley Hill and there was hardly any traffic on the road, which pleased me. I kept thinking to myself, I hope to God he doesn't ask me to drive through Brentwood High Street.

'Straight over the lights please,' the examiner said. His voice made my stomach turn!

Without realising it, I was saying all the procedures through my head. Mirror, mirror, don't cross your hands and don't leave your hands on the gear stick too long. And certainly don't drive on the clutch. Mick had drummed these words into my head.

I had got as far as the Robin Hood shops just using the indicator. 'I would like you to start using your hand signals now please,' said the examiner.

'Yes, OK,' I said very quietly in a somewhat shaky voice.

I unwound the window so I could get ready for the next instruction. I started to use my hand signals as well as the indicator, which we had to use at the same time. This I didn't find very easy at all, especially with the nerves.

'Can you stop on the left, please?'

'Yes,' I replied. I wasn't quite sure whether just to say, 'Yes,' or, 'OK!'

'I would like you to do your three-point turn here when you're ready.'

I'd been dreading this part, but the quicker I got it over the better, I thought.

After I had done my three-point turn and all my other tasks we made our way back to the test centre where he asked me some questions on the Highway Code. By this time the sickness had gone, but I was feeling light-headed.

After the questions, my hands and forehead were really sweating. I was so nervous. The examiner went to shake my hand.

'Congratulations,' he said. 'You've passed.'

Goodness knows what he thought about my hand, which was horribly wet. There was no expression on his face as he opened the car door and said, 'Goodbye and good luck.' Then he was gone.

The next thing I heard was, 'Well done.' I looked up and there was my instructor.

'Stay in the seat. You can drive home.'

'No thank you. I feel too sick inside to drive.' With that I was out of the seat and round the other side of the car.

I never opened my mouth all the way home to Janet's house. Once we were there, I turned and said, 'Thank you very much.' Then I shut the door and walked away.

Then I did all the usual. By that I mean jumping up and down and waving my paperwork in the air. I got in my car and took Janet and the children out for the afternoon, which was very pleasant.

But I still had that sick feeling in my stomach.

Tops jumping out of the bedroom window

It was a beautiful summer's day. It was a weekend, so Brian was at home which was quite nice. He had been doing gardening most of the day. And I had been quite busy cleaning the house. It was so warm that I had most of the windows open.

'After lunch, shall we go round to see your mum and dad for a while?' I asked.

'If you like,' said Brian. 'We can't take Tops because of John's dog Skipper. As you well know, they don't get on. So if they should clap eyes on each other, there will be a fight.'

Anyway, we all had our lunch, cleared away the dishes and got ready to go to see Brian's mum. We left Tops indoors. I knew he would cry, quite loudly as well, but nevertheless he couldn't come with us. As we were walking out the gate we could hear Tops making a dreadful noise, just like a wolf.

'Will Tops be alright?' Katy asked.

'Of course he will. He'll get fed up and lay down in a minute,' replied Brian.

'You'll be lucky, Brian,' I said. 'He'll go on for ages, and that I do know from what the neighbours told me.'

'Maria, look out! Your Tops is jumping out your bedroom window,' said Dawn.

Brian and I turned round and sure enough there was Tops flying through the air. His ears were out like wings on an aeroplane.

'Oh God, Brian. When he lands he's going to break his legs,' I said.

We ran back to where Tops had landed, and there he was standing on all fours, shaking himself.

'He must have broke his legs, Brian, or hurt himself in some way.'

'Is Tops alright, Dad?' Katy was asking as she was lying on the ground stroking him.

'He seems to be,' said Brian. 'He's standing well and he isn't making any noise when I feel his body.'

The next thing I saw was Tops making a getaway. Straight through the gate he went, and he was making his way to Brian's mum's house which was only around the corner from us. Brian was running after him, with Katy not that far behind.

I followed quickly, and as I approached Brian's mum's house I heard, 'Quickly! Put Skipper away. Tops is here.'

Once we were in the house, Brian's dad made us a welcoming pot of tea. Oh, did we need it!

We all sat down around the table and listened to Brian telling this story about Tops. Even Tops had a dish of tea that Brian's dad had given him. I could hear him lapping away and thoroughly enjoying it. Well, he did deserve it after his ordeal flying through the air.

Dad's waistcoat

My dad loved smoking his Woodbines. There he would be, sitting in his arm chair, enjoying this quiet smoke.

Dad never once finished a cigarette. His habit was to dab it out and save the end in his waistcoat pocket. Then he would put his head back and drop off to sleep, not checking whether he had put the cigarette out properly.

One day, my children were playing on the floor while Mum and I were in the kitchen, having a piece of cake and a cup of tea and quietly talking away so as not to wake Dad up. I heard the children giggling away in the other room.

'They sound happy, Mum,' I said.

'They are being really good,' said Mum. 'They're not being noisy and won't wake Dad. Once he's asleep that's it. The only thing which will wake him is calling out, "Cuppa tea Ambrose."'

From where I was sitting in the kitchen I could see Shane playing with his cars, and Katy playing with her dolls.

'I love watching the children play, Mum. It's really a warm feeling, you know.'

'I used to watch you children play when I could but I didn't always have the time. Life was so hard in my day. Not that I'm saying you have it easy, Maria, what with Brian being away all week and you having to go to work and look after Shane and Katy.'

Suddenly, Shane shouted out, 'Granddad, you're on fire! Get up! Your waistcoat has got a lot of smoke coming out of its pocket.'

With that Mum and I jumped up out of our chairs, and went into the front room. There was Dad, brushing rather quickly at his waistcoat to try and stop the smoke.

'Ambrose,' said Mum, 'take your waistcoat off and shake it outside. The way you're going at it you're going to set your chair on fire.'

Myself and the children stood by the back door watching Mum shake the living daylights out of Dad's waistcoat.

'I've told you so many times, Ambrose, not to put your cigarette ends into your pocket before you make sure they're totally out.'

'I thought it was, Luvvie,' Dad said, trying not to laugh.

'Look at the state of this,' Mum said, showing Dad the hole in his pocket. 'That waistcoat wasn't cheap, either. I'll have to get Anne to take me to the shops tomorrow to get you another one. And if you put any cigarette ends in the pocket, Ambrose, God help you.'

'I think I've learnt my lesson, don't you Luvvie,' Dad said, smiling all over his face.

The children thought it was hilarious.

'Come on, let's go and have a cup of tea,' Mum said, with the waistcoat tucked under her arm. We had our tea, and no more was said.

Shopping in Tesco

My sister-in-law, Janet, always went shopping with me on a Friday, and we would push our prams into Brentwood in the morning. This particular morning while we were in Tesco's, I had Katy in my trolley and Janet had Donna in hers. Both children were giggling away while we were putting our shopping in the trolleys. In those days I only had five pounds for all the family food for the week. I used to try and keep ten shillings back just in case I needed anything extra. If I didn't use the ten shillings I would put it up in my savings for our holiday.

Anyway, I was merrily shopping away, looking for good buys. As we were walking around the shop a man stopped me.

'You're selling her, are you?' he said, pointing to Katy. Then he turned to Janet and said the same thing while pointing to Donna.

Janet and I looked at each other. 'What a funny man,' I said. The two girls were stacking the shopping so neatly as we were putting it into the trolleys.

'You'll have a problem once you get to the till with those two girls,' various people were saying.

'Well Janet, I think I have all my shopping. How about you?'

'Yes, I think I have as well.'

We then made our way to checkout. While we were in the queue, people were smiling. When it was my turn I bent down to start putting all my shopping onto the counter. Katy then turned and faced me. All I could say was 'Oh no!' I looked up and noticed that the checkout lady had her mouth open. She had already called the manager for help, and by this time I was feeling sick.

It was going to take ages to take the price tags off Katy's face and put them onto the right items!

I turned and called out to Janet. By this time she had noticed that Donna had put all the sticky price tags on her face as well.

In those days there weren't that many tills to go to. Anyway, the other shoppers were taken to another queue while we were sorted out.

The manager stood there with her note pad with all the prices on, and one by one the tags were taken off Katy's face and put onto the right items and rung up on the till. Every so often I looked up at Janet and bit my bottom lip. We never said a word to each other. Once they had taken all the price tags off the girls' faces we got out of there as quick as possible. Janet and I didn't say anything to each other until we had got quite a way down the road. Then we turned to each other and laughed.

'The next time we go into Tesco's you're going to face me,' I said to Katy. 'That way I'll see what you're up to!'

'That goes for you too, Donna,' Janet said.

Bless them, they didn't really understand. They were only three. It was our fault. We should have noticed what they were up to. Still, never mind. We can look back and laugh about it.

Granddad's mushrooms

Beside my parents' caravan was this rather large field in which there were usually quite a lot of cows. This meant nice fleshy mushrooms, my dad used to say!

We used to visit my parents on Saturdays. When we arrived, my dad would always greet us. 'Come on Shane,' he would call out, and the pair of them would go looking for mushrooms. I don't think Shane was all that keen really. He knew he had to tread very carefully not to put his foot into a cowpat.

I can remember Mum and I sitting outside in the summer. I heard Dad calling out, 'Come on, Shane. There's some nice ones over here for picking.'

'I'm coming, Granddad. I just don't like the cow muck.'

'Don't walk too near it then. You don't want to fall in it.'

It was so funny to see Shane holding onto his bag of mushrooms, and walking so gingerly.

'I think I've got enough, Granddad. I'm going back now.'

'All right, mate, and mind the cowpats. I don't want to have to hose you down.'

It didn't take Shane that long to get out of the field. He was under the fence in no time.

'Put the frying pan on, Luvvie,' said Dad. 'We can have some nice mushrooms to go with the bacon and eggs.'

We had our egg and bacon with our mushrooms, which was very nice. Once the children had their breakfast they went out to play. I certainly don't think they went picking more mushrooms, judging by the size of those cowpats in the field!

I noticed Katy was walking towards Anne's house where she loved to go. Dad got up and went outside to see Shane.

'Come on, mate,' I heard Dad call out to Shane. Away they went across the fields. Shane loved being with Dad.

They would talk for hours. Mum and I got on with the washing up. All we did was talk about our housework and shopping. One thing Mum would keep on about was that I was working too hard, working too many nights and not getting enough sleep during the day.

'I'm alright Mum. I always have my sleep in the mornings.'

'You make sure you do have plenty of sleep,' Mum said as she was washing up the dishes. 'I don't want you knocking yourself up through tiredness, because you wouldn't be well enough to go to work.'

As I was wiping the dishes, I glanced up at Mum. She still looked lovely. Her skin was so soft and smooth. She was always so clean and tidy and her hair was so nice. I never did see my mum or my dad untidy.

Also, Mum kept the caravan spotless, and Dad kept the garden around the caravan immaculate. In the spring and summer the garden would be ablaze with flowers and looked wonderful.

Dad loved working in the garden, and Mum loved doing her housework. All this meant so much to them. Once Dad had finished in his garden, he would sit on the caravan step with a cup of tea, enjoying the view.

Granddad's socks

When we used to visit my parents at weekends, Shane always went out with his granddad, both with a catapult.

My dad thought he was an excellent shooter, but the thought of a catapult made me feel sick. I never saw Shane with one at home. He probably had one hidden away somewhere where I wouldn't find it.

Anyway, when the pair of them had finished mucking about outside, they would come in for a nice cup of tea. Granddad would sit down in his armchair and start to take his socks off. Shane and Katy loved watching him take his socks off just so they could count how many he had on. My poor old dad suffered terribly with cold feet.

'Take them off slowly Granddad, so we can count them,' Shane and Katy would say to him.

First he used to count them before he took them off, then he would start taking them off one by one.

My mum and I used to sit and watch the children count the socks as they came off Granddad's foot.

'Oh Ambrose, it's a good job I buy loads of socks for you. If people see the rows of socks on the line every day they must think that I have more than one man to wash for, or I have got a fetish for washing socks.'

In the background while my mum was talking to me I could hear the children counting away, one, two, three, four and so on. Then the children would call out, 'Nan, Granddad has got seven pairs of socks on.'

Granddad would get up out of his chair, walk into his bedroom and get his clean socks for the next day.

'How many have you got, Granddad?' the children would ask him.

He would throw them onto the floor so they could count them, and there would always be seven pairs of socks, but his feet did look blue with cold. He used to say that although they looked cold and blue they felt hot.

My poor Katy has got problems with her feet as well, bless her. If Granddad was here now he would say to her, 'Put plenty more socks on, my girl. That will help your feet.'

Shane the pen pusher

Anything to do with lorries Shane just didn't want to know. I asked him once if he wanted to be a lorry driver like his father. The reply came back rather quickly with a sharp, 'No way, thank you.' Sometimes he would sit in his dad's lorry or stand beside it, and pretend he had just come back from abroad.

At this time he was working in the AA office in Romford. He started off stacking shelves with brochures every Saturday. Then he went on to the insurance side with the help of a good friend of ours who worked in insurance with the AA.

For many years, Shane worked at Epping in Ongar at one of the AA mobile sales points. Before he could drive he would take his bike on the train. He cycled from Priest Field, Ingrave to Brentwood railway station. Then he would travel to Epping where he worked.

Then one day Shane came home and said he would like to learn to ride a motorbike. The thought of it turned me cold, especially as Shane was only seventeen.

'I'll be alright, Mum,' he said.

'But Shane, they're evil things. If you fall off you don't stand much of a chance.'

'No, Mum, but I'm fed up with going by bike to work.'

I was glad when no more was said about motorbikes that evening, but one weekend Bruce Webster, a friend of ours, came to see us. I felt he was going to ask us something. He did alright. He asked us if he could loan Shane the money for a motorbike. Brian and I just looked at each other. I was speechless.

Shane said he would be able to get to work far quicker than on his bicycle, and he wouldn't have to take a test straight away. Although you can't just get into a car and drive it off without passing your test, you can ride a motor bike as soon as you feel comfortable with it. Not for me, though. I don't like them. I would much rather have something with four wheels!

Well, they agreed to Bruce's suggestion and Shane bought his motorbike and off he went. But many a night when Shane came home the keys would fly across the kitchen with anger because he had come off his motorbike.

'You alright, Shane?' I would say, looking at his helmet with more scratches on it.

'Yes, I'm alright,' he used to say as he walked through the hall to go up to his bedroom.

Shane never spoke about work or his drive home. I knew he couldn't wait until he had his driving licence. Shane never went out much on a weeknight. But on a Friday evening there he would be in the bathroom smartening himself up. The smells that came down from the bathroom were wonderful.

I used to say to Shane, 'Don't forget your dad comes home tonight, so don't bring the milk in when you come home.'

'Why can't I bring the milk in when I come home, Mum?'

'If you bring the milk in Dad will know roughly when you came home. So if I were you I'd leave it.'

'But what if Dad is home when I get in?'

'I would be very quiet if I were you.'

'Oh I will, don't worry. I've even trained Sach how to be quiet. She's a good dog, Mum. She knows just what to do for me.'

'Go on with you! Go and enjoy yourself, but be careful.' Shane gave me an old fashioned look.

'I'll be careful,' he said, smiling all over his face.

I looked at him and thought, time goes by so quickly so go and enjoy yourself.

As he was going out the door he shouted out, 'See you later, Mum.'

He must have come in late, I didn't hear him.

Every morning when I woke up I always looked into Shane's room to see if he was there. He was there, curled up in a ball, which was the usual way he slept. Oh well, I thought, it's seven thirty, I'd better wake him up. This was always a task with Shane as he hated getting up. Mind you, neither do I like getting up in the mornings. It puts a cold shiver down my spine when I think about it.

However, he did get up that morning. Not looking too good, I might add. His hair was all over the place. He had two shredded wheat and two slices of toast and went back upstairs to get ready to go out. It didn't take him too long. I think it was the shredded wheat that gave him the energy to move himself!

'Bye, Mum,' he called out, and away he went.

'Be careful,' I replied. 'I'll see you tonight.' I turned around and there was Brian.

'Cup of tea?' I asked.

'Yes please. Have the children been good?'

'Yes,' I said, which was the truth.

'Good,' he said as he was sitting down at the dining room table.

'Would you like breakfast?' I asked.

'Yes please.'

I went into the kitchen to make our breakfast. While I was cooking I asked Brian how his week had been.

'Ok, really,' said Brian. 'It's all much the same when you're a lorry driver. The only thing I really look forward to is coming home to see you all.'

'Do you think that Shane will ever become a lorry driver, Brian?'

'I don't think so, Maria. He's a pen pusher. And he certainly likes his bed at night. With our job you have to get into your bed when you can. I don't think for one minute that would suit Shane.'

'I think you might be right.'

I placed our egg, bacon and fried bread on nice warm plates and walked through to the dining room. We sat down and started to eat our breakfast in the comfort of peace and quiet. Mind you, our house was never noisy really.

'It's a lovely breakfast, Maria.'

I looked up at Brian and said, 'Good. You enjoy it, love, and no more thinking about pen pusher.' We looked at each other and laughed. Then we promptly got on with our breakfast.

It was a cold winter's night

It was a very cold November night when Brian came home with this funny look on his face. I was sitting by the fire reading. Yes, you've guessed. It's a baby book. I was six months pregnant, and not feeling too good at all! I heard the back door open and in walked Brian, looking rather pleased with himself.

'What's with the smiling face?' I asked.

'I've bought you something which will hopefully keep you company while I'm at work.'

He started to unzip his coat and lifted out a little black bundle of fluff. It was so tiny; it had the blackest eyes you ever did see. Brian handed me this ball of fluff, which was wriggling about all over the place. Its little tail looked just like a powder puff. I don't know if it was pleased to see me or just pleased to be out of Brian's coat.

'Well, what do you think of your little poodle then?' asked Brian.

'Oh he's lovely! What's his name?'

'I thought we could call him Tops. What do you think?'

'That's fine by me, but why the name Tops, Brian?'

'Well, when I was abroad in the army we had this beer called Tops, and by God that was strong stuff.'

I chuckled. 'Oh, so you think this little thing is going to be a strong bit of stuff do you, Brian?'

'I hope so because he's got to look after you while I'm at work,' Brian replied with a half smile.

'I need looking after then, do I?' I said, looking down at this tiny little thing running around.

Suddenly, it squatted on the floor and did this rather large wee! As I was mopping this mess up I asked Brian, 'How big will he grow then?'

'Not that big because he's only a miniature poodle.'

'Well, if he isn't going to grow that big, I'd better teach him how to be sharp then, hadn't I!'

'There is one thing I'd suggest, Maria.'

'Yes, what's that then, Brian?' I replied with a bit of a sharp tone to my voice.

'I wouldn't sit and cuddle him too much, otherwise he'll grow up to be a lapdog!'

'Is that so?' I didn't dare look up at Brian or he would have seen the smile on my face and he would have certainly been able to read my mind!

He probably knew what I was thinking anyway, but I certainly didn't want to have a discussion about it. Knowing Brian, he would have gone on and on! Meanwhile, little Tops had made himself quite comfortable on my lap. In fact he had gone to sleep, and I was beginning to like this already.

That evening we decided to visit my parents, who lived at Warley Hill, Brentwood, to show them my little pride and joy - Tops!

While I was getting ready, Tops was finding his way around his new home quite nicely. He was running from the kitchen, through the dining room and into the lounge. He had not only found his legs, he had also found his bark, which was coming over quite loudly. I wondered how long it would be before one of the family from next door poked his head outside. They were normally very nosy when anything different was going on. But this time they didn't come out. Very unusual.

It took us quite a time before we caught Tops and he thought it was a great game! Eventually, we were on our way to my parents with Tops snuggled inside my coat. Tops sat on my lump, and every so often the baby would move and Tops would just move himself so he could get comfortable again.

When we arrived, Brian said that he would go first so he could open the gate for me. I climbed out of the van with great difficulty. It was one of those old Thames vans, not at all comfortable, but it got us around, and we were a lot better off than some people.

Brian started to walk in front of me. I couldn't see that well as it was so dark. Usually my parents left a light on in the kitchen or the dining room, but tonight of all nights there weren't any lights on.

The next thing I knew, something had hit me on the head and knocked me sideways into my father's flowers! Oh, no, not the flowers I thought! He loves his flowers! Tops hadn't even moved in my coat. Thank goodness I fell on my side, and not my stomach. I would have squashed him, and God knows what I would have done to the baby! I rolled over on my side and was calling but nobody heard me. Brian didn't even know that I had fallen.

My parents and Brian were sitting down indoors waiting for me. When I did eventually manage to get up from amongst the flowers, I couldn't see what damage I'd done as it was so dark. I made my entrance in a right old mess, with my little Tops still inside my coat. Well, I certainly gave my parents a surprise.

'Oh my God!' my mother said. 'Whatever's happened? I was wondering where you were!'

'I tripped on a piece of wood on the path.'

'Ambrose!' Mother called out. 'I told you to put a light out there in case Maria came up this evening. But no, you said they wouldn't be here tonight. Now look at her! She's covered in mud and cement.'

Poor old Dad. All he kept saying was, 'Are you alright, my girl? Come and sit down.'

Father helped me to the chair, and in the middle of all this commotion I could hear Brian saying, 'Whatever's happened? Didn't you see the plank of wood out there?'

'Of course I didn't see it,' I replied. 'If I had I wouldn't have landed in the flower bed.'

Mother decided to make a cup of tea, and in the background I could hear her telling Father off.

'I told you to put a light out there. But no, you knew better, didn't you? Anyway, Maria, whatever made you come out on this cold old night? It won't do you any good. You should be resting in your condition.'

That was a good cue for Brian to put his tuppence worth in! 'Resting! She's resting all the time.'

That was definitely the wrong thing to say while my mother was around, especially considering the state I was in at the time. I was feeling quite sick and I didn't need any sarcasm from Brian! I couldn't be bothered to answer back, but I gave him one of my famous looks. He knew then to keep quiet! I started to unbutton my coat, to show them my little dog.

'What have you got there?' my father asked.

Mother had come in with the tea and was standing over me, wanting to see what I had in my coat!

'Ah, show us,' she said. 'What a dear little dog. It's like Peppi, the other poodle you had. When did you get it?'

'Brian bought him for me today,' I said, 'and I thought it would be nice to bring him up to see you this evening.'

'Yes, but I think you could have waited until tomorrow afternoon. By that time the cement would be nice and dry!' my father replied.

Mother jumped in. 'Yes, Ambrose, and if you'd put a light out there she would have seen the bloody plank, and this wouldn't have happened.'

'Luvvie, don't keep on. It happened and she's alright. I feel bad enough as it is about the situation.'

We had a couple of cups of tea. Tops had some as well and made himself quite at home. My parents' little dog, which was a Yorkshire terrier, was sitting on the windowsill wagging her tail. Not that she had much of a tail. The windowsill was her favourite place, by the look on her face. I am staying here thank you very much, she seemed to be thinking.

'I don't think you two should stay out too late,' my father announced.

When it was time in my father's eyes for you to go home, whether you wanted to or not it did no good to argue. You just got ready and home you would go. One of my father's old sayings was, 'Come on togethers, it's time you were off.'

We put our coats on, and back inside my coat went Tops. 'Mind the plank of wood this time, Maria,' Mother said.

'That's alright,' I heard Father call out. 'I've put one of my old road lamps out there, which is giving a bit of light.'

'We can see nicely, thanks,' I said.

'If you'd put the bloody light out there in the first place the girl wouldn't have fallen over, would she!' shouted Mother.

'Thank you, Luvvie. We've already been through that conversation once tonight,' replied Father.

Bless him. I do miss him, and Mother as well. I know we can't have them forever, but wouldn't it be nice if we could!

We all said good night and Brian and I set off on our way home, with our new addition to our family.

'I do hope that Mother doesn't keep on about the fall to Father,' I said. 'It's done with and I feel OK.'

'Oh, by the way, Maria, my mum has given us her old washing machine,' said Brian, interrupting my train of thought.

'A washing machine? Where the hell are we going to put the washing machine? Our kitchen isn't big enough to swing a cat.'

'I'll get an extension lead and you can wash outside.'

'Oh you must be joking, Brian. Wash outside!'

'Well you can't put it in the kitchen, can you? There's no room,' Brian replied with a smile on his face.

All I could think of was that I would be going back in time, washing outside.

Going back to school

My children came home from school one evening, laden with homework. After they had their tea, they both decided to start on it. I could hear them both huffing and puffing. When I asked them what was wrong, they replied, 'Nothing, we are just trying to do our homework.'

After they had gone to bed, I decided to have a look at their homework. I wish I hadn't. It was quite frightening. As I was sitting trying to go through it all, I suddenly remembered about adult education classes that were being held in Brentwood.

I was beginning to think to myself that I could join a class and start to learn all over again. The next morning, after the children had gone to school, I decided to go and find out about the classes. I joined a class, and I didn't realise how much I had missed out on when I was at school.

My class started on the following Wednesday. I arrived in the evening at seven p.m. sharp, quite frightened. Clutching my writing pad and pen, I sat very quietly in the classroom. I couldn't speak as my mouth was too dry.

Our teacher was called Zane. She asked us to write a piece about ourselves, and to bring it in next week so as not to rush it in one evening. That evening went quite well. We discussed what we wanted to learn, and all in all it was a pleasant session. I went home quite pleased with myself for actually having made the move to learn again.

The next day I started on my homework. I decided to write about the time when my mother was working on Mr. Payne's farm at South Weald. My mother and my sister-in-law were stacking hay, but while they were having their lunch they sat by one of the haystacks where chickens were laying their eggs. Mother had decided to take some of the eggs, and hide them in her bag. However, she never gave it a thought that I would go rummaging in her basket for a drink as I was so thirsty. On catching me searching, she said, 'Maria, mind those *youries!*'

What she meant was, 'Mind those eggs!'

Our family had kept many Gypsy customs, and often spoke among ourselves in Romany.

Mr. Payne was driving the tractor and had heard her call out. Mother didn't think for one minute that he had overheard any of the conversation and anyway she didn't think he would understand it.

It wasn't long before Mr. Payne got off the tractor and came to where I was sitting. While I was rummaging in Mother's basket he said, 'Mind those eggs. They're really coosty ones.'

I was speechless to think that he understood the word *youries*.

I didn't get up. I just stayed put. Mother didn't notice what was going on, thank goodness. If she had, she would have gone the colour of a beetroot. There was Mother, working away in the field, oblivious to what Mr. Payne had just said.

'I'm going for lunch now Mr. Payne,' I said.

He just smiled. Then he winked at me and walked back to his tractor.

The following week I handed my homework in, thinking it would come back with lots of lines through it, but Zane was really pleased with it. In fact she read it out to the rest of the class, and I was really pleased. She kept a copy, and from time to time she read it out to the group.

I am so pleased that I went to evening class, and have learnt so much over the years. All I can say is, if you are thinking about it, don't think about it too long.

My heritage

Gypsies and non-Gypsies have different cultures and in the past tended not to mix with each other. More recently, however, Gypsy parents have been encouraged to send their children to school, particularly now that many Gypsy families have settled down. This is good for the children as they have started to mix with non-Gypsies. Better school attendance has also improved their literary skills.

You don't often see the older generation sitting reading a book, but they love listening to the radio, which can be very stimulating and exciting. One of my mum's favourite programmes was Woman's Hour. Gypsies and travellers have always learned about their history by storytelling. They need their history to pass on to their children who in turn pass it on to their children.

Gypsy people, myself included, don't like letting non-Gypsy people know our language. It's always been kept a secret from the non-Gypsy population. When I was a child and was out with my mum, it was our way of letting each other know what each other was saying. My father always told me not to let any non-Gypsy know what you were saying. There are fears that the Romany language and culture will disappear.

In the eighteenth century, English Gypsies were generally lumped together with Irish travellers. But by the nineteenth century a series of powerful romantic notions about Gypsy life began to predominate, with a new interest in Gypsy 'lore.'

When the Gypsies first arrived in England in the early sixteenth century curiosity was soon followed by hostility. It is said that Gypsies formed the largest single ethnic minority in Kent and this is also the case for other eastern and southern counties such as Cambridgeshire and Essex.

It's more difficult for a Gypsy woman to marry a gorger man and accept the non-travelling way of life than it is for a gorger woman to marry into the Romany way of life. That's why years ago they never intermarried.

By the mid 1960's, all hops were picked by machines and Gypsies were not needed anymore. As the farm work dried up, so did the travelling way begin to die out. Gradually, the small sites became large permanent settlements. The nomadic way of life was further hampered by legislation preventing roadside stopping and caravan dwelling.

I was so lucky really, because I was brought up in a bungalow and never knew the inside of a wagon. My parents were all for settling down and giving us an education. I'm so grateful to them, although I will never forget where I came from. My heritage and my culture mean a lot to me.

Shane and Matthew

We had this wonderful caravan, and most weekends we would go away to a camp site near Billing in Northampton. The children really enjoyed it as there were plenty of amusements, and also a wonderful river. Shane had this rather nice rubber dinghy, so all in all they had a lot with which to occupy themselves.

Matthew, my nephew, came one weekend. He was about the same age as Shane. As soon as we got to the site, Shane and Matthew were wanting Brian to pump the dinghy up. Once it was pumped up, off the pair went to have fun on the river.

Brian and I used to watch them, and there were always plenty of other people on and around the river, so the children were quite safe. The fun they had just paddling up and down.

Shane had taken his tent, which he used when he was young. It was like one of those army tents. This meant that the two boys had their own space. They both ate well, which was lovely to see. They had a full English breakfast. I think it was the fresh air, or perhaps it could have been that they were burning up a lot of energy.

I must say their tent was kept tidy. They kept a bowl on their table, which was their washing area. It did look good for first impressions. They used to tidy it up every morning and evening supposedly after they had their wash.

The laughter which came from Shane and Matthew in the evenings, while they were in the tent, was great to hear. In the morning, they were up and dressed and waiting for their breakfast. I don't think they washed at all over the weekend, and I don't think they had much sleep either. Still, I know they had good fun. One thing I did insist on was for them to change their clothes as they had plenty. I don't think they would have changed or washed themselves if I hadn't prompted them.

Katy wasn't that keen on getting in the boat. She was quite happy playing with her friend whom she used to meet up with. Her parents would try and park near us so their little girl and Katy would be able to play together. They were such a nice couple. The father had a false hand, but it never stopped him from doing anything.

In the evening, we used to go to the amusements, and the children used to go on the rides. There weren't that many they couldn't go on, except poor old Katy. She was so small in build that the rides seemed far too big for her. So Brian and I went with her. No way was she going to be left out. She was so headstrong and strong with it as well.

Tops wearing sunglasses

We had a miniature black poodle, and he used to come everywhere with us. Most of the time we would go down to our caravan, which was at Walton-on-the-Naze.

On this particular occasion it was a really hot sunny day and we had got up early. Well, we had no choice with two children who always awoke at the crack of dawn. I had packed our bags for the beach, and we had put bottles of water in the fridge, so they would be nice and cold. Tops liked his cold water as well. Brian packed the coldbox and put the rest of our things under the pushchair. We had a lovely full English breakfast and warm bread, which I had gone and got early that morning.

'Mum!' I heard. 'Come out here and look at Tops.'

'I'll be there in a minute,' I said. 'Just let Dad and I finish off what we're doing.'

'No. Come quick,' Shane called out.

Brian and I looked at each other, and went straight to the door. 'What's wrong?' we both said sticking our heads out the door. There sat the two children on the step of the caravan with Tops.

'Come outside and look at Tops.'

We looked straight at Tops and burst out laughing. He was wearing a pair of sunglasses and looked so funny.

'Take them off him. They might hurt his eyes. Anyway, who put them on?'

'I did,' Katy shouted out, smiling all over her face.

Katy tried to take the sunglasses off Tops, but no way was he having it. As soon as she got them in her hand, Tops started to jump up at her. He wanted them back on, and that's where they stayed for the rest of the day.

To see a black poodle wearing sunglasses walking down the road on a lead really made people laugh. There were times when he got sand on them, and he sat beside me while I was cleaning them. Once they were nice and clean he would let me put them back on him again.

Tops was so mischievous. He used to watch the children make their sandcastles, then he would run up to them and put his paw on them to break them down. One of his other tricks was to run around and collect all the childrens' buckets. We never heard any child cry. Most of them would laugh, and then Tops would do it all the more. The funniest thing was he always brought the buckets back to us, and then he would run off for more. He never carried one bucket in his mouth. He always carried two or three back to us.

The children and their parents would come to us for their buckets. We always had a heap of them beside us.

Some of the children would make sandcastles just so Tops could knock them down. The fun we had on the beach. Shane and Katy made so many friends, and so did we. What wonderful times they were.

After our day on the beach, we would walk back with the children in the pushchair. Once back at the caravan, Brian and I would take the children to the washrooms, to clean all the sand off them. Even Tops liked going to the washrooms so he could get all that sand out of his coat.

After the children had their dinner, it was never that long before they were in bed asleep. That's when Brian and I would sit back with a nice glass of wine and some peace and quiet. Shane and Katy were not noisy children but it was just nice to be able to relax. Tops used to be stretched out on our divan bed after he had his dinner, and that's where he would stay, fast asleep after his busy day. Probably dreaming about how many buckets he could get!

'Brian, I wonder if Tops will want the sunglasses on tomorrow,' I used to say.

'He will, because he thinks he's one of the kids,' said Brian. 'I've put them beside the children's clothes for the morning.'

Appleby Fair

Always held during the first and second weeks in June, Appleby Fair is known to be the largest of its kind in the world, and is said to have existed under the protection of a charger given by James II.

The fair has existed since 1685 for the purchase and sale of all manner of goods such as horses, mares, geldings, and also chinaware. As long as money changes hands there will be a fair! I do hope it carries on for many years to come.

Appleby in Westmoreland is in Cumbria. The town is normally quiet and peaceful, but this usually changes overnight. The Gypsies, travelling people as they are known, descend on the town three or four days before the fair opens. I suppose that's to make sure they get a good place to park. The Gypsies travel from various parts of the country, and for many of them the journey would take several days, involving overnight stops. Often they would meet up with their own people en route who would travel with them the rest of the way. They probably hadn't seen each other since the previous year, unless there had been a funeral or some other important event.

The day prior to the fair, Gypsies can been seen at Sandford, Hilton and Mallerstand, and also in the Sedbergh area. They can be seen in groups of ten or more, usually in flash caravans which glisten in the sunlight. There are many types of caravans, from Gypsy vardos (horse drawn vans) to very luxurious living ones. Even their motors shine. And when I say motors, I mean motors! Range Rovers, Mercedes and even Rolls Royce cars can be seen.

The traders set up their stalls on Fair Hill, hoping to sell a great variety of goods from horse brasses, to carpets, to china and many other things. If you are looking to know what the future holds, there's even a fortune-teller waiting for you to hold your palm out and cross the Gypsy woman's hand with silver.

The campfires are lit in the evenings, and you can hear the singing of traditional Gypsy songs from field to field.

The horse traders conduct their business throughout the day from sunrise to sunset, if there's money to be earned. The horses are tied up along the side of the road for several miles around Fair Hill. Hundreds of people stand by the roadside watching the horses being run up and down the road. This is not just for show but also for selling purposes.

On the day of the fair, there are police everywhere. The nearer you get to the middle of the town the more crowded it becomes with vans, cars, horses, horseboxes, Gypsies and loads of children. In the town centre, everything comes to a standstill while the police try to sort out the traffic. They direct you to a car park which consists of many fields. So there is plenty of room and everything is well organised.

It's a wonderful feeling, being among your own - true Romany Gypsies. All you can see is thousands and thousands of vans, cars, Gypsy trailers and real old Gypsy wagons, all in superb condition. You'll never see so many Gypsies in one place at one time.

I can say from personal experience that you don't want to stand too close to the road. Believe you me, the travelling men and young boys race their horses, and their traps and carts, up and down the road at a tremendous speed.

On one occasion I was just walking and watching what was going on when suddenly I felt a terrific thud on my back and nearly fell to the ground. Everybody shouted. The horse and rider had nearly run me down! All I got from Brian was, 'I told you not to stand too near the side of the road.' I was no nearer the road then he was. I must say I felt the pain for a few days at the back of my head.

No one wears a hardhat, or rides with a saddle. There were children as young as seven riding up and down the road. They would ride their horses from the hill down to the river to wash their horses. Cars and vans would be coming up and down the road, and the children don't seem to have any fear at all.

When the riders reach the river, out comes the Fairy Liquid bottle to wash the horses down. Once the horses are washed, they are ridden into the water to rinse off the Fairy Liquid. There were always travelling men standing by the water's edge, just in case there was any trouble.

The horses are in wonderful condition. They have to be because there are plenty of RSPCA officials walking and riding around, inspecting all the horses. And my word - they inspect them really well. Of course, horses are a Gypsy's livelihood so, if you think about it, they would take great care of them anyway.

I have been going to the fair for a few years now and yet I haven't seen any trouble. I was probably in bed when fighting started! I did ask a police officer whether there was much fighting, but he said that all in all most years were quiet and trouble free.

The people who have stalls usually start packing up very early because they want their pint of beer!

The women usually have their night out around their trailers but the men go off to the pub!

Visitors come from all over the world to see the fair and join in the fun. Many hotels, guesthouses, and pubs that do bed and breakfast are fully booked weeks beforehand. Restaurants and cafes are filled from morning till night with the sound of Gypsies singing and tap-dancing. There is an air of exhilaration about the town as traders celebrate successful business. Even around the caravans the women sing and dance and tell their stories from years gone by.

This is today's generation telling the stories which our parents told. I do hope the Gypsy way of life never fades away. I know things will change, but as long as they keep up the traditions there will always be Gypsy people, God bless them.

The very first time I went to Appleby fair, I met up with my cousin Jo, Bluey and Tiddler's son, from Swanley in Kent. I was walking down the hill, watching the horses being ridden, when I heard someone call out, 'Maria.' I didn't bother to turn around, because I didn't think they were calling me.

'Maria, the chap behind you is calling you,' Brian said.

I turned, and there stood this chap holding a black and white horse. He was smiling and I walked over to him, trying to think who he was.

'Hello, Maria. How are you?' he said, putting his arm around me. Then it clicked. 'You're Bluey's boy,' I said.

'Yes, that's right,' he said, laughing.

I couldn't believe it. 'How on earth did you recognise me - from the back as well?'

Jo was eight when I last saw him, and that was at our wedding. So, you see, we all recognise our own!

Jo told me that my cousin Becky from Kent was also somewhere about. She is my Aunt Becky's and Uncle Elijah's granddaughter.

'She's over there,' he said, pointing to a field.

So we started to walk across the field. Well, we walked and walked. Then, all of a sudden, we saw her.

'Becky, look who's behind you,' Jo called out.

We recognised each other straight away. 'Maria! Oh, my lord, what a lovely sight,' she said hugging me. I thought my ribs were going to break.

We had a wonderful evening. It was exhilarating for me, and I think even Brian enjoyed the occasion.

The next day I bought myself some traditional china to take home. We couldn't go all the way to Appleby and not buy any china. I didn't want a horse. The grandchildren would have loved it, but not us. We decided on china, which would be easier to get home.

Celia and Maria learning to sew

Celia and I were sitting on my mum's back doorstep, and feeling so bored. There was plenty to do if we had put ourselves to do it, but no. All we wanted to do was sit and moan.

'Come on, you two,' said Mum. 'Get up and go and play. Every time I go in and out of the backdoor, you're in my way, and I have loads to do. You can't sit there all day.'

Without answering, we got up and walked away, heads hanging low in a real sulk and feeling quite sorry for ourselves. As we walked around the front of the bungalow we noticed Anne.

'Come on Celia,' I said. 'If Anne notices us she will want to know what's wrong, and I don't really feel like telling her, do you?'

'No, I don't,' Celia said.

With that we both jumped over the front garden to try and get out of her way. But it didn't work, because the next thing we heard was, 'Maria! Celia! Come here. What you two up to?'

'Nothing,' we shouted out as the two of us tried to get through the gate at the same time.

'If it's nothing, why are you both wanting to escape so quickly?' Anne called out.

'They're bored, Anne,' Mum called out.

'That's done it, Celia. Anne will give us something to do, and we won't like it you know.'

'How do you know we won't like it? It might be something nice, and we might enjoy doing it,' Celia said.

Celia was all for it, but I wasn't. I knew my sister Anne and her bright ideas. I had this gut feeling it was going to be sewing, and I hated sewing.

'Come on, you two. I'll give you something to do,' Anne said all cheerful.

We were told to sit on the back doorstep and wait for her to come back. Without smiling we looked at each other.

'Maria, I feel like going home,' Celia said.

'Don't, Celia. I'll be all on my own if you do.'

'All right then, I'll stay. But if I don't like it, I'm going home,' Celia said.

'Come and watch me, and I'll show you what to do,' said Anne when she returned.

Anne sat on the lower step with this piece of material. She turned the bottom part up to make a hem, sewing neatly along the edge. Celia and I sat on the top step looking over her shoulder.

Celia and I looked at each other, wide eyed. I certainly knew what she was thinking. How can we get out of this one?

'There you are, you two. Do you think you can do what I've just done?'

'Don't know,' we both said at the same time.

I didn't want to be shown again. All I wanted to do was to go and play. It would teach me next time not to sit moping about.

'Celia's got the hang of it. Look, she's sewing small stitches, Maria,' Anne said.

I looked across at Celia. She was smiling all over her face, and probably feeling so proud of her piece of work. I just didn't want to be sitting on the back doorstep sewing. But I knew, if I played up, Anne would make me sit longer, and no way did I want that. So I decided to get my act together and start to sew, well try to anyway.

'That's it Maria. That's looking nice, isn't it Celia?' Anne said.

We had been sewing for some time, and I was wondering when Anne was going to let us stop. Celia had finished the bottom part of her hem and so had I.

'Look, Anne.' Celia held her piece of work up to show it to Anne. 'Look, Maria. Celia has finished her piece,' Anne said.

'So have I, Anne. Look?'

Anne looked down at my piece of work. 'Well done, Maria. That looks quite nice. I think you and Celia have done well. Would you both like to finish it off tomorrow?'

Celia and I both said in a squeaky voice, 'Oh.'

With that Anne took our work from us, got up from the doorstep, said, 'Bye' and walked away from us.

'Come on, Celia. Let's go before Anne gets us doing something else.' I said.

With that we jumped up, walked quickly away from the back door and disappeared around the front of the bungalow and out of the gate as fast as our legs would take us.

'What shall we do now, Maria? Celia asked.

'Well, you know those hand puppets you've got, Celia. We could have a puppet show in your front garden. You've got that nice front wall, which would be really good for a puppet show. What do you think?'

'Ok then. What shall we charge then, Maria?'

'Whatever they can afford. It's better than sitting on my doorstep sewing.'

'I think you're right. I'm not into sewing, are you?'

'No, and I hope Anne forgets about it. She goes out with Peter most evenings, so let's hope she wants to be with him and not us,' I said, looking at Celia.

We had a lovely hour with our puppets. Then all of a sudden, I heard Mum calling me to go in.

'I have to go now, Celia. It's my tea. I'll see you at school.' I handed my puppet to Celia, and away I went. As I started to walk out her gate, she called out,

'Maria, what shall I do with the money?'

'Put it in a tin for next time,' I replied. 'Ok then. See you,' she said.

As I was walking up the road to my bungalow I was thinking, please let Anne be out, as I didn't want to do any more sewing.

When I arrived home, I caught sight of Anne all dressed up. Thank goodness, I thought. She's off out. There won't be any sewing for me this evening!

All that week, Anne never mentioned the sewing. I was so pleased and so was Celia when I told her. I'm sixty four and Celia is sixty three now, and we are still not interested in sewing. I'm into reading and I like working on my computer. I also like being in my garden. Celia likes reading as well and we both live happy lives.

Prince the horse

One Saturday my sister telephoned me to make sure we were coming over to see Mum and Dad as they had a surprise for Shane and Katy, but I did tell Brian.

That afternoon we made sure we went a bit earlier. When Brian turned into the driveway where my parents lived, there was my father pacing up and down. When he saw us he waved to us to park up. We always parked in the same place.

'What's the matter with Dad? I do hope nothing is wrong,' said Brian.

'Well,' I said, 'let's hurry up and get out and find out why he's pacing up and down like a pregnant father.'

Dad walked over to the children and pointed to a lovely grey horse with a slight black patch on its coat. It was such a pretty little thing.

Dad walked the children over to the horse, which was in the paddock beside my parents' caravan. By this time, my mother had come out to see the children's faces, which lit up. They were so excited and Katy couldn't wait to ride the horse. But my father said it would be better to get to know the horse first.

'What's its name, Granddad?' Shane asked.

'Prince. Do you like him?' Dad said, looking at Shane and Katy.

'Come on, let's go in and have a nice cup of tea and a piece of cake,' Mum said.

With that we all went in. Shane and Katy made sure that they were near the front window so they could see Prince through the window.

We were all sitting around having a laugh, when all of a sudden my dad said, 'Oh, my lord! Katy's in the paddock with Prince and she's walking him towards the fence. Everyone stay where you are.'

I was so frightened my stomach was going over and over. I could hear Dad calling Katy over to the fence. Prince was walking so nicely with her, and she wasn't a bit scared.

'Hello, Granddad. Wasn't Prince good walking with me?' we heard her say.

'Don't you ever do that again, Katy. You could have been hurt,' Dad said with a very stern look on his face as he brought Katy back into the house.

'Katy, you were brave going in there with Prince when he doesn't know you yet,' Anne said. 'Would you like to take him down to the other paddock? Then we can put reins on him. That way he can start to go round and round, and get used to people, especially us. Would you like that?'

Both Katy and Shane jumped up out of their chairs and followed Anne. Mind you, I wasn't far behind.

Anne put Prince on a lunging rein, and he seemed to like it. Anne was calling out to him to walk on, and he was doing it nicely.

'I'll work on him this week,' said Anne, 'and perhaps next Saturday you might be able to ride him. But you won't be able to ride on your own for a while. Someone will have to be with you at all times. You must never be left alone, because you could get hurt.'

'Come on, we ought to put Prince back in his paddock now,' Dad said.

Anne led him out of the other paddock, and started to walk him back to his own paddock. Katy was holding onto his rein, and Shane was walking beside Dad. By the look on Katy's face, she couldn't wait to get on and have a ride, but she knew that she wasn't allowed to. And she knew that she wasn't to go into Prince's paddock without telling someone.

Shane and Katy thanked Granddad and Nanny for a lovely afternoon, and said that they would see them next Saturday. They said their goodbyes and climbed into the van. I could see that they had had a brilliant afternoon just by looking at them.

'Granddad, do you think I will be able to ride Prince next Saturday?' Katy shouted out.

'We'll see. If he's quiet enough by next week, perhaps I'll walk him up and down the yard with you on his back,' Granddad said.

All that week the children kept talking about going over to Granddad's and Nanny's. Well Saturday afternoon came and was I pleased. We had our lunch, cleaned away and got ourselves ready to go.

'Come on Shane and Katy. We're going now,' I called out. They came down the stairs four at a time, rushed out the door and climbed into the back of the van. For once they didn't need telling. All they had on their minds was Prince.

'I expect Dad will be ready for us when we get there. I know he'll be just as excited as us to have the children over so they can ride the horse,' I said.

'Do you think so, Maria?' said Brian.

'Yes, I expect Dad has worked so hard so the children will be able to ride Prince,' I said.

'They won't be able to ride him on their own, you know, if he hasn't been ridden before,' said Brian.

'I'm just as excited as the children are, really,' I said.

Brian turned into the driveway where my parents and Anne and Harry lived. Anne has two boys, Wayne and Matthew. Wayne didn't ride but Matthew did.

We parked in our usual place and the children were out before Brian turned the engine off.

'Granddad! Nanny!' Shane and Katy shouted out. 'We're here.' When my parents saw them they put their arms around them straight away and gave them a hug, which they always did. It was lovely to see.

'Cup of tea and a piece of cake everyone?' Mum called out.

'Yes please,' we said and sat down to a very enjoyable cup of tea. There is nothing nicer than your own parents' cup of tea and a piece of cake is there, I thought to myself.

As we were having our cup of tea, Anne came in. 'Hi everyone. Oh Mum, is there any more tea left in the pot for us?'

'Yes, but it'll be too strong for you two girls. I'll make you another pot. I really don't know how the pair of you can drink such weak tea - without milk as well!' said Mum.

'I like strong tea, Nanny,' Katy called out.

'I don't,' said Shane.

'I know just how you two like your tea,' Mum said.

'Granddad, when you've finished your tea, can we go and get Prince and have a ride on him?' Katy asked.

'I expect so, but you have to do as you're told. He's a quiet horse, but I don't want anything to frighten him at this early stage,' Granddad said to the children.

Anne jumped up. 'Come on everyone. Let's get going, otherwise it will be evening before we know it,' she said, walking out the door.

It wasn't long before the children were up and following Anne. Katy was having a job keeping up, because she had little legs and Anne walked so fast. Shane was walking with Granddad and Nanny.

I wasn't quite sure if Shane really wanted to ride as much as Katy did, even though he was always with Matthew riding Sherry. They used to go off for quite some time and looked really good riding.

Prince was in the paddock and waiting for us. When he saw us he came straight over to greet us, which was really lovely. Anne went into the paddock to bring him over to where we were. There was Katy right behind her. She was never far from Anne when we used to visit my parents.

'Who's going to have their first ride on Prince?' Anne asked. 'Me!' Katy shouted out and with that she was lifted onto the horse.

'Hang on, Katy. Anne, don't you let her go, will you, as anything can happen,' Dad called out.

Once Katy had had her ride, Shane was ready to have his. Brian went into the paddock to help him on to the horse. Prince wasn't a big horse but the children still needed help getting on. Once Shane was on, Brian walked him around.

'Brian, don't you dare let go of those reins as Prince might not like being ridden,' Dad called out.

Brian was laughing, and I didn't like it at all. By this time I was beginning to feel quite worried. The next thing I saw was Prince bucking away with Shane on his back, and Brian wasn't holding the reins.

'You bloody fool, Brian. What the devil did you go and do that for. You could have killed Shane,' Dad shouted out to Brian.

There was Shane lying on the grass. Anne ran over to him and picked him up. All I could hear from her was, 'You could have killed him. Whatever made you do such a silly thing?'

I looked across at Brian and he didn't look too good. In fact, he looked quite sick. Mum got hold of Shane's hand and walked him slowly back to the house.

After that, there wasn't much said. I think enough was said down by the paddock.

We didn't stay long after that. Dad suggested that we went home, and that Shane should have a nice hot bath. We all said our goodbyes and away we went. I didn't speak a lot to Brian on the way home. I couldn't find the words. And if I had, they wouldn't have been that nice. I thought it better to keep my mouth closed for once!

When we arrived home and got indoors, I heard Brian apologising to Shane about the incident. I didn't interfere; I just let them have their talk.

The next thing I heard was Shane in the bath, and that's where he stayed for quite some time, which did him good. I knew he had been very frightened with the whole situation.

That evening, I wondered if Shane would ride again with Matthew. When he was in bed and watching his television, I asked if he was OK, and whether it had put him off riding with Matthew on Sherry.

'No. I'll ride with Matthew next Saturday, but no way am I going to ride on Prince. I'll let Katy ride him,' said Shane.

That was a very sombre evening. Brian and I didn't say too much to each other. But in the morning, all was forgotten and life went on as usual.

Charlie Jo in the bowl

It was a lovely summer's afternoon, the sun was shining, and Brian and I had decided to have our lunch outside. I telephoned Katy to see if she would like to come round for lunch. She said that she would love to, and within half an hour she was at ours with her baby, Charlie Jo. He was eight months old and always laughing. He was such a happy little baby.

I had made a lovely chicken salad lunch which we all enjoyed. As we were sitting under the trees, Katy decided to take Charlie's clothes off for a while. He was covered well in sunblock. As he was so fair, Katy wasn't going to take any chances.

Brian had brought the washing up bowl out. I noticed that there was water in the bowl, assuming that this was for the dishes. Brian put the bowl down on the floor, and then sat back down in his chair to finish off his glass of beer.

'Shall I take the dishes in, Dad?' Katy said.

'No, that's alright. I'll do that in a minute,' Brian replied. After we ate our dessert, I noticed Brian getting up out of his chair. He reached over to take Charlie Jo off Katy.

'Ah, that's nice. You're going to have a cuddle with your grandddad,' Katy said smiling.

With that, Brian bent down and put the baby into the bowl and placed a beer bottle in with him. I got up and ran indoors to get the camera so I could take a photo of Charlie Jo in the bowl. Here he is and doesn't he look good. He has such lovely big blue eyes and gorgeous blond hair. He is going to be a stunner when he grows up, bless him. So all I can say is watch out girls, here he comes!

TDT number plate

Brian and I were at the cinema one evening, watching a good movie. Well, it seemed alright at the time. I didn't really see that much! Romance blossomed, especially in a picture house, for most of us when we were young. I can't even remember what it was called. Still, that doesn't matter.

All I know is that we were sitting comfortably, when all of a sudden an announcement came up on the screen.

'Would the owner of car TDT 3 go to the front desk as your car is blocking the side up.'

Well, we didn't move, we just sat there. Brian never gave it a thought that it was his car, and neither did I. Then Brian suddenly turned and looked at me, and said, 'That's my number plate. You wait here while I go and see what's happened.'

Off he went, leaving me to watch the film by myself. I was quite worried, because if someone had marked his car he wouldn't be in a very good mood. Plus the fact I wouldn't see the end of the film!

'Hello. I'm back. Here, I've bought you a nice ice cream,' said Brian on his return.

'Thank you,' I said as he passed it to me. 'How did you get on with the car?'

'Oh, it was alright really. I just moved it over a bit. They could have got a lorry through the gap.'

'It was nice of the person to have called into the cinema and mentioned it. They could have just marked the car and gone off.'

Because Brian drove lorries, he thought everyone could get into any small gap. I couldn't, and I still can't even today.

The film hadn't finished, and by now I was quite interested in it, which made a change for me, especially when the cinema lights were turned down. I wonder how many of you girls in the sixties remember the picture house? Most likely, quite a few of you. I wonder if it's still the same in the cinema. But nowadays DVDs seem to have taken over. The first thing I would do after the film was to go to the ladies and tidy my hair and freshen my make-up.

Well, I will close now with wonderful memories floating around my head of cuddling up in the cinema.

Peter Brown being bitten

John, my brother-in-law, had a dog called Skipper. He was a very friendly dog. In fact when anyone came to John's other than us he had to put Skipper in the other room.

If we went for walks and I was with my dog Tops we would let them off their leads and they would play nicely. However, when we got home things changed. Skipper didn't like Tops at all, so if they met up it wasn't nice. Sometimes Skipper was so good but we could never stroke him, just in case.

Brian and Peter decided to go and visit John. While they were there, all Skipper did was just walk around the garden, good as gold. Then Peter bent down and stroked Skipper, who suddenly jumped up and bit Peter in not a very nice place! They did no more but decided to come back around to see me.

When they came around to see me, I was in the kitchen preparing dinner,

'Cup of tea?' I asked them.

'Yes please,' Peter said.

'John's dog has just bitten Peter,' Brian said.

'Oh no. Are you all right Peter? Show me and I'll clean it for you.'

'No, it's all right Maria. I did clean it round John's.'

'Oh, of course. John would have seen to it for you.'

'No. I cleaned it myself. It's a bit stingy, but I'll be all right,' Peter said.

'You don't look all right. You ought to show me where he has bitten you. I'll clean it again, and then I think you ought to go to the hospital and let them have a look at it,' I said.

But Peter was still unwilling to let me examine his bite. 'Why won't you show me your bite, Peter?' I asked.

Brian burst out laughing.

'It's not funny, Brian,' Peter said holding himself between his legs.

'Oh no! I am so sorry for asking you to show me your bite when you've been bitten in that place! No wonder you didn't want me to see it,' I said with a chuckle. I felt awful.

Peter never said a word. He just stood in my kitchen, leaning against my kitchen cupboards and holding on to his bite!

'Thanks for the tea, Maria. I think I'll be going now.'

'OK mate,' Brian said as he walked to his car with him. I could see that it was very painful the way Peter was getting into his car. Shortly after Peter had gone, Brian came in.

'I hope he goes to the hospital, Brian, to get it seen to. I felt awful after he told me where he had been bitten, and you never said a word. You just stood there smiling.'

'I didn't know what to say did I? It was personal really. Especially in that certain area,' Brian said with quite a serious face, which is unusual for Brian.

Peter didn't come over for a few days, and didn't go to work either. I didn't comment on anything as I really didn't want to get involved, just in case I said the wrong thing.

That weekend we went out with Peter and his wife Linda for a meal. I never said a word about the bite. I thought it was best to keep my mouth shut. Even Brian never said anything, which was rather nice! All in all we had a very nice meal, but when we decided to go I did notice that Peter was getting up rather slowly from his chair. We said goodbye to them and we went and got into our car.

'Peter looked all right,' I said, biting my bottom lip so Brian wouldn't notice that I was smiling. I didn't hear anything more about Peter's bite, which was good. Eventually he did walk better!

Finding the Street family

At last I have finished off researching my family history. Finding my Nanny Street's grave was wonderful. At least I know where she is buried, but not my granddad.

As I laid flowers on my nan's grave, I felt emotional. Because I didn't know where my granddad is, I laid flowers on Nan's grave for him as well. It brought a lump to my throat.

However, I will not give up on tracing my granddad Street's grave. He has got to be somewhere, hasn't he! Many years ago, Gypsy people were left in their caravans when they died. Then it was burnt, caravan and body. Not a very nice thought, considering Gypsy people don't believe in cremation.

Myself, well I'm being buried, and I know where I will be laid to rest. So Lord help the person who goes against my wishes! I'm going to be buried with my husband. He has a nice headstone, so the only thing to be done is to put my name on it (Just a little cost for the children - not much! Hope that's OK with you Shane and Katy!). You can put 'The Hills are Alive' at the bottom if you like, as you know I'm always singing this song.

Having these few days away in a hotel has done me a power of good. Going back to Brentwood and visiting family and friends has been lovely, plus all the churchyards (there are a few of those, I might add). I have never been in so many churchyards in my life looking for relatives, and I found everyone except my granddad Street, bless him.

My little dog Betsy walked round the churchyards with me. Up and down the rows we went, looking for relatives. Not once did my Betsy complain. Then when I found one of the graves, I would stand and think about old times.

I had tears in my eyes and a smile on my face as I chatted to them about the days gone by.

I have brilliant memories of my childhood. Once I had finished visiting a churchyard, we got back into the car. As she lay on the seat beside me, I looked down at Betsy. She looked up at me with her cute face and big brown eyes and long eyelashes. She must have been thinking, not another bloody churchyard to walk round looking for people!

When I came to the grave of my Aunt Gentellia (Genty), I said to Betsy, 'Look, that's my aunty.' She was such a nice lady. She would sit in her chair by the fireplace eating orange peel. If we ever had an orange I would always save the peel for her. She used to say, 'Thank you my love. I will eat that tonight with enjoyment.' Whenever I went into my aunt's bungalow I could always smell oranges.

Not far from my aunt's grave my Uncle Riley (Gentellia's husband) is buried. There I stood looking down at the grave and telling Betsy that this was my Uncle Riley. He had a lovely garden at the bottom of which was a rather large greenhouse.

Uncle Riley used to grow tomatoes and cucumbers, and they were magnificent. They tasted nice as well. If we were lucky and he left the door open, his daughter Celia and I would sneak in and take a couple of tomatoes to eat. We never let him see us. Well, that's what we thought, but he probably did! When I think back I can see Uncle Riley riding up and down the Marlborough Road on his penny farthing bike, laughing all over his face.

When I stood by my Uncle Jim's and Uncle Major's graves, memories came flooding back to me. My Uncle Jim had a horse and cart in which he would collect rags. My Uncle Major used his cart to sell dung to various people. And that stunk! He used to torment me by calling out to me when he came to visit my parents. He would say, 'Come on my girl. Jump on and I'll take you home.' I wasn't getting on his cart with the stench of rotten dung. However, my Uncle Jim with his rags, that never bothered me at all. I would jump on his cart and he would take me home.

My Uncle Jessie carried logs on his cart, and yes I would get on his cart with no problem. My Uncle Jessie looked so much like my dad. Even my son Shane would call him Granddad. When we went to see my parents, Shane never asked Granddad about his horse. Yet if we ever saw my Uncle Jessie, Shane would call out, 'Granddad.'

When I visited my nan's grave, I noticed that there wasn't a blade of grass on it. I turned to the warden and asked him, 'Why doesn't my nan's grave have any grass on it? Also, it looks as if it hasn't long sunken.'

'Well, your nan had a curb stone all around her grave, which didn't belong to her. It belonged to the person next to her. There was another person buried in the grave next to your nan's. The curb stone was moved and put on your nan's grave. The people who moved the curb stone never came back to the other person's grave to put their curb stone back. So your nan, bless her, had a curb stone around her grave for many, many years, right up until now. We had to move it as we found out that it belonged to the people in the grave next to your nan. That's why it looks like it does.'

I looked at the other person's grave, and said, 'I bet they were pleased to get their curb stone back.'

I also visited my parents' graves at Wickford, Essex. I sat down between the two graves and spoke to my parents as if they were there. I spoke in great detail all about my wonderful grandchildren, and what they were up to. I told them that my son Shane was in the haulage business and that he drives an articulated lorry. I said that Katy my daughter is a hairdresser and owns her own salon.

As I sat on the grass I could feel the sun on my back. A lovely warm feeling came over me. I knew they were listening to every word I said. I laid flowers on their graves, got up and said my goodbyes to them, and walked away. I know we can't have our parents forever, but I still feel lost without them.

I got in my car and went to visit my sister Anne who only lives down the hill from the church. I didn't tell her that I was coming so it was a surprise for her. I hadn't seen my sister for four years and we certainly had a lot of news to catch up on. Although we talk on the phone every week, it's not the same as seeing her.

We had a lovely afternoon and evening together, and we went to see my nephew Wayne's house to see his wife and girls. Wayne's daughters have grown into really nice young ladies. Wayne showed me around his wonderful garden. He has a fantastic aviary, and always liked birds as a young boy.

Matthew, my younger nephew, wasn't in so I didn't see him, but next time I will make sure I do. I won't call as a surprise. I will tell him I'm coming. If I never visit Brentwood again, although I hope I do, at least I'll have something to talk about. I shall say the last time I went to Brentwood I went to churchyards on a family history hunt for the Street family on my mother's side of the family. I think it will keep the grandchildren and Shane and Katy quiet for a while! I hope I can make the talk enjoyable for them to listen to.

A piece of fat

I used to love the fat on all meat, especially when it was slightly golden brown and crispy. But these days they say it's bad for us. I ate quite a lot of it when I was young. I do still like a bit of fat, but don't eat as much as I used to. Finding out about cholesterol (and I'm prone to high cholesterol) has put a stop to me having too much fat.

My mum used to say that a bit won't hurt you, and would help to keep the cold out. How they came up with that idea I'll never know! My sister Anne never really liked meat and certainly not the fat. She would give the fat to me.

I never got fat though. I was really slim as a young girl. My brother Patsy used to say that I had legs up to my armpits. Years ago cholesterol was never mentioned to us. I eat more fish than meat these days. I have always liked fish. My father used to take me down to Leigh-on-Sea, Southend, Essex. I loved going to Leigh to get round the cockle sheds. The smell was delightful and mouth-watering. I would sit on the wall eating my cockles. They always had plenty of pepper and vinegar on. The thought of them now is making my mouth water.

Giving Kieralea Lucozade

Brian and Katy and I decided to go and get some shopping in. Well, Kieralea was pleased as she liked shopping.

We set off and Brian put the radio on in the car as usual. Kieralea loved music as a baby and still does. Anyway, off we went with the music on. Kieralea was singing and rocking to and fro on the front seat with Brian. Katy and I were in the back of the car.

When we got to the supermarket, out we all got. Kieralea went off with her granddad to get their drink and sausage roll and chips.

'We won't be seeing them for a while Kate,' I said.

We didn't really want that much shopping. It was the trip out which we all liked. Katy would go off in one direction and I would go off in another. If I couldn't find Katy sometimes I would go to the help desk and ask them to call out her name to say that her mum was looking for her. She hated it, but I loved doing it. Although she used to tell me off, she always laughed, which then made me laugh. I felt like a naughty child.

'It's not funny, Mother,' she used to say.

'Then why are you laughing?' I asked her.

'Get your trolley and finish off your shopping Mother, but don't leave my side,' she would say.

I love going shopping with Katy. We have such good fun. She makes me laugh with her giggle. Shane will laugh at anything as well.

As I am sitting writing this piece of work, I am laughing just thinking of Shane and Katy. I know when I have done wrong. I just keep my mouth shut. I have learnt when to keep my mouth shut. I have had good practice over the years!

As Katy and I were walking towards the lemonade aisle, we noticed Brian and Kieralea walking towards us.

'Hello. Have you had a nice time?' I said looking down at Kieralea.

'Yes.' She got hold of my hand. 'Nanny, can I come with you now and hold your trolley?'

Brian and Katy went one way and we went the other way. 'Mother, don't go wandering off over the other side of the shop, will you. Dad and I would like to be able to find you when we want to go home. And don't think about getting people to call my name out,' Katy said.

I knew she was trying not to laugh by the look on her face. I got Kieralea a small bottle of lemonade, and myself a bottle of Lucozade.

I spotted one of the ladies who work in the shop and asked if it would be OK for us to open these bottles for a drink.

'Yes, only make sure you pay for them at the till, won't you,' she said.

'Yes, I will, thank you,' I replied.

With that I started to open Kieralea's bottle for her to have a drink. Once she had got her drink I opened my bottle of Lucozade and started to drink it.

'Nanny, what does yours taste like?' Kieralea asked.

'Well, it's a lot different than yours, darling.'

'Can I taste some please Nanny,' she asked.

'Of course.' With that I held the bottle for her so she could drink from it.

Well, within three minutes she was spinning around like a spinning top. Whatever is wrong with her, I was thinking. Then suddenly it came to me. It's the Lucozade I gave her. It had lots of E numbers in it. Oh God, her mother is going to kill me. I turned around and there stood Katy and Brian.

'By the looks of her she's got loads of energy. Whatever have you given her, Mum?'

'Nothing, only a couple of mouthfuls of my Lucozade.'

'That's what's making her high, Mum.'

'Actually, it could be the lemonade and not the Lucozade, because she has been drinking lemonade as well,' I said to Katy. I felt like a naughty child all over again. I was sure I would be sent to bed when I got home. Well that's how it felt!

We went to the restaurant and had our cup of tea and cakes, which was rather nice. Kieralea was beginning to calm down by this time, which was pleasing me.

I don't think I'll be giving her that drink anymore. It has taught me a very big lesson! I got told off in the car on our way home, but I just kept very quiet. I wasn't going to say anything, as I didn't want it to blow up all over again. I felt bad as it was. It was a long time before I even bought Lucozade again, and I loved that drink. It used to give me energy!

Yolk drink

I needed to go shopping. Shaun and Danielle, my grandchildren, were with me this particular day.

'We will have a nice drink in Tesco if you like, children,' I said. They both smiled and grabbed their coats.

'Come on Nanny,' they both shouted out.

'Wait a minute. I must put some make-up on first,' I said.

I walked into the bathroom and got my make-up and started to put it on.

'Nanny can I have some make-up on please?' Danielle asked me.

'Ok, but only a very little, and I will put it on for you.' I said. After I had put on my make-up, plus Danielle's as well, I called out to Shaun to say that we were ready to go.

Danielle walked off in front of us with her head held high. I think she felt quite grown up.

'Can we have our sausage roll in the car please, Nanny, like we always do?' Danielle called out to me.

'Yes, of course you can. Would you like a drink as well? If we get our eats and drinks first for the car, we won't forget it, will we?' I said.

'We won't let you forget, Nanny,' Danielle called out.

As soon as we got to Tesco and I parked up, Danielle nearly fell out of the car with excitement.

Once we were in the shop, we headed towards the counter where the sausage rolls were. The children both chose a large sausage roll. I let them have them because I knew they would eat them. I chose a samosa, a lovely lamb one.

'Right kids, let's go and get the shopping now,' I said.

'Do we need much, Nanny, and can I hold the list please?' Shaun asked.

I passed him the list, and I noticed that he was reading it.

'Let's go and get the vegetables first, Nanny, then we can work our way around the store.'

I looked at him and thought, he has got his head screwed on right. He knows what he's doing, and I'll just follow him. I handed him my pen so he could cross things off as he got them.

'Nanny, can I go and get our drinks please for the car?' Danielle asked me.

'Off you go then, but don't run.'

'I won't, Nanny.'

While Shaun and I were casually shopping, I heard Danielle's voice. 'Nanny, I've got the drinks for when we are in the car.'

I looked down, and there she stood with a rather lovely smile on her face.

'You've got three small bottles of juice. That's good, but why have you got a bottle of chocolate yolk, Danielle?'

'I like it, Nanny, and I was wondering if I could have it now. I didn't have much breakfast. This will stop me feeling hungry, and my tummy is making a noise,' she said, looking up at me trying not to laugh.

'Ok then, you can have it, but when you've finished it you must put it in the trolley because I have to pay for it. Also, you stay with me and don't run off while you have the drink in your hand. You can have a mouthful, then you must put it back into the trolley,' I told her.

All the while I was talking to her Shaun was trying to say something to me, but I knew that I had to speak to Danielle first.

'OK Shaun, what is it that you wanted me for?' I asked.

He was giggling away. 'Well, Nanny, I was trying to tell you about Danielle with the yolk drink. She gets really high on it, and you've given her the chocolate one as well. You won't be able to hold her down.'

By this time Shaun was not giggling. He was laughing, and when you see Shaun laugh you want to laugh yourself because he is so funny. But right now I was not laughing. Danielle had nearly drunk the whole bottle. I put my hand to my head and thought, dear God what am I going to do now!

'Shaun, let's do the shopping quickly and get out of this store.'

I took the bottle from Danielle and put it straight into my trolley. But unfortunately the drink had started to work on her. I got hold of her hand and away we went. I went around that shop in record time.

I could hear Shaun laughing behind me, and in between his laughs he was saying, 'I did try to tell you, Nanny, but it was too late. She had drunk quite a bit of it. She only needs a sip.'

Even Shaun was beginning to look worried, but by this time I had got what I wanted. I hoped that when we got to the car, the sausage roll would soak the chocolate drink up. But Danielle was already beginning to jump about and laugh. She wouldn't stop. It was lovely to hear her laugh, but not like this.

As soon as I had paid for my shopping, we were outside and in the car, I think in record time. Shaun got into the back of the car, and Danielle was getting into the front seat.

'Would you like to stay here and eat your sausage rolls, or would you like them at home?' I asked.

'No, we always eat them here,' they shouted out, Danielle the loudest, which didn't surprise me really!

We sat and ate our goodies, in between laughs. It was funny really.

I certainly learned my lesson, and never gave Danielle another drink after that!

Anne going out with our lodger

We had a lodger called Eddy at one time and he was really nice. My dad thought the world of him. In fact, he was like one of the family.

Eddy was Irish and quite nice looking. Well, I thought so. Celia, my cousin, and I used to say he was nice. I think that must have been the time when Celia and I started to notice boys! I know we used to giggle a lot when he was around us.

When I think back, whatever must we have looked and sounded like. Anyway, Anne was getting ready for her date with Eddy, doing her hair and make-up which had to be just right. I sat and watched her that evening get ready, thinking one day I'll be doing my hair and make-up for going out. I wondered if I would take as long as Anne. All this was going through my head as I sat watching her.

Anne wasn't late when she came in from her date. I had lain in bed that night trying my best to keep awake, which was difficult for me as I loved my sleep. Whenever my head hit the pillow I would shut my eyes and be fast asleep in no time at all.

The next thing I heard was the noise of Anne's high heels clicking on the path as she walked around to the back door.

'Did you have a nice evening, and do you think you will be going out again with Eddy?' Mum asked Anne.

'No, he is younger than me. He was good company though, and we did have a nice evening,' I heard Anne say to Mummy.

I jumped out of bed, I couldn't wait to find out more and rushed to the lounge where Mummy and Anne were standing.

'What are you doing up? You should be asleep by now, not listening to what we are saying,' Anne said, looking at me with not a happy face on.

'Anne,' Mummy called out, 'why is he too young when he's a nice lad?'

'He might be, Mummy, but he's not my type.'

'That's the trouble with you. You prefer older men,' Mummy said, looking at Anne and trying to keep a straight face. I noticed that Mummy had got her lips tightly pressed together, trying not to laugh.

I was sitting beside the fire with my head down and trying my best not to laugh as well.

Anne burst out laughing. She has got such a giggle, my sister has.

'I don't like older men Mummy,' Anne said.

'Anne, don't think you can pull the wool over my eyes. I know more about you than you think,' Mummy said. 'So you won't be going out with him again then, Anne? I think you might find that a bit difficult to explain, don't you my girl?'

'No, not really. I will say that I am not ready for a relationship at the moment,' Anne said.

With the look on her face, I don't know if Anne was smiling or thinking deeply as to what she would say to Eddy.

How could she not want to go out with him, I sat thinking by the fire.

The next thing I heard was, 'Maria, get yourself to bed. It's late, and what are you doing up anyway?'

'I was waiting for you to come home,' I said to Anne.

'No you weren't, you stayed awake to be nosey, didn't you?'

I didn't answer. I just got up and walked back into my bedroom. I knew when to keep my mouth shut. Well I tried to!

When I think back, my daughter has the same laugh as my sister Anne. Katy giggles just like her. She takes after Anne in so many ways, which is really lovely actually.

Feeding Nell our horse sugar lumps

Most days Mum and I would go out on the horse and cart selling logs. I was probably only about four or five years old, but I remember it so well.

Mum was such a strong lady. When she got to the house where she would sell her logs, she would get on the cart and move one of the sacks of logs. Then she would jump down and, standing with her back to the cart, reach up with both arms and pull the sack of logs down onto her back.

They weren't small sacks. They were the large ones, and the logs which were in the sacks were large and unevenly cut, which meant they would be digging into Mum's back when she lifted them. I never heard her complain.

While Mum was delivering her logs, I would be feeding Nell, our horse, with her sugar lumps. I used to say to her, 'Would you like another sugar lump, but first you have to show me your teeth.'

Nell could roll her lips right back. She looked funny and people walking by would stop and laugh at her. Once I had given a lump of sugar, she would go straight to my pocket and gently nudge it with her nose to ask me for more.

I could get quite a few people around me, especially the children. They loved watching her roll her lips back. The children would call out, 'Make her do it again.' Nell knew what she was up to. She was a very intelligent horse.

'Would you like some more? Say please then.' Straight away she would nod her head up and down for yes. Then I would place the sugar on the palm of my hand and she gently took it from my hand. As soon as Nell had eaten her lump of sugar, I would say to her, 'Now what do you say?' At once she would pick her foot up from the ground and scrape it along the concrete on the road. Then the children would clap their hands.

'Come on Maria. Jump up on the cart. It's time to go,' Mum would call out to me once she had made her delivery of logs.

'Goodbye,' she would call out to the people on the side of the road who had been watching me feed Nell. Then off we would go. I would sit beside Mum. I used to feel so proud sitting beside her on the cart. I never once felt ashamed of being with Mum out selling logs. In fact I loved it.

It never took Mum that long to sell all the logs because she had her regulars to go to. Then it was time to go home.

'Come on Nell, let's go home.' Nell knew those words. Straight away she would get a move on, and she knew where she was going as well. She was very good on the roads. She would listen to every word that Mum would say to her.

Once we were home, Mum would take Nell's harness off, and feed and water her. Then when everything was done for her, Mum would put Nell in her stable.

Nell loved her bed. Dad used to put plenty of hay in her stable for her to lie on. In fact she was spoilt. Dad used to say that she should have the best as she did a lot for us. If it wasn't for Nell, we wouldn't be able to sell our logs. 'So we must look after her, my girl,' Dad used to say.

Dad grinding his teeth

We usually had our meal in the evening around six o'clock. When I think back and close my eyes I can still hear us around the table. It would only be the sound of knives and forks, because Dad didn't allow us to talk around the table. He used to say that there is plenty of time to talk after you have eaten. Also, when you are talking you are taking in air, and air will fill you up and you won't want your dinner.

'Taking in air don't fill you up Dad,' Anne said.

'Don't you be so sure, my girl. Come on, just eat your dinner,' Dad replied.

Our dinner was never rushed. We had to take our time and eat slowly. Patsy and Anne were terrible at winding each other up at the table. Although they never spoke, it was the way they looked at each other. They would try their best not to laugh. All my dad had to do was look at them both. Not a word would come out of his mouth.

Once they had finished their meal, Patsy and Anne used to ask to get down from the table. (As old as they were, they still had to ask.) Then it would kick off outside.

'Patsy, you nearly got me told off at the table,' Anne would say. Then Patsy would start to sing, with a song which would relate to Anne. At the same time, you could hear the sound of his shoes as he tap-danced, which he could do very well. We loved watching and listening to him. He would be singing every moment of the day.

After my dad had finished his meal, he would say to my mum, 'I'll only be a minute. I'm just going to sort Patsy and Anne out.'

I would be sitting at the table with one ear open and trying my very best to hear what was going on outside. All I could hear was my dad telling them off, but never a word did I hear from Patsy and Anne. Mind you, they knew better than to answer my dad back. They were in their teens, but they had respect for Dad in that way.

Once Dad had said what he had to say, he was sitting back at the table drinking his tea and talking to Mum. Then Anne would come in, face like thunder. I would look at Anne and smile, biting my bottom lip and trying not to laugh.

'That's it Maria, you sit there. It won't be long before it will be your turn and you will be coming to me for help,' Anne said.

I turned to Dad and noticed he was frowning. Then the frown turned to a smile and he winked at me. 'Well, Luvvie. It's about time I made tracks for my bed. I'll have a wash and a shave, then I'll bid you all good night.'

Mum and I sat for a while talking. I loved sitting and talking to Mum. I found her so interesting to listen to. I felt my dad put his hands on my shoulder. He leaned over and kissed me good night. It had only just gone seven, but Dad liked to be up at four in the morning, to be at work by five thirty.

Dad was a really early bird. If it was a particularly nice morning he would have done some gardening before he left for work. He used to work at the London Annex, which was no distance from us. By bike you could do it in less than ten minutes.

Dad walked towards Anne's bedroom door and called out, 'Good night and God bless. I hope you have a good day tomorrow, my girl, at work.'

'Thanks. Good night, Dad.'

Anne came out to be with us. I was sitting at the table reading, and I could hear Anne talking to Mum about Dad. I could hear every word that they were saying.

The very next thing, Anne was standing beside me. 'Don't go tell Dad what you have just heard me saying to Mum, will you Maria.'

'I never heard you say anything. I was reading my book.'

Anne made a slow, deliberate movement of her head towards the window, and then back towards me. It was about Peter, her boyfriend.

I looked at Anne, and said, 'Would you wash and plait my hair tonight, so it looks all nice and wavy for the morning when I go to school please, Anne?' I said with my head slightly tilted to one side.

Anne stared straight into my eyes, her voice becoming softer towards me, but I could see by the look in her eyes that she was none too pleased with me. She didn't believe me when I said that I hadn't heard anything that she had said in the kitchen to Mum.

'Come on, then, if you want your hair washed and plaited tonight. I haven't got all night, you know,' Anne said to me.

When Anne had washed my hair, and was just about to comb it to get it ready for plaiting, I put my hand around the back of my head and held on to my hair. Then I turned to face Anne.

'When you comb my hair you won't hurt me, will you?' Pressing both my lips together and squinting my eyes, I looked at Anne. One ouch from me and Dad would be out of bed like greased lightning.

Anne started to comb my hair very gently. She wasn't always rough. I couldn't blame her at times for being rough with me, as I wasn't always that nice to her!

Mum walked into the room with two cups of tea and put them down on the table.

'Don't let your tea get cold, the pair of you, will you,' Mum said. 'We won't,' Anne said and passed me my cup of tea.

'Thank you,' I said. 'Can you do my hair really nice and tight for me please, Anne. Then tomorrow it will look really lovely and wavy. And can I have a ponytail in the morning for school please,' I asked her.

'OK, I'll do it in the morning before I go to work.'

'You're joking. I'm not getting up that early in the morning. Mum, will you do my ponytail in the morning, please?'

'OK then, but no moaning saying it hurts when I have to pull your hair so the pony tail will be nice and high like you like it,' Mum said as she stood in front of me drinking her tea.

'Whatever is that noise, Mum? It sounds like a rat gnawing at a piece of wood,' Anne said.

'That's your dad grinding his teeth together. He does it all the time,' Mum said.

'The rate he is going, he won't have any teeth left in his head. They will be tiny little stubs in his mouth,' Anne said laughing.

'Mum, do you hear that noise at night, and doesn't it keep you awake?' I asked.

'I just turn over and put the covers over my head. That way it shuts the noise out,' Mum said.

'You can get up now, Maria. I've done your hair. It will look lovely in the morning for you,' Anne said.

'Thank you,' I said and got up and walked over towards Mum and Dad's bedroom door. Anne was right. It sounded like a rat gnawing at a piece of wood.

'Does he snore as well as gnawing his teeth, Mum?' I asked.

'Come away from that door before you wake your dad up, Maria.'

I wanted to stand there and listen. I found it quite entertaining. I was trying to think of a tune that would go with the noise of Dad gnawing his teeth.

'Maria, it's time for bed,' Mum said.

'Oh do I have to? Can't I sit by your bedroom and listen to Dad?' I asked Mum.

'No. Come on, it's bedtime, and you don't like getting up in the mornings, do you,' Mum said.

'OK I'm off.' Mum came over and gave me a kiss. Then I walked over to Anne for my kiss good night, which I got but I do think it was half-heartedly. Anne could be very lovely to me. She never let me go without anything. She was very kind in lots of ways, and I love her dearly for it.

'If someone snores, Mum, you can tell them to turn over. That way they usually stop snoring. What do you do if someone is gnawing their teeth?' Anne asked.

'Nothing, my girl. Just leave it alone, will you. You're just like a dog with a bone,' Mum replied.

I stood by my bedroom door, looked back at Anne and noticed that she was trying her best not to laugh. I pointed at her, and really wanted to say, 'Ha ha! You've got told off.' But I knew I had better keep my mouth shut this time.

The next night at dinner time I knew full well Anne would come out with some remark, which would set Patsy off laughing. Poor old Dad. He tried so hard to keep the peace at the dinner table. We were never noisy. It was just a little bit of teasing really. We did respect Dad's wishes though. But like all children, we couldn't help ourselves sometimes, could we!

Bowling day

Brian and I were staying down at Walton-on-the-Naze for a weekend. It was beautifully hot, and we could not have wished for any better. We had been on the beach most of the day, and after we had our dinner Brian suggested that we could go bowling.

'That would be nice. I think we'll enjoy that,' I said to Brian. After washing up and clearing away, we got ourselves ready and then set off for an evening of bowling. We walked down to the sea front where the place was. When we arrived we noticed that there was a rather long queue.

'Oh, Maria, look at the queue,' said Brian. 'Do you want to queue up or would you rather go for a drink instead?'

'I don't mind waiting. I was rather looking forward to having a game of bowling,' I replied.

'OK then. Let's line up behind those people,' Brian said.

As we were lining up, the queue was going down quite quickly, I was thinking to myself. I kept feeling someone pushing me. I didn't like to say anything for a while, but then it got the better of me. I just couldn't stand it anymore. So I turned round and said to the chap, 'What's your name? Shover?'

'No. Gary Dun from Sweden.'

Well, that put me in my place. Brian and I couldn't help but laugh. In all the years I have never forgotten it. Brian and I laughed about it for ages. The chap didn't take offence to what I said to him. Thank goodness he didn't, really, as I suppose it could have been worse thinking back. He could have given me a right mouthful, which would have been not nice. But as it was he carried on talking to me. I had a job to keep a straight face.

Eventually we were at the door, and Brian gave the money to the doorman, who then said, 'Is she with you?'

'Yes, why?' Brian replied.

'Well, I'm sorry but she can't come in because she's wearing jeans.'

'You are joking,' Brian said.

'I'm not, mate. It's club rules.'

Brian put some extra money into his hand, and with that he let us in. They weren't heavy looking jeans. They were a nice soft pastel colour. In fact they didn't really look like jeans. Anyway we got in and had a smashing game. Brian won though, which he kept telling me all evening.

After we had our game, we sat in the bar and watched the other people play theirs.

'Look over there, Maria,' said Brian. 'There's your friend Gary Dun waving to you.'

'Oh Brian, perhaps he has just realised what I said to him, and he is going to come after me when he has finished his game.'

'Don't be silly. He's just waving to you to be polite,' Brian said, smiling all over his face.

'I'm a bit worried, Brian. Can we go now?'

'Oh all right then. If you like, we could have a drink at one of the other pubs. Then we can get some fish and chips on our way home.'

'Could we sit on the wall and eat our fish and chips, Brian? I love my fish and chips out of the paper. They taste so much nicer,' I said.

Once we got our fish and chips, we sat on the sea wall and ate them. The sea was quite rough, but beautiful to look at. After we had eaten, we walked back to the caravan. It was a pleasant walk home, and the smell of the sea was really nice. Once we got back, I made a nice cup of tea and we sat outside drinking it in the cool of the evening, which was wonderful.

I always felt healthy after I had been down at the caravan, with the lovely sunshine and the vitamin D which my body needed. We tried to get down to the caravan once a week as we so enjoyed our time, and when the children arrived it just made everything complete in our lives.

Sometimes difficult to understand these people

It is sometimes difficult for non-Gypsies to understand this hard working, resilient, independent, close knit and caring group of people. But, by working together, barriers can be removed and Gypsies live in harmony with gorger-bred people.

You have to be born to a Gypsy family to be a true Gypsy person. They are often confused with the tinkers of Ireland. There is good and bad in every community, but Gypsies have been subjected to negative stereotyping and harassment. Gypsies are self-employed and have lots of different skills and recycle materials. The majority are law-abiding, tax paying citizens who would like to see their lifestyle and culture respected by the rest of the population.

The reason why some of the children don't go to school is that their parents feel that they might be bullied. I was bullied by a few of the children, but I must state that many of the children were very nice and friendly to me, and they are still friends to this day. If I had not had those few children who were very nice to me, I don't know how I would have managed!

Gypsy people all over the world have always been a persecuted people, and that includes in Britain and the rest of Europe. They have been mistrusted and blamed for anything that goes amiss in whatever area they are in at the time. This is such a shame, as they are not all bad, and there is good and bad in everyone.

The Gypsy community, like any family, doesn't like trouble, and there is always an elder of each family who usually takes stock of the troublesome ones. Believe you me, if they do take stock of the one who is making trouble, he will be put through his paces, as my father would say!

My father always said, if you continually play up outside, one day you will find your match!

I often used to think as a child that many years ago Gypsies seemed strange to other people. They must have had a great store of strange secrets which they held tight in their hearts and never spoke of outside their family or friends within their community. This I can say is this is very true as I have secrets which are close to my heart, which are only told to my own family!

These days, as well as the traditional horse drawn wagon, Gypsies can be seen travelling by car or truck with their caravans being towed. They have smart motors such as Mercedes. When they are on the move, they do look wonderful. The caravans cost thousands of pounds and all this is paid by cash. You never see a Gypsy person with a cheque book. However, I am a true Gypsy woman and although I sometimes use cash, most of the time I pay by cheque!

I do not hold with the Gypsies who leave their rubbish, which is just scattered around. There are plenty of places for it to go, and they are not short of trucks to take it to the proper place!

Gypsy people are robust, healthy and strong. They are usually of light build with dark expressive eyes and swarthy complexion, ranging from deep brown to olive. However, fair skinned Gypsies are not unheard of. I can speak from experience, because as a child I was very fair skinned with very blond hair. I think it came from my mother's side of the family. My mother was slightly fair skinned. My Aunt Becky in Kent said to me once that Gypsy people have a timeless face, which is always fixed against the wind and open sky.

Someone told me once that Gypsy people are hard looking, with onyx eyes, and that they belong to a long line of secret ancient Gypsies. I have never forgotten what that person said.

The River Medway

On Thursday October 20th 1853, a wagon full of hop-pickers toppled into the swollen river Medway and thirty people were drowned. The harvest was late that year. On this particular day, some Gypsies were crossing over the old wooden bridge at Hartlake when suddenly one of the horses stumbled and fell through a rotten section of wood, taking horses, riders and human cargo with it.

People reported that you could hear the screams as far away as East Peckham. People came from miles around to help with the rescue, prodding the riverbank with hop poles to find survivors. The conditions were so bad that one body was not recovered until the Monday.

The bridge badly needed repair. After the incident, it was replaced with a stone bridge, but some of the old wooden posts are still there today. The victims were buried in one grave at Hadlow Church and a memorial was erected in memory of those who died. Inside the porch of the church is a plaque on the wall. The names and ages of all the people lost are listed, including a child from the Hearne family who was only two.

All this must have lain really heavy on their hearts throughout that season, and many years after that.

I am so glad my parents decided to settle down rather than travelling around the country. When all the family used to meet up at various houses, I can still hear the infectious laughter. This is one of my treasured memories. We have our treasured memories which we hold dear to our hearts.

My mother was pleased that she gave up the Romany way of life, but my father always seemed as if he missed the travelling ways. I could sense it through his stories which he used to tell me. As young as I was I could see it in his eyes. These days there is no land to park up on. Also, the land work is done by machines, so there is no work for them. It has all disappeared.

When I meet up with my family and friends there are lots of storytelling of years gone by, which is lovely. I love listening to the stories. To me, there is nothing better.

Shaun gardening

My grandson Shaun is now sixteen, and he has become quite a good gardener. Brian showed him how to mow the lawn when he was thirteen years old. I am so glad he did. Shaun mows my lawn every weekend, and he does anything else that might need doing in the garden. He just gets on and does it, bless him.

Shaun patterns the lawn just like Brian showed him, and no way will he do it any other way. He takes real pride in his gardening. And he doesn't just cut my lawn; he also cuts a couple of neighbours' lawns as well. When I watch him through the window he is just like his dad.

We have only just thrown away our other mower, which Brian had for twenty-six years. Brian bought it for twenty pound, and it was second-hand then. We gave it to the man opposite us, and he is still using it.

Brian bought a lighter mower as the other one was far too heavy for Shaun. He loves this one. He cleans it every time he uses it, and tells me when it's ready for service. He's quite a little handyman. He sorts things out when I wouldn't have thought he would be able to. But he gets on and does it and makes a good job of it as well.

Shaun saves up all his gardening money and then he buys himself something. The latest thing he has bought is a large two-berth tent, which is in my garden at the moment and the grandchildren are sleeping in it every weekend. I don't know they are there as they are so quiet.

On one occasion I was sitting on my garden bench in the middle of the night because my little dog Betsy wanted to go out and have a wee. Suddenly I heard this flapping of wings. When I looked up there was an owl sitting on my wooden frame amongst the grape vine which is over my back door. It is growing beautifully at the moment so there is plenty of hiding places for the owl and other birds. There he sat quite happily looking down at me. Then I thought of Betsy. I called her over to where I was, and for once she did as she was told. The owl just sat there.

Then I suddenly thought, if it should fly off and land on Shaun's tent it could wake the grandchildren up. But there was no noise from the tent. Then the owl took off and went and sat on my conservatory roof. It was such a beautiful bird. It's such a shame that birds get killed on the road.

Early hours of the morning, the garden looks and smells so nice. That's all thanks to Shaun, my grandson.

Snobby Sue

As a family we always ate at the table, even when Brian wasn't at home. There was far more enjoyment from the meal, plus we could all talk about our day, which was so important for the children as well as ourselves. The little things that the children would talk about were really brilliant. All their little troubles would be spoken about.

This particular day I was feeling so tired as I had just finished my four nights of work. While the dinner was cooking, Shane came in shouting that snobby Sue had hit him. Well, that didn't please me. I turned the gas down under the saucepans and straight away I went to see what had gone wrong. I don't think my feet touched the floor until I got to her house. All the children on our small estate used to call Sue that, and it stuck. By the time I had got to her house everything looked quiet. Dawn and Sid, who lived next door to her, were in their garden. There were many other children all standing around, I think waiting to see what was going to happen.

'Have you come to see what happened, Maria?' Dawn said.

'Yes,' I replied.

'Apparently the children were going round the estate on their bikes for a bit of fun. Then Sue decided to come out and stop them by shouting at them. They weren't doing any harm. Then all of a sudden Sue put her hand out to stop one of them when they were passing her gate. And it was your Shane that got her hand across his face. Then he fell off his bike and came straight home to you.'

With that I went and banged on Sue's door. It was a while before anyone came to the door, but I stayed there until someone showed their face. Eventually, the door started to open slowly. Then there was this very low voice.

'Hello. What do you want, Maria?'

'What do I want? I would like a very big apology from you for hitting my son around the face. He wasn't doing any harm. In fact, none of the children were. So why did you do it?'

'I don't know. I just did it,' she said.

There was silence, and then she turned to go in. 'Where are you going?' I said to her.

'I'm going in. Why?'

'Well, don't you think you ought to give Shane and myself an apology?'

'Not really. They were all making rather a lot of noise. That's why I came out to them.'

'Yes, but you hit my son, didn't you?'

Sue looked straight at me and said, 'Sorry,' in a rather flat tone. With that I turned and walked away from her. I heard her shut her door with quite a bang.

Sid and Dawn were still in their garden. 'Oh well, I didn't get much of an apology from her, did I?' I said.

I went home to finish off getting our dinner ready. That evening at the dinner table none of us spoke of the incident, but I could still see a mark on Shane's face where Sue hit him. I don't think Shane stayed clear of her when he was playing around the block as well as the other children did.

And yet, her daughter sometimes came to play with Katy. She was a nice little child, and so was Sue's son.

The next morning, just as I was about to take my children to school, there was a bang on my front door. I walked up and opened the door and there stood Sue.

'Yes?' I said, looking at her.

'I've come to say that I'm truly sorry for what I did to Shane, and it was wrong of me to have hit him.'

'You're a teacher as well, Sue. Is that how you carry on at school?' I said. 'Don't you ever lay a finger on my children and if I were you I wouldn't do it to the other children either.'

With that, I told her I had to go to get my children to school.

We never really spoke after that, not that we spoke much before. We were both pleasant to each other, and that was about all.

The children did play around the block after that on their bikes, and so did her son. Nobody else ever complained about the children for playing on their bikes. We were all young once.

The pork chop

It was such a lovely day, so Janet and I decided to walk into Brentwood with our prams, me with Katy and Janet with Donna, who were both about a year old.

We used to walk into Brentwood quite a lot as it was a pleasant walk. We strolled around the town and bought a few things, plus we had our coffee in Bonmarché, which we always did. This was our treat once a fortnight.

On one occasion I went to get some meat. While I was in the shop, Janet was outside looking after the prams. After I bought the meat, I laid some on the bottom of the pram in the rack and the rest I laid on top of the pram.

We had got as far as the Robin Hood shops when I decided to go into the sweet shop to buy some sweets for the children when they came out of school. Janet again waited outside with the prams. I was always afraid that someone would run away with my baby. In those days people used to leave their prams with their babies outside the shops.

I had to wait in the queue for quite some time. All I kept thinking about was the children in the nursery as time was getting on and they had to be picked up by twelve o'clock. Eventually I was served, and I paid my money and walked outside.

I noticed Janet was laughing and I could hear her saying, 'Give it to me, Katy. You can't eat that.'

There was Katy, hanging on to this raw pork chop with her teeth. She didn't have that many teeth but what she did have were strong.

I put my hand out to her and she just took the chop out of her mouth and handed it to me. I placed it back into the bag, and then I wiped her face.

'I only turned my back for a minute to look in the shop window and when I turned around there was Katy with the pork chop in her mouth,' Janet said.

'We had better go, Janet, because we are getting a crowd around us.'

I released the pram brake and away we went. We didn't walk that slowly. All we wanted to do was get away from the shops as quickly as we could. We laughed all the way home.

When I told Brian, he just laughed and said, 'We ought to give her the nickname Pork Chop, not Katy which Anne gave her.' But we didn't, and she is still called Katy today. A lot of people don't even know her real name.

Janet and I laughed about the pork chop. I never put anything on the pram again after that. I always made sure it was out of Katy's reach.

Times gone by

In the forties and fifties, hardly anyone owned a thoroughbred dog. Dogs would roam the streets all day until the owners came home. Then late in the evening you wouldn't see a dog on the street. The poor things were tired probably, asleep from all the walking which they had done throughout the day. It was sad really. People just used to open their doors in the mornings and let them out. Thank goodness it's not like it today.

In those days, you'd even reach into a muddy gutter for a penny. Children would play cricket in the road, and no one would shout at them. Not like today. If they played in the road they would be told to clear off.

When you went to the garage to get petrol, they sometimes automatically checked the oil and cleaned your windscreen. Also, you got trading stamps, which was good. No one ever asked where the car keys were because they were always left in the car overnight. People did not drive as fast as they do today. They just can't wait to get there. Or should I say they should have left earlier.

When the Ford Zephyr came out, it was everyone's dream to own one. They were so roomy inside, and so comfortable.

I can remember the time when Green Shield stamps came out. They were everywhere. Whatever you bought you would get the stamps. It was great because you could save them up and then go to the Green Shield shop to collect your item which you had saved for.

What about peashooters? We don't see children with those these days. They have even changed Andy Pandy. The sweet cigarettes which you could buy even came in a packet just like real cigarettes.

I loved going to my local coffee shop. The jukebox would be in the corner playing our favourite songs. There we would be snuggled up at one table by the window. The coffee shop was called Wen Jo. So many happy hours were spent there, talking about everything and anything. Happy Days!

The only weapon that was found on someone was the catapult. If you had done something wrong at school, and you were sent to the head teacher, you would have been punished. And when your parents found out it was a far bigger punishment.

The television was quite ugly really. We didn't have a remote control, and it took five minutes for the television to warm up.

We were asked to get up and change channels, and we only had two! We would be sitting so close to the television, and Father kept turning the knobs to see if he could get a better picture. But the picture was fine. It was his eyes that needed seeing to.

What about those ugly gymslips, girls, which gave us no shape at all? Still, we all looked the same, which was nice. No one had better than anyone else.

All those games we played together, riding on our bikes, the hula hoops, and the visit to the local swimming pool. Whatever we buy today, nothing tastes the same as it did all those years ago. Everything is smaller these days, and there is less in the packets. I could go on and on, but to me that just felt good going back in time. What about you? How did you feel?

My first date with Brian

I felt really nervous on my first date with Brian. We went over to see his friends at Ongar in Essex. In the boot of the car was a load of apples, and the smell was coming into the car. It wasn't a nice smell at all.

When we eventually arrived, Brian got out of the car. Bending down to look at me he said, 'Stay there while I unload the apples. Then I'll come and get you.'

I heard the door shut. Then out came a rather plump man with a sack barrow. How many apples has Brian got in the boot, I thought? There can't be that many, surely. I could feel the car going up and down. Looking in the wing mirror, I could see quite a few boxes piled up on the pavement waiting to go into the person's house.

Brian and the other man were laughing away to each other. I do hope Brian doesn't forget me sitting in the car. It's rather cold as well. I don't feel like sitting out here while they drink tea. If he does forget me there won't be another date.

Soon I couldn't see anything through the window as it was dark. I was sitting all huddled up, trying to keep warm, when Brian made me jump by opening the car door.

'Come on,' said Brian. 'They've made a pot of tea for us. It's nice and warm in there as well.'

I'm really cold. I do hope I don't look blue in the face. If I do, whatever will my make-up look like? Bloody awful, I reckon. I got out of the car feeling rather shy as I had never seen these people before.

Brian reached out for my hand.

'These people are really nice, and they are waiting to meet you.'

'That's nice,' I said in a squeaky voice, walking behind him and holding his hand.

'Come on in, my dear,' this rather nice lady said.

I felt really at ease with her. She had such a wonderful smile that lit her face up.

She was rather a chubby lady, wearing a flowered dress and an apron which nearly covered her dress. Mind you, all elderly ladies wore aprons in those days. Nowadays we don't wear them or, if we do, they are very small and our clothes would not be properly protected.

'Have a nice cup of tea. You must be frozen sitting out there,' said the lady.

'Thank you,' I said as I followed her through to their sitting room. It was a really cosy room with a lovely log fire burning. There were two armchairs either side of the fire and a settee was against the wall. In one corner of the room there was a table with the tea pot and cups laid out which looked rather nice.

'Do you take sugar, my dear?'

'No, I don't take milk either, thank you,' I said really quietly.

The cups and saucers were a pretty blue with tiny flowers. I watched myself all the time while I was holding the saucer and drinking the tea. It wasn't strong tea, thank goodness, as I just can't drink strong tea. The weaker the better for me. I always say, when you have made the tea pour it straight out for me with a nice slice of lemon.

They had a daughter with lovely black hair who sat very quietly on the settee. They were all talking about many years ago. I was lost so I just sat quietly drinking my tea. I hoped they wouldn't ask me any questions as I hated questions, especially when I don't know the people.

I couldn't wait to go. It was rather rude of me to think that, but I just couldn't seem to blend in with the family. They were really nice, but I didn't know what they were talking about, so I felt rather left out.

'We must get going as Maria has to be in by ten o'clock,' said Brian.

'I certainly don't want to be late. My dad is a real clock watcher, as you know, Brian,' I said. 'Thank you for this evening.' I shook hands with everyone. Mind you, I wasn't sorry to go. As much as they were nice people, my stomach was tying itself in a rather large knot.

We all walked to our car and Brian got in after shaking hands with everyone. He started up the engine and away we went. I gave them a smile and wave through the window as they had been so nice to me.

Weekend caravanning

We decided to buy a new caravan, as the one we had was quite small. Although we had the awning, which gave us more space, Brian and I thought it would be nice to have a new one.

We went out the following weekend to look for a caravan, and we saw some really lovely ones. The only thing was the money. John, Brian's brother, came with us and he certainly fell in love with them. He was opening all the cupboards and looking inside.

'Now that's good,' I heard from John. 'It's certainly something we don't have in the caravan we have at the moment.'

'What's that John?' I heard Brian say.

'It's an oven. Look, and it's quite a nice size too.'

The pair of them were kneeling down looking inside the oven.

'It also has two stoves on top for putting saucepans on for cooking. The caravan actually is a nice size. And plenty of room to walk about in, which we need,' said John.

'Well the oven is a bonus,' said Brian. 'This time, Maria, I won't have to go looking for it. Do you remember that Maria? When we wanted to cook that meat pie we were looking in all the cupboards for this blessed oven, which wasn't there. I tell you what. Those birds that day had a really good feed, and it smelt and looked so nice too.'

'Brian, your mum would have been devastated about the pie, and what we had to do with it.'

'No she wouldn't. She'd laugh because we thought we had an oven in the caravan, and there we were looking in all the cupboards trying to find it. As if this oven was going to suddenly emerge! Still, we managed, didn't we, that weekend even though it was somewhat cold? So this time when we buy a caravan we must make sure that the one which we are having has an oven in,' Brian said, laughing.

'Nice warm pies to go with our dinners. I can cook nice portions of chicken as well. We'll be in heaven, Brian.'

'Come on you two let's go and see how much they want for this one,' John called out.

With that Brian and I were soon following John. I thought it best to leave the business to Brian and John while I looked around some other caravans. But it wasn't doing me any good, because they were all more expensive than the one we had already decided to buy!

Well we did buy the one that we had been looking at. We had some wonderful weekends away in the caravan, plus many wonderful holidays.

There weren't that many places that we didn't visit in this country. We went to Scotland one year. It was in June and it was hot. All the children wore were shorts and little tops, and I thought it was going to be cold. I took Wellington boots, rain coats and warm jumpers. And we never had to wear any of those as we had beautiful weather, and the sun shone all the time.

Thank goodness for the camera, as we took loads of photos, which has given us wonderful memories. The scenery was breathtaking, and the mountains were amazing. I had never seen so many mountains and I don't think I'll ever see so many again!

'Look out of your window, Shane, and look at those wonderful mountains,' I said to him one day.

'Yes Mum. When you've seen one mountain you've seen them all,' he replied.

Brian and I looked at each other and smiled. I bit my lip as I really wanted to laugh out loud. But it wouldn't have been right, as Shane was getting quite fed up with just travelling around.

All in all we did have a fabulous holiday.

Feeling so ill

On one occasion when Brian and I were down at the caravan I was about four months pregnant and it was such a nice day that we decided to walk to the amusements.

The walk along the sea front was quite nice, and I wasn't even feeling sick. When we got to the amusements, Brian decided to go on the one arm bandit. As he was putting his money into the machine, I was beginning to feel sick.

'Brian, I'm going to stand outside for a while,' I said.

'OK, take care,' he said.

With that I started to walk outside, and I was feeling worse by the minute. I thought I ought to go to the toilet just in case I was sick. I would be so embarrassed if I were sick outside. I turned round and quickly went back to Brian to tell him that I wasn't feeling too good, and that I was going to the toilet. Brian was not too pleased because the machine that he was playing was just spilling money out every time he pulled the handle down.

'Will you be alright on your own, Maria? This machine is giving me money without me having to put any in,' Brian said.

'I'm going now, Brian, I'll be over in the toilets, so don't go away, will you,' I said, holding my stomach.

I didn't wait for Brian's reply. I just ran off towards the toilets. When I arrived, there was this long queue. I'm not going to be able to wait in this queue, I was thinking to myself. I must have waited for only a couple of minutes when all of a sudden I felt worse. I just said sorry to everyone and pushed my way through.

With my hand tightly clenched to my mouth, I stood at one of the toilet doors waiting for someone to come out. Then I was going to make a bolt for it. I was praying all the time that I wouldn't be sick where I stood. Then a door opened and out came this lady.

I just pushed by her saying, 'I'm so sorry, but I'm pregnant and I'm going to be sick.'

I never even shut the door. I just got on to my hands and knees, with my head over the toilet. Thank God, I thought, I've made it in time. I stayed in the toilet for quite some time. I was too frightened to go outside. I don't know how long I stayed in there, but suddenly I heard someone calling out.

'Are you alright, love? Do you need help?'

'I'm alright,' I called out. I just wanted to stay a bit longer. I was sitting on the floor, not even bothered whether it was dirty or not.

'Maria, are you in there? Are you alright?' Brian shouted out.

'I'm coming out now, Brian,' I called out.

I slowly got up from the floor and pulled the door open, and there stood Brian. I put my hand out for him to hold.

'Come on, let's get you home. You don't look good. What's brought this on? You were alright when we were walking down to the amusements,' Brian said.

'I know. I think it was to do with the smell of the amusements. I've never liked that smell. I don't want to talk about it anymore. I just want to go back to the caravan,' I said to Brian.

With that we just carried on walking. I didn't say another word all the way back. Mind you, I didn't feel like talking. All I wanted to do was get back to the caravan, have my night drink and go to bed, which I did. And Brian came with me as well.

'Are you sure you're alright?' Brian kept saying to me.

'I'll be alright in the morning after a good night's sleep,' I replied. And with that I turned over and went to sleep.

How did they manage?

You never see a travelling woman wearing glasses. Most of them can't read so they don't need them for close work. They would tell you that they could see into the distance, and that's quite enough.

Mind you, whenever they were making their flowers inside or outdoors, they always had a cigarette in their mouth. They would be drawing on the cigarette and the smoke would be going up into their eyes, which would be making them squint. I don't think they could really see that well. They were so used to making their flowers that they knew just what to do.

'Luvvie, if it rains tomorrow we've had it.'

'It won't rain, Jenty. It's going to be a really nice fine day because I told the good Lord to give us a fine day for our flowers. Otherwise, they won't be flowers. They'll look like a soggy piece of tissue!'

'Well I hope he listens to you, Luvvie, because my Celia needs new shoes!'

They used to say that if they hadn't had their ears pierced they would not have such good eyesight! Therefore, if you think about it, the women must have better eyesight than the men. The women have both ears pierced, but the men only one!

My mother wore glasses, but not until her later years. She could read and write quite well, so she was not afraid to go to the optician. It's quite frightening really, if you can't read properly. There you are in front of a load of letters and what do you do? I suppose if you know what is coming you wouldn't go to the optician would you!

My father used to say, 'Luvvie, where are your glasses? I want to look at the paper.' He couldn't read or write, but he got by. Very shrewd was my father. He had no problems with adding up, which he taught himself. I don't think you will find a travelling man who can't add up.

The way they learnt to add up was by playing with stones, my father told me. This they used to do in the evening around the campfire, while the rest of the family would be telling stories, possibly singing and dancing as well.

When I was a child, there were some Gypsies who used to come to our estate. My cousin Celia and I used to play with them. Oh, what fun we had. We used to go home smelling of burning wood, Mother used to say.

'Where have you been? Don't tell me you've been playing with the Gypsies down the lane?'

'Yes,' I used to say, with big beaming eyes and a big smile. 'They won't take me away, will they?'

'What gives you that idea, they won't take you away'

'Well, I'm a Gypsy and they only take the gorger-bred children away. Anyway, they wouldn't want another one like me would they Mum?'

'No, I suppose not,' she said smiling.

When my son Shane was at school he had his ear pierced, and the school tried to make him take his earring out. But no way was he going to. He got away with it by saying it was his religion. In fact, he's right, because all Gypsy children have to have their ears pierced. It's their way of life, and what they believe in. Shane told his teacher it helped eyesight. We never did hear any more about it, and he kept his earring.

Eunice Attridge

Eunice lived on the school grounds. She was always a friendly girl. Whenever we played in the school grounds she would come out and have a chat with us all. Sometimes we would hide so her father wouldn't find us. She never split on us.

Eunice always looked so smart, and was a couple of years older than me. So when she went out, she wore different clothes, which made her look much older.

Myself and my friends Shirley Alexandra, Jennifer White, Dulce Harvey, Rosemary Sells and Barbara Pratt would be sitting on the green on the corner of Pilgrims Hatch talking away to each other. Then Eunice would be coming down the road, all dressed up and looking very lovely in her pretty dress and cardigan, with her white high heels clicking away. We used to call out, 'Where are you going, Eunice?'

'I'm going to the pictures with my boyfriend,' she used to reply. We never did ask who the boyfriend was. We were just interested in the clothes that she was wearing. I couldn't wait for the day that I was allowed to wear slender high heels. I could see on the other girls' faces that they were thinking the same. We watched her walk into the distance towards the bus shelter. Then she was out of sight.

Then we all turned and faced each other. We were all pulling pieces of grass up, so we could put a piece between our two thumbs to make a noise.

Then I said, 'It won't be long before we will all be able to wear high heels.'

'I can't wait,' said Barbara Pratt, and the others all agreed.

We used to have such fun together playing and laughing, and it didn't cost any money either. These days all they want is expensive games to play with. How times have changed. I do hope it changes back. But on the other hand I really can't see it happening. More likely they will want more expensive games to play with.

Betsy

My little dog Betsy was such a sweet gentle little dog, full of fun. She loved to be around the grandchildren. I think she thought she was a child.

Once I had finished my housework, Betsy would make her way into the front room and pull the throws off the settee, and then she would pull the cushions off the chairs. I have a large rug on the floor which is quite heavy for her little teeth, but she always managed to pull it into a heap.

When I eventually went into the front room and saw what she had done, she used to jump up onto the settee into her usual place. She had three lovely large cushions which were placed on the settee where she would lie and look out the window, or perhaps have a sleep. She used to look so cute when she turned her head towards me and wagged her tail, much as to say ha ha! Brian and I never told her off for doing it. We just wondered how on earth she managed to pull the settee cushions off with her tiny teeth.

Once I had put everything back in its place, with her watching me, Betsy would settle down and go to sleep until I started preparing the vegetables for dinner. It didn't matter how quiet I was, she always knew when I was chopping the vegetables. She loved her cooked vegetables which she had every day with her dinner.

If I went shopping, I had to make sure I bought her fresh runner beans. As soon as I had put my shopping down she would be in the bags looking for the runner beans. Once she got hold of one she would run into the front room with it in her mouth, and no way would she let you have it. She would eat it with so much enjoyment.

If I gave her a pea which was in its pod, or a broad bean, she would pull the pod apart until she got the peas or the beans out, and then she would eat them. She never ate the outer part of the pea or the broad bean, but she ate the whole of the runner bean. She loved her meat and veg every day.

I have an electric buggy which I use to go out on, and Betsy loved to sit on the platform of the buggy. She would sit on the buggy until I got to our local church, and then she would get off and walk beside me. No way would she get back on, unless it was raining. Then on she would jump again and home we go.

She didn't like the rain, bless her. She didn't mind the wind and often stood facing the wind so it blew into her face. She would have her little legs firmly on the ground, enjoying every moment of the wind in her sweet little face.

My neighbour Maggie has fish and chips for her lunch on a Thursday, which is delivered to her by her local fish and chip shop. Betsy knew when it was a Thursday and would sit by the lounge window looking out, waiting for the fish and chips to arrive. Any other day of the week, although she would sit by the window, she would be on and off the settee. But on a Thursday, no way would she move until the fish and chip man came down the path.

Once the man had delivered the fish and chips, Betsy would bark at my back door to be let out so she could go to Maggie's bungalow for her lunch. You wouldn't think that a dog would remember a day, but she did. She knew when it was Thursday, and even knew the time of day when the fish and chip man arrived.

I noticed lately that she was looking very tired, and her eyes had a glaze over them. When Shane and Katy saw her, they always remarked how tired she was looking as well. I didn't want to hear those words and tried not to listen.

Then one day I noticed that she didn't look too good, so I decided to take her to the vets for them to check her over. I had taken her a fortnight before as she didn't look well then. The vet looked at me, and I knew in my heart that the time had come to say goodbye.

She left me for a while so I could have my special time with her. Then she came back and took her out to another room. When Betsy came back to me I noticed that the vet had put a line in her leg, so when she put the medication in it would go straight into the vein.

The vet said to me 'Are you ok?'

I looked up at the vet and just nodded. Thank goodness I was sitting down because I knew my legs wouldn't hold me up. Then the vet put Betsy in my arms and I lowered my head to kiss her.

'I loved you Betsy so much,' I said with tears running down my face. The nurse was standing beside me with her arm around me.

I felt Betsy go limp in my arms. It was so quick. Then I started to cry. I was having problems with my breathing because I was gasping for breath. I held Betsy so tightly saying to her 'I love you so much darling. You've been a wonderful pet to me, and I feel blessed that I had you for all of fourteen wonderful years.'

By this time my sobbing had gone into a very loud cry and, when I say loud, by God did I cry out loud. The lady vet and the nurse held me so tightly. My legs were like jelly and I was shaking all over. They were so kind to me.

The vet said, 'You did the right thing. She was tired and worn out, it was her time.' The last time I cried like that was when I lost my Brian.

I telephoned Shane and Katy when I got home that evening.

Over the phone I could hear Katy sobbing. Shane came home that evening to see me. He didn't usually come home on Friday evenings, and I wouldn't see him until Saturday morning. When he walked in the door I noticed that his eyes were red. The first thing he said to me was,

'You should not have gone on your own. You should have waited until tomorrow so I could take you.'

'I wanted to be on my own with her. Don't tell me off for going on my own. Katy has already done so.'

I still feel sad and lonely without Betsy. Writing this piece of work is bringing the tears back, and I have got a lump in my throat as big as an orange. Well it feels that size anyway. Brian and I loved her so much and so did all the family.

To me she wasn't a dog, she was my little girl, my baby and I adored her. So did Brian when he was alive, bless him.

My great-grandchild Savannah being born

It was the 18th June 2012 and my granddaughter Kieralea has had this very beautiful little girl. She was born in Doncaster. All the grandchildren have been born in Suffolk.

When Kieralea was in labour it was awful. Just me and my little dog Betsy were at home waiting for news. I was so worried. Every time the telephone rang I practically jumped on it. Katy was wonderful keeping me informed as to Kieralea's progress all the time, bless her.

I had cleaned the whole bungalow and packed my case for my journey to Doncaster. I was all ready to go the next morning.

When Katy telephoned me to say that Kieralea had given birth I just burst into tears, I was so relieved. Katy was crying with joy. Betsy and I will be up on the first train in the morning, I told Katy.

That night I didn't sleep that well but I was up at the crack of dawn, to catch the early train. My good friend Jean took me to the station. She is brilliant to me and is such a kind lady. Anyway, I was on the 10.15 train. Betsy was a happy dog, cuddled up on my lap. She loved a train ride and knew where she was going.

When I got to Doncaster, Katy was there waiting for me with a big smile on her face. Once Betsy was settled at Katy's and we had had a very refreshing cup of tea, we set off for the hospital to visit Kieralea and her baby.

Kieralea and her other half, Charlie, named the baby Savannah Rose. I think it's such a pretty name. I'm so proud of her and only wish her great granddad was here to enjoy everything.

As I held Savannah Rose in my arms I was thinking of Brian and felt he was with us. Katy and Kieralea said that they felt that he was with them all the time.

Shane was pleased as well. I think he was just relieved that it was all over, and the baby had arrived safely.

Savannah Rose was so tiny. Although she weighed six pounds she was a tiny six pounder, but a very pretty baby. She was just like Kieralea when she was born, although she has her daddy's chin. Kieralea and Charlie are both good looking, so I think we are going to have a very pretty girl when she grows up. I think they will have to watch the boys with her!!

I stayed with Katy and her husband Ray for a few days, and then made my way back home. It will be so nice when Kieralea comes to stay for a few days. I'm so looking forward to laying Savannah Rose in the family heirloom, our crib!

The Gypsy vardo

The Romany Gypsies and their vardo caravans seem to have taken to the roads about the middle of the nineteenth century. I can remember my parents telling me that in the 1870's not many caravans were on the roads.

They used to live in benders which were like tents. They were made with willow sticks, which were bent over and dug into the ground (they used willow sticks because they were easy to bend). Tarpaulin sheets were then placed over the top to keep them dry. This would be where the older ones would sleep and live, until they could afford their own wagons. The girls and boys always had their own separate bender. To buy a wagon would have cost a lot of money, far too much for the young couples when first starting out in life. They always cooked and ate outside unless it was wet.

It is said that Gypsies never learnt the trade of making wagons. However, my uncle Elijah was always telling me about the wagons which he had made in his younger days. However, in the middle sixties my Uncle Riley made a Gypsy wagon in his own back garden. When it was finished, a couple from America came and bought it, and took it back to America.

The wagons were warm and very strong, and they lasted many years. They had to last; no way could they go out and buy another one just like that! The very young would live inside the wagon, and their sleeping place would be under their parents' bed, which was a drawer. One wouldn't know there was a bed there. The front of the bed would be very colourful painted doors, which would hide the bed.

In the evening the bed would be pulled out just like a drawer. The child or children would be tucked up in their drawer bed. Then in the morning the bed would be made, then pushed back out of the way. And no one was the wiser that there was a bed hidden away. A good hiding place when the school board man in those days came around. They hoped and prayed that the school board man would not stay too long, because when the children came out, they were quite red faced.

The last chapter of my wonderful memories

Well, I have eventually come to the end of my book. I have really enjoyed writing my memories. Sometimes it's been quite a sad journey, but other times I have felt happiness in my heart, with a tremendous amount of laughter, and remembered old friends on the way.

I have two wonderful children, Shane and Katy, five beautiful grandchildren and two great grandchildren. I love each and every one of them dearly.

I loved my childhood thanks to my parents and my brother and sister. When I got married to Brian on the 27th. March 1965 at the age of nineteen life completely changed.

But I was happy to be with Brian, and when the children arrived it was such a wonderful feeling. Shane was born on the 27th. March 1966, when I was twenty. Then, on the 9th. August 1967, I had Katy when I was twenty-one. I felt grown up - I was a mummy with two beautiful children whom I adored and loved dearly.

I do hope you all enjoy reading my book.
God bless.
Maria Hearne

Great Grandchildren
Savanah-Rose
Junior

Grandchildren
Kieralea
Charlie-Joe
Shaun
Chantelle
Daniella

Acknowledgements

I would like here to express my gratitude to my proofreader and editor, Jeremy Ratcliffe without whose advice, enthusiasm, diligence and constant support I would have struggled to publish this book.
Thank you Jeremy.